THE ENGLISH CIVIL WAR AND REVOLUTION

The English Civil War and Revolution offers a wide range of accessible source material covering the principal aspects of the mid-seventeenth century crisis, and a guide to the progressive, revisionist, post-revisionist and other historiographical debates involved.

The source material offers different perspectives from various levels of society, drawing on controversial literature, official records, private correspondence, diaries, reports of grass roots reactions, minutes of debates, contemporary illustrations and petitions. Each document has an introduction which provides contextual information. The book also contains a comprehensive glossary of seventeenth century terms appearing in the source material and a chronology of events for reference.

Whilst familiarising students with some of the main sources used in contemporary historical debates, *The English Civil War and Revolution* contains many extracts from unpublished, manuscript sources. Source material is grouped thematically in relation to six key questions, thus aiding understanding of this complex period and providing a useful reference tool.

Keith Lindley is Senior Lecturer in History, University of Ulster.

THE ENGLISH CIVIL WAR AND REVOLUTION

A sourcebook

Keith Lindley

Routledge
Taylor & Francis Group

LONDON AND NEW YORK

First published 1998
by Routledge
2 Park Square, Milton Park, Abingdon, Oxon, OX14 4RN

Simultaneously published in the USA and Canada
by Routledge
270 Madison Ave, New York NY 10016

Routledge is an imprint of the Taylor & Francis Group

Transferred to Digital Printing 2005

British Library Cataloguing in Publication Data
A catalogue record for this book is available from the British Library

Library of Congress Cataloguing in Publication Data
A catalogue record for this book has been requested

ISBN 0–415–17418–x (hbk)
ISBN 0–415–17419–8 (pbk)

CONTENTS

CONTENTS

ILLUSTRATIONS

Figures; from the Thomason Tract collection by permission of the British Library

ACKNOWLEDGEMENTS

I am grateful to Heather McCallum, the editor at Routledge, for originally suggesting this volume and for showing patience and understanding as I worked towards its completion. Ian Roy gave me some valuable advice and assistance on the royalists and drew my attention to the British Library manuscript describing resistance to the royalist excise in Somerset. Bob Hunter was, as usual, an inexhaustible fund of information, and an ever-critical eye, on the Irish dimension to this book. I am also very grateful to Gillian Coward, who worked wonders on her computer with the illustrations drawn from the Thomason Tract collection, and Joanne Taggart, who 'surfed the net' in search of the sources for some of the biblical allusions.

I would also like to record my thanks to the staff of the British Library, the Coleraine campus library of the University of Ulster, the Corporation of London Records Office, the Greater London Records Office, the Guildhall Library, the House of Lords Record Office, the library of the Institute of Historical Research, the Public Record Office and Dr Williams's Library.

All the dates given in this book are in the old style, except that the year is taken to begin on 1 January and not 25 March. The spelling and capitalisation of all contemporary texts have been modernised as too has the punctuation when needed to aid clarity.

INTRODUCTION

There has been much lively controversy among historians about the origins, nature and consequences of the English civil war and revolution. Rival inter-~~pretations of these events may be roughly grouped under three main~~ headings: 'progressive', revisionist and post-revisionist interpretations, although in no case do all the historians so classified invariably advance identical views. Progressive (mainly Whig and Marxist) interpretations, whose historiographical roots stretch back into the nineteenth century, view the civil war and revolution as a crucial landmark in English history with long-term causes and an outcome that was virtually inevitable. For Whig historians, it was a vital stage in the emergence of modern liberal democracy and the rise of religious toleration. A constitutional and political struggle was waged between, on the one hand, an authoritarian monarchy with abso-lutist ambitions and popish religious tendencies and, on the other, staunch parliamentary defenders of liberty, property and Protestantism. An increas-ingly influential and assertive House of Commons (rather than the Lords) held centre stage. Puritanism had an absolutely central role to play (hence the label, a 'puritan revolution') and the struggle and outcome were distinc-tively English, with the kingdom stealing a lead over the rest of Europe in its progress towards a modern democracy. Similarly, Marxist interpretations view England as more 'advanced' than the rest of Europe with a capitalist economy and society, and political structures to match, the ultimate goal. In the original Marxist formulation, mid-seventeenth-century England witnessed a bourgeois revolution in which a traditional 'feudal' society, led by a restrictive royal government allied to a declining aristocracy, was over-thrown by a new capitalist class composed of enterprising peers, gentry and merchants. The latter moulded the political system to protect their interests, thereby ensuring that England developed as a constitutional monarchy and a market economy. The whole process was inevitable as the increasing disparity in sixteenth- and early seventeenth-century England between those who wielded economic power and those who retained political power was unsustainable, and only revolution could resolve the tension by placing the economically dominant in power. Puritanism remains important in this analysis as providing the new religious values and attitudes that both harmonised with, and encouraged, capitalism. Recent Marxist-influenced writings on the period have seen less concern with a rising capitalist class, and more interest in the supposedly radical values of those drawn from the middle ranks of society (the 'middling sort' of people) and their failed attempt at social revolution.

Revisionist interpretations see few, if any, long-term origins of the conflict in mid-seventeenth-century England and emphatically deny that it was inevitable. Social and economic explanations are relegated to the status of minor contributory factors, if not dismissed out of hand. There was an ideological consensus, it is argued, in early Stuart England and an almost total absence of principled divisions so far as politics and the constitution were concerned. It was a profoundly hierarchical and deferential society in which the aristocracy, far from being in crisis or decline, wielded enormous political influence, including dominance over the House of Commons. An adversarial view of politics as a conflict between crown and parliament, government and opposition, or 'court' and 'country', was wholly alien to this society where the emphasis was on cooperation, consensus and unity. Any idea of resisting the crown or of seeking to limit royal power was anathema. Furthermore, it was the county community, rather than the nation, which provided the principal focus for political and social loyalties and ambitions. England was becoming a more law-abiding and stable kingdom; regional rebellions were a thing of the past and popular unrest was limited and easily containable.

Similarly, religious consensus prevailed in England until the accession of Charles I, according to some historians, or much later, according to others. The former argue that most educated English Protestants were theologically Calvinist and were content to have a Church governed by bishops until the promotion to power by Charles of William Laud and his allies. With few exceptions, puritans remained within the Church supporting preaching and other godly concerns and, far from being alienated malcontents or potential revolutionaries, were upholders of order. Laudianism, with its anti-Calvinism, sacramentalism and ceremonialism, split the Church and allowed extremist minorities to gain a disproportionate influence. Other revisionists see no serious religious tensions in England before the late 1630s, and play down the importance of both Laudian innovations and puritan opposition.

Religion features centrally in revisionist explanations of why Charles's government collapsed and civil war was its eventual outcome. This is linked in turn with the crucial British and Irish dimensions of the conflict, Charles's drastic shortcomings as monarch, the twists and turns of high politics (as the king and senior figures negotiated and made decisions) and the stubborn localism of county elites. Short-term and contingent circumstances are highlighted, and progressive and traditional roles are reversed, with Charles I and his government as the innovators and his critics the defenders of conservative political and religious positions. The resort to arms was hampered by the neutrality of some and the reluctance of many others to be drawn into the conflict, and the experience of war and its burdens, and exposure to the forces of godly reformation, broadened and intensified the desire for a return to normality. The political revolution of 1649 was the work of a small minority led by army leaders and was contrary to the wishes of the great mass of the population. Those who had been working for a social revolution as well were also relatively small in number and could in no way claim to be representative of the interests and convictions of the middle and lower ranks of English society as a whole. The civil war and revolution had only a limited (and, in political terms, largely negative) influence on post-Restoration England. The social and economic changes that did come after 1660 were more the result of developments begun before 1640 than the product of the revolution itself. It was in religious and intellectual developments that the civil war and revolution made its greatest mark with the post-Restoration rejection of religious enthusiasm, a Church placed firmly under lay control and the gradual emergence of a new rational and empirical intellectual climate.

Post-revisionist historians seeking an explanation for the mid-century crisis have restored long-term origins, principled divisions over politics and the constitution, the importance of puritanism and the significance of the interactions of social and economic change with politics and religion. They do not return to the notion of an 'inevitable' conflict but stress that the form it actually took was shaped by long-term political, religious and social developments. Revisionists are attacked for placing too much stress on political consensus and high politics. Although consensus was the ideal, there was ample room for division and conflict beginning with rival views on the constitution. The royalist/absolutist view had kings subject only to God and not bound by law or the need for consent while its opponents derived royal power from the people and believed it should be exercised according to the law and, especially where taxation was concerned, with consent. A parliament was normally the body which gave that consent and there was a widespread belief in the importance of parliaments generally. However, this does not mean a return to an older thesis that the civil war was fought between promoters and opponents of arbitrary rule. Many were only prepared to rally to the king after he had conceded constitutional ground in the reforms of 1641–42, yet memories of earlier excessive royalist claims remained to poison the political atmosphere. It is also argued that the 'political nation' was much wider than the aristocratic and gentry elites of much revisionist writing. The 'middling sort' of people (modest freeholders, smaller merchants and artisans) were well-informed and, far from being voting fodder, could exert political influence. 'Court' and 'country' have been rescued as meaningful political concepts and employed to help explain the emergence of rival conspiracy theories, one obsessed with popular sedition and the other with popish plotting.

3

There is general agreement with revisionists that religion is crucial in explaining the conflict but there are some major differences on the shape of religious developments and their wider impact. There was a serious divide, it is argued, among English Calvinists in the early seventeenth century. The central Calvinist doctrine was that only a minority of mankind (the elect or godly) had been singled out by God for salvation, while the rest (the reprobate) were predestined for damnation, but only God knew for sure who were among the elect. Most English Protestants would have subscribed to this belief but this did not mean that there was a 'Calvinist consensus' in England prior to the advent of Laud. Conformist Calvinists fully accepted that it was not possible to distinguish between the godly and the reprobate in this world and believed that the Church should foster order and conformity. However, a rival strand in Calvinism, to which the term 'puritanism' can be largely applied, believed it was possible for the elect to obtain some assurance of salvation in this life through an examination of conscience, attending sermons and generally living a godly life. This led them to seek out the company of their godly fellows and to work for the eradication of popery and superstition in the interests of defending true religion. Puritanism is therefore restored by post-revisionists as a well-supported and dynamic movement with a wide social base and plenty of activist potential to disturb the current order. The rise of Laud and the anti-Calvinist theology of Arminianism, and the association of both with authoritarian views about Church and state, unlocked this potential in puritanism with the result that godly zeal played a central part in moulding events in the 1640s.

Social and economic factors, assigned to the background by revisionists, are reasserted as important in explaining the crisis. Over a century of population growth and price inflation had encouraged commercial farming and the expansion of overseas trade. Both the numbers and the overall wealth of the gentry increased and they provided most local government while their leading figures sat in the Commons when there was a parliament. At the other end of the social spectrum, there were increasing numbers of the landless poor and those dependent on poor relief. Probably most of the 'middling sort' prospered, and they too were involved in local government, but some fell upon hard times. The trend was towards increasing social differentiation in which increased rents and the enclosure of previously common land soured relations between rich and poor. Yet serious social unrest was prevented by ameliorative action and especially the Elizabethan poor laws. This did not prevent governing elites from fearing that popular disorder might run out of control, and riots in fens and forests and mass demonstrations outside parliament had important political effects in the early 1640s.

Finally, post-revisionists find themselves drawn towards a recent analysis that seeks to explain the civil war as a conflict between 'cultures', as expressed in the contemporary stereotypes of austere, repressive and kill-joy Roundheads and frivolous, vain and pleasure-seeking Cavaliers. Parliamentarians were

4

engaged in a struggle for godly reformation and the removal of the menace of popery from Church and state. Royalists were rallying to the defence of the traditional social order and valued the harmonising role served by those parochial rituals and festivities which puritans were targeting for attack. However, post-revisionists find themselves less convinced by a line of argument that gives this cultural conflict a social and regional dimension, with arable regions (with their settled villages presided over by parson and squire) providing fertile territory for royalism while parliamentarianism's appeal was to the more mobile, socially polarised and less ordered wood-pasture and cloth industry regions.

Many of the issues raised in the above discussion of rival interpretations of the civil war and revolution will be returned to in the course of addressing six central questions: why did Charles I's government collapse?; why did a subsequent political settlement prove impossible?; what determined alle-giances in the civil war?; what impact did the war have?; why was it not possible to conclude a settlement with the king after the war and why did revolution become an alternative possibility?; and why did the revolution take the form it did?

WHY DID CHARLES I'S GOVERNMENT COLLAPSE?

Historians are in general agreement that Charles I was a lamentable failure as a monarch and by 1640 he had alienated most of his subjects. While far from being a stupid man, Charles was temperamentally authoritarian, holding to an exalted notion of the nature of kingship as God-given and denying opposition any legitimacy. Cold and aloof, he lacked basic political skills and judgement and came increasingly to be seen as untrustworthy. He made concessions with the greatest of reluctance, and sought to reverse them later, and gained a well-deserved reputation for deviousness by negotiating with opponents while, at the same time, planning to use force against them. He pursued unpopular policies, none more so than his disastrous religious policy, and he was personally responsible for the decision to impose the Scottish prayer book which set the whole chain of events that would eventually lead to civil war in motion. Yet the entire responsibility for the conflict cannot be laid at Charles's door even though he had an important part to play in making it possible.

The king's character and personality were important given the nature of the 'ancient constitution', England's revered unwritten constitution that had emerged out of the mists of time. That constitution combined the features of a 'personal monarchy' with that of a 'mixed monarchy'. Government, administration and justice were all conducted in the monarch's name and monarchs were free to choose ministers and advisers. Much political activity was centred on the court because parliaments met only periodically and had not yet become regular parts of the country's government. Monarchs possessed key powers and initiatives, including the power to summon and dissolve parliaments and make war or peace. Yet there was also a widespread belief in 'mixed' or 'limited' monarchy – that a monarch's powers were limited by the law of the land and monarchs should seek to govern by consent in the interests of national harmony and unity. Revisionists argue that almost all members of the political elites subscribed to this view and that there were few if any absolutists in early seventeenth-century England. However, as has been seen, critics of this notion of an elite ideological consensus have demonstrated the existence of rival absolutist views, especially but not exclusively among some of the clergy, which see monarchs as accountable to God alone and not 'limited' in any way or obliged to rule with consent.

A parliament was the chief body in which monarchs sought the consent of their subjects. For an eleven-year period, the 'personal rule' of 1629–40, Charles did not summon a parliament. This was the longest period without a parliament since the beginnings of that institution and perhaps (we cannot know for sure) Charles intended to dispense with parliaments altogether. Revisionist historians, rejecting the notion of 'the eleven years tyranny' gradually building up to crisis and conflict, present the 1630s in a much more mellow light than previously. These were years of peace with no foreign wars or serious domestic disturbances, beyond the occasional forest or fenland riot, comparing favourably with the troubled 1620s or the 1590s. England was well on the road to recovery from population growth and price inflation, sea-borne commerce was expanding, and levels of national taxation (but perhaps not local taxation) and the national debt were low by continental European standards. The nation was generally law-abiding and politically stable. At the centre, the court contained within it critics of royal policies, some of whom were to be prominent in reformist circles in the early 1640s, alongside the more subservient or convinced advocates of those policies. In the localities, the insensitive interventionist line adopted by the government in the drive for efficiency and uniformity was resented by many, yet not enough to forfeit their cooperation. The absence of a parliament meant that there was no national arena in which grievances could be aired and reforms advocated. Dissident voices were largely silent, there was no underground resistance plotting to bring down the personal rule by force, and there were only a tiny number of political and religious prisoners. The main alternative to conformity was not rebellion or revolution but emigration to New England, with a despairing John Pym and Oliver Cromwell contemplating it in the late 1630s. Even religion would have lost its divisive potential in the long term as people became accustomed to the changes, and the influence of the godly gentry is easily exaggerated. The internal discontent in England in 1637, therefore, would not have brought about the collapse of the personal rule and it was the events in Charles's Scottish kingdom that were to bring it to an end. The king's fatal weakness was that he lacked the resources to fight a war and the Scots war was the basic cause of the collapse of the personal rule.

Critics of this sanguine view of the personal rule argue that it is a mistake to interpret the lack of overt resistance or opposition – in an authoritarian society where censorship was in operation, letters were opened and people were naturally cautious – as evidence of basic stability. Where private sources do exist they show serious concern over issues such as ship money or religious policy. Leading figures who were to be at the centre of reforming initiatives in the early 1640s maintained contacts and exchanged views through regular meetings of the Providence Island Company and other colonising ventures. In the country as a whole, networks of the godly were established as they sought to defend themselves against Laud and these too were ready for mobilisation once a parliament met.

parliamentary taxation, which could undermine the constitution by removing one of the main reasons why monarchs called parliaments, and fears that the Church was being returned to popery. The levying of ship money, a rate imposed by virtue of the king's emergency powers to meet the costs of the navy, was eventually to prove one of the most contentious issues. Ship money was an onerous national levy that widened the tax net appreciably and its regularity was resented. Yet almost all the money was collected from 1634 to 1638 and most public protests centred on local rating objections and the amount of the levy rather than its constitutional implications. Nevertheless, such protests could also cloak deeper concerns and private sources reveal real anxieties among some of the gentry about the prospect of arbitrary taxation once it had been conceded that the king could impose levies, in what he regarded as emergencies, without the consent of a parliament. The decision in Hampden's case (1637–8) went in the king's favour yet, significantly, five of the twelve judges failed to uphold the king's case and, in its aftermath, resistance to ship money and refusals to pay mounted and became widespread once fresh burdens (coat and conduct money) were added by the Scots war [ch. 1, pp. 35–7]. Support for, or opposition to, ship money did not provide a clear divide separating future royalists from future parliamentarians. Moderate royalists in the Long Parliament recognised the constitutional dangers of ship money and supported the impeachment of the Hampden case judges who had found for the king.

By the end of the 1620s, Pym and other militants had come to the conclusion that there were moves afoot to 'recatholicise' the Church and that Charles or his advisers wanted to dispense with parliaments because they would stand in the way of this transformation. The fact that Charles was married to a Catholic French princess, Henrietta Maria, whose attendant clergy celebrated Mass in her Westminster chapel, and that in the later 1630s there was a papal agent, George Con, resident at court actively

7

encouraging conversions to Catholicism, gave credence to the belief in a popish plot. In these circumstances, the king's anti-Calvinism, and the rise to power of the Arminians with the favour accorded to Laud and his allies, were bound to have a crucial impact on both religious and political developments in the 1630s. The Laudian ascendancy in the Church meant the eclipse of Calvinism, a switch of emphasis from preaching to the sacraments and a reverence for ceremony. It brought controversial changes to church interiors and none more so than the conversion of communion tables into railed altars [ch. 1, pp. 39–41]. It was accompanied by efforts to enhance the status and role of the clergy both by restoring their wealth and independence from secular authority, and by securing their promotion to secular office, while at the same time imposing sanctions on laymen who trespassed into the clergy's domain. Fears about property rights were also aroused by clerical hopes that the Church would regain secularised church property. It was authoritarian, meddlesome and vindictive, stressing hierarchy and obedience to superiors in Church and state and seeking to impose a rigid uniformity on a Church purged of dissident elements [ch. 1, pp. 37–9]. Godly ministers and laymen were driven into forging defensive alliances which were to be of crucial importance in radical politics in the early 1640s. A tiny minority of the godly became separatists and some left for New England, but probably most settled for a sullen conformity, seeking solace from surviving godly preachers and praying to God for the deliverance of his Church from popish error. But opposition to Laudianism went much wider than the ranks of the godly, as many people were repelled by its divisiveness and its clerical pretensions and there were anxieties over property. There was no need, therefore, to subscribe to a popish conspiracy thesis to find Laudianism objectionable and, significantly, beyond the bishops, no one was prepared to stand out in its defence in the Long Parliament.

It was Charles's determination not only to impose religious change on England but also to unite all three of his kingdoms in the new orthodoxy that was eventually to spell the end of his personal rule. The British and Irish dimension to the conflict, which had formed an important part of an earlier Whig analysis, has recently been restored to prominence by revisionist and other historians. Charles was in the unique position in seventeenth-century Europe of ruling over three kingdoms all of which had religious divisions and within each of which there were dissidents who preferred the religion of one of the others to their own. The end product of the king's attempts to bring his three kingdoms into religious conformity was armed resistance in all of them with the defence of true religion a main battle-cry. Scotland led the way in 1637 when an attempt to impose a new prayer book on the Scots led to protest and riots in Edinburgh and the subsequent drawing up and circulation for signatures throughout Scotland of a national covenant pledging to defend the Scottish Church against popery and superstition. Scottish pride in their Church as superior to its

English equivalent, and a careful wording of the covenant to conciliate moderate opinion, ensured widespread support. The covenant had wisely avoided an outright attack on episcopacy as potentially divisive but over the following months, faced by an intransigent king, who regarded the covenant as a threat to his authority, the covenanters were gradually turned into a Presbyterian movement. In December 1638 the Glasgow general assembly abolished episcopacy and established a Presbyterian system of government. By this stage, both the covenanters and the king were making preparations for armed conflict.

Both sides sought support outside Scotland and thus events in one kingdom came to have an impact on the others in what has been described as a billiard-ball effect. There had been contacts between opponents of royal policy in Scotland and England perhaps as early as the mid-1630s and the covenanters were able to draw encouragement from the fact that they had friends south of the border. A large amount of covenanter propaganda was printed and circulated in England through godly networks, and intelligence from some senior English sources was to reach the Scots after the outbreak of war. The king had hoped to obtain help against the covenanters from his army in Ireland (largely composed of Catholics) and the Catholic earl of Antrim and his followers in Ulster but it never materialised. Had it done so, it would have encountered strong opposition from Antrim's clan rival in Scotland, the earl of Argyll, as well as Scottish Protestants who had settled in Ulster. There was some potential support for Charles in Scotland but it would have required as yet unacceptable royal concessions before it could be mobilised. Few in England had any enthusiasm for going to war with the Scots and the English army was under strength and ill-prepared for combat. The covenanters also experienced problems in raising an effective army although they did have the great advantage of superior morale. The first bishops' war, therefore, ended in a treaty signed at Berwick on 18 June 1639 before the two armies had joined battle. By this stage lack of trust in the king, and fears that once he had recovered his authority in Scotland he might reverse all the gains the covenanters had made and punish their leaders, led to radical civil demands. A remodelled Scottish parliament, freed from royal control, was to meet regularly to ensure that there would be no return to pre-1638 rule in Scotland. Various measures passed by the Scottish parliament in 1639 and 1640, such as a triennial act (laying down that future parliaments were to meet at least once every three years), anticipated the English parliament's constitutional reforms of 1641. Yet it was not simply a case of the English aping Scottish initiatives for there were generally English precedents too for those measures.

The decision made in December 1639 to renew war against the Scots, and assurances from Wentworth (based on his relatively successful experience with the Irish parliament in 1634) that he could manage an English parliament effectively, persuaded a somewhat sceptical Charles to call a parliament (the Short Parliament of 13 April to 5 May 1640) to raise the money needed to fight the Scots. Elections to this parliament, and its successor the Long Parliament, have been seen as marking the beginning of a changeover from deferentially selecting MPs on the basis of their superior status to the modern notion of choosing them on a partisan basis. Certainly those associated with unpopular royal policies could face a rough ride in these elections and there were probably more godly MPs returned than in previous parliaments. The king's sole concern in summoning the Short Parliament, to gain a vote of supply for a new war against the Scots, clashed with parliament's priority, remedying the grievances that had accumulated over the previous decade or more. In a celebrated speech delivered on 17 April Pym formulated a comprehensive indictment of those grievances, including a Church threatened by popery, and identified a need for frequent parliaments [ch. 1, pp. 51]. Pym was part of a significant minority in parliament who could be described as pro-Scots at this time, and he and his allies were possibly acting in collaboration with the Scots. The abrupt dissolution of parliament was followed by arrests and the searching of homes and studies, no doubt partly in the hope of uncovering some damning evidence of such treachery.

The Scots could take great encouragement from the fact that parliament had refused to finance a fresh war against them and in the future they would insist on the English parliament's involvement in any peace settlement made with the king. The presence of Scottish negotiators in London during the Short Parliament enabled the covenanters to keep in close touch with their English friends, and valuable intelligence and advice continued to reach Scotland. Lacking funds and effective organisation, the second bishops' war (July to September 1640) was a disaster for the English army which retreated after its defeat at Newburn leaving the covenanters free to occupy Northumberland and Durham. On the same day as the battle of Newburn, twelve English peers petitioned the king to summon another parliament [ch. 1, pp. 57–9].

There has been much stress recently in some revisionist writings on the importance of the peerage as a social and political elite and even a suggestion that behind the events leading up to the outbreak of civil war lay an attempted aristocratic coup. Leading Commons figures such as Pym, it is argued, were following the lead of aristocratic patrons such as the earl of Bedford who were ultimately responsible for policy initiatives in the Lower House. Such peers were not so much concerned with enhancing the role of parliament as with achieving a political settlement that would place them in dominant positions around the king. Even after the outbreak of conflict, politics continued to be dominated by rivalries among parliamentarian peers until 1649. This recognition of the peerage as key political players, rather than declining feudal magnates, is a valuable addition to an understanding of the nature of the conflict, but taken too far it over-emphasises the political dependency of other members of the governing elite, and discounts religious and political principles as factors binding peers and their followers to one another.

All but two of the twelve peers who petitioned for a parliament were future parliamentarians. Some of the peers, and Lord Brooke in particular, had become deeply involved with the Scottish covenanters and their collusion with the Scots during the bishops' wars was technically treasonable. It has been argued that awareness that the king knew of this collusion had the effect of binding those peers concerned closer to the Scots as their only hope of protection from a treason trial. Any future political settlement with Charles would also have to have sufficient safeguards to prevent him using this knowledge later to avenge himself on his political opponents.

WHY DID A POLITICAL SETTLEMENT PROVE IMPOSSIBLE?

Charles accepted the advice of his privy council and called a new parliament (the Long Parliament) which convened in November 1640. Most people, including future royalists, welcomed the news that a parliament was to be called, and expectations of what it might achieve ran high. There was a general recognition that many grievances had accumulated over the previous decade or so and that reforms were needed to restore harmony and unity in the kingdom. It was the responsibility of Charles and his parliament to reach a viable settlement and restore political equilibrium. The king began in a relatively isolated position but by the summer of 1641, having made important concessions to his critics, he was beginning to pick up wider political support and by the following summer he was able to put an army on the battlefield. Political eventually gave way to military manoeuvres for a number of reasons, not least of which were Charles's failings as a monarch, the fears aroused by demands for further reforms (and especially those concerned with religion) and, linked to both, the disruptive influence on England of Charles's other two kingdoms. Elections to the new parliament in the autumn of 1640 saw a marked increase in the number of seats being contested (yet it remained the case that most MPs were still returned unopposed) and much more in the way of partisan electioneering. Alongside more traditional local grievances, national issues emerged in these elections with religion and resentment against courtiers coming to the fore. Men who had gained reputations as opponents of unpopular royal policies were more likely to be returned while court-backed candidates faced rejection. Even those of the latter who managed to secure a seat could soon find themselves ejected when the House ordered the expulsion of monopolists and the staging of fresh elections in their constituencies [ch. 2, pp. 60–1]. Most MPs arrived at Westminster determined that there would be no return to the policies of the 1630s and there was a sizeable minority of MPs who were fired with Protestant zealotry. In the House of Lords too there were many peers who

Seating in Parliament

were thoroughly partisan but this fact was obscured behind a tradition of compromise and an illusion of consensus. The number of godly peers was tiny and a programme of radical religious change would never command many votes. An exceptionally long parliament meant that levels of attendance in both Houses could shrink at times, and this was particularly true of 1642 as members left to join the king or simply returned home.

Both Houses were kept aware of the strong feelings in the country by the presentation of mass petitions to parliament. There were well-organised petitions for the root and branch abolition of episcopacy, beginning with the London petition of December 1640 [ch. 2, pp. 61–2]. Other petitions called for the execution of Strafford, constitutional reforms, action against papists (including popish lords), religious reforms to remove Laudian innovations and safeguard Protestantism, the removal of scandalous ministers and action to reverse the decay of trade. However, by late 1641 the Houses were also beginning to receive petitions in favour of episcopacy and the prayer book [ch. 2, pp. 62–5], although they were usually careful to disown Laudianism. In addition, they received a few of the growing number of petitions in 1642 calling for a negotiated settlement, most of which were addressed to the king. Some of the petitions were accompanied by large numbers of supporters when they were presented to parliament, and mass lobbying could occasionally appear threatening and even exert an influence on parliamentary decision-making.

Up to the summer of 1641, there was a large measure of agreement about what needed to be done to restore harmony. There had to be a purge of those 'evil counsellors' responsible for the policies pursued in the 1630s; those measures and institutions that sustained the personal rule had to be dismantled; and there had to be guarantees of regular meetings of parliament in future. The imprisonment of Laud and Strafford pending their trial, and the exile or disgrace of other key councillors, satisfied the first requirement. The declaration of the illegality of ship money and other extra-parliamentary taxes, and the abolition of star chamber, high commission and the other prerogative courts, met the second. The triennial act (requiring a meeting of parliament at least once every three years), the act against the dissolution of the present parliament and the tonnage and poundage act (in effect making the collection of customs duties conditional on regular parliaments) addressed the third. Action and legislation on all this had received the royal assent no matter how reluctantly granted. Even in the much more problematic area of religion there was considerable common ground with general agreement that Laudian innovations and increased clerical authority had to be reversed and steps had to be taken to control popish recusants. On all the above matters agreement and cooperation were to be had from future moderate royalist leaders such as Hyde, Culpepper and Falkland.

In early 1641, there were also moves by the king to make a settlement with the twelve peers who had petitioned for a parliament in 1640 and their associates, the key figures involved being Bedford, Pym and St John. Of seven new privy councillors created by Charles in February, six were from the ranks of the petitioning peers, yet none of them were as yet given any major office of state, and the privy council itself was declining in frequency and influence. Hopes of a settlement being concluded in this way were effectively dashed even before Bedford's sudden death in the following May. After the revelation of the first army plot, plans to exert control over Charles by capturing the major offices of state substituted coercion for persuasion as their means.

From the summer of 1641, serious divisions began to appear among those who had up to now backed the changes and reforms. These centred on three main issues: whether Charles could be trusted to honour these reforms; whether parliament's extension of its powers had grown excessive; and what kind of religious settlement would be acceptable. As previously noted, there is universal agreement that Charles was a disastrous and extremely unpopular king. The Scots had already experienced his duplicity in offering concessions to the covenanters while at the same time preparing for war and there is no doubt that their English friends were fully apprised of this. That Charles could not be trusted, that he conceded reforms under pressure and then sought to recover his authority by force, was a clear lesson that could be drawn from the politics of 1641–2. The two army plots of the spring and summer of 1641 (involving the possible use of the English army remaining in the north to overawe parliament), the 'incident' in Scotland in October 1641 (a conspiracy to seize leading covenanters), the outbreak of rebellion in Ireland later that same month (soon rumoured to have had royal encouragement) and the attempt at the beginning of January 1642 on the 'five members' (an attempted coup against the parliamentary leadership) all fatally undermined confidence in the king and rendered the prospect of a peaceful settlement increasingly unlikely. Yet distrust of Charles and despair of him as a monarch was not so all-pervasive as to convince most contemporaries that he should be stripped of power or even deposed. The remarkable fact remains that he managed to recruit a sufficiently strong following in 1642 to be able to put an army on the battlefield, and an explanation of that is to be found in the remaining two issues.

On 21 April 1641, Strafford's attainder was carried in the Commons by an overwhelming majority of 204 votes to fifty-nine. Yet, on the following 22 November, the grand remonstrance detailing all the grievances of Charles's reign and justifying past and present measures to remedy them, passed the Commons by just eleven votes (159 votes to 148). The king was well on the way to recruiting a 'party' and part of the explanation for this is to be found in the anxieties raised by the further novel measures that the Commons leadership were prepared to adopt and their consequences. The fifty-nine 'Straffordians' included future steadfast royalists but not men such as Falkland and Culpepper who supported the attainder, and opinion in the Lords too

13

was far from synchronising with later political alignments. Animosity towards Strafford in fact stretched from inside the privy council to politicians in all parts of Britain and Ireland. Yet the highly questionable justice of the proceedings against him, and the accompanying mass lobbying by godly Londoners of the Lords and the king, created dilemmas for some defenders of the law and the constitution. The presence of crowds of demonstrators at Westminster also produced some tensions between the Houses over what attitude should be adopted to them, with the Commons taking a conciliatory, and the Lords a condemnatory line [ch. 2, pp. 72–3]. Out of Strafford's attainder and the first army plot (which aimed to rescue him from the Tower) came the Protestation, an oath to be subscribed by all; the dissolution act, a major encroachment on the royal prerogative; and defensive measures which anticipated in some respects the militia ordinance of the following year. Strafford's execution also made the prospects for a settlement with Charles more remote by poisoning relations between the king and his critics, and raising the spectre of the queen suffering a similar fate.

The grand remonstrance, like the Protestation, was a direct encouragement to people at every level to concern themselves with matters of state. Furthermore, the decision to go ahead without the Lords' assent raised constitutional objections and revealed differences between the Houses which Charles could seek to play on. The recent emphasis by some historians on the dominant role of the Lords is difficult to square with a Lower House at this stage taking radical initiatives and dragging a generally reluctant Upper House, still intent on searching for consensus, in its wake. The proposal to print the remonstrance, thereby appealing to the people, was attacked by some MPs as a dangerous novelty and for several weeks it circulated in manuscript until Commons approval of its publication was finally given. The actual debate on the remonstrance had teetered on the brink of violence and it was an issue that two days later brought a thousand pro-remonstrance apprentices down to Westminster. Events on the streets of the capital were shortly to confirm the worst fears of those who warned against drawing the people into Westminster politics. The mass demonstrations and confrontations that marked the last weeks of 1641 and January 1642 were accompanied by far from groundless suspicions of collusion between godly MPs and like-minded Londoners, and the possible orchestration of demonstrations from within the House.

There is general agreement among historians that it was religion that proved the most intractable problem in 1640–2 and that strongly held religious positions were to be one of the central determinants of party allegiance in the civil war. The British dimension is also crucial within this context. There were few people prepared to defend Laudianism; there was no need to subscribe to the full popish conspiracy thesis to find it offensive as a divisive, meddlesome and clericalist movement. A return to the Church of Elizabeth I and James I would probably have satisfied most people but the problem remained that the Laudian faction had gained ascendancy in the Church with the favour of its head, Charles I, a king with as deeply-held religious convictions as any godly Englishman. The main radical solution on offer was to follow the Scottish example and adopt a Presbyterian system of Church government and complete the unfinished work of religious reformation in the Church of England. Naturally this was the course favoured by Scottish covenanters who for the first six months of the Long Parliament had great political leverage. The Scots had concluded that a durable settlement in Scotland, including the vital protection of their Church from future attempts at Anglicisation, depended on bringing the English Church into conformity with the Scottish Church. With an army occupying north-east England, and treaty commissioners accompanied by some Scottish divines enjoying direct contact with godly allies in London, the Scots wielded considerable influence which they used to back a campaign for the root and branch abolition of episcopacy.

How extensive opposition to the government of the Church by bishops had become by 1640 is open to debate among historians. What is much clearer is that by the end of 1640, with strong encouragement from the Scots in London, there was an active and well-organised root and branch movement in the capital [ch. 2, pp. 61–2] which was to draw support from other parts of England during 1641. It is equally clear that there was a strong body of opinion in the capital and nation opposed to root and branch, and positively in favour of a Church governed by bishops, and by 1642 it had moved very much onto the offensive [ch. 2, pp. 62–5]. Freed from external pressures, and especially from the Scots, most members of both Houses would probably have settled for some form of reformed episcopacy, with greatly reduced powers, which would have prevented any future royal moves to change worship and belief.

Presbyterianism as such had few principled supporters in parliament and there was considerable resentment at any prospect of the Scots dictating an English religious settlement, as their own recent history should have made the Scots only too aware. Those members of both Houses who eventually came round to supporting root and branch did so for mainly political reasons, to maintain the essential support of their Scottish allies and to keep control of the Church out of Charles's hands. This did not prevent some of them from sharing with others general anxieties about the clericalism of the Scottish Church. A majority of the Commons, on an average attendance, could just about be found for root and branch and a bill passed the House in the summer of 1641. However, it was never presented to the Lords where there was no prospect whatsoever of it being passed. The votes of no more than a dozen or so lay peers could have been enlisted for the bill and the bishops were certain to vote against it en bloc. An earlier attempt to exclude bishops from the Lords had foundered in a House that was not prepared to allow its membership, including bishops and popish lords, to be decided by

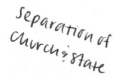
Separation of
Church & State

15

outsiders. Only in a House marked by high absenteeism in early 1642 did a bishops' exclusion bill pass the Lords and even then a root and branch bill, if one had been introduced, would almost certainly never have gained a majority. By this stage, county petitions had been received in favour of bishops and the prayer book [ch. 2, pp. 62–5] and future royalists were rallying to the defence of their traditional Church.

The whole debate over Church government had much wider secular implications, linking religion to constitutional, political and social issues, and these have to be recalled when claiming that it was 'religion' that provides the key to the conflict. Royal authority and political patronage were at stake in any attack on Charles's governorship of the Church, and his ability to appoint bishops and other key clergy. The end of bishops would complete the secularisation of the House of Lords with possible ramifications for its place in the constitution. Relations between the Houses became strained when divergent views about religious changes opened up between them. Root and branch, bishops' exclusion and the question of how far should reformation at the parish level be encouraged all led to tensions between the Houses arising from different opinions and priorities. Fundamental changes to the Church's structure would, on past experience, lead to further confiscations of its property creating opportunities for some and major problems for others. The mass demonstrations at Westminster against bishops and popish lords, with frightened bishops at their height abandoning their seats in the Lords, greatly added to other concerns about constitutional propriety and the maintenance of order. When London artisans and apprentices could freely abuse bishops social deference and hierarchy were clearly under threat.

WHAT DETERMINED ALLEGIANCE IN THE CIVIL WAR?

One influential trend in recent writings on the civil war has been to emphasise the reluctance of most people to be drawn into the conflict. Up to the very outbreak of hostilities, it is argued, there were major efforts in England to avoid war but these were all stymied by the determination of militant minorities (usually fired by religious enthusiasm) to confront one another. There were, therefore, committed royalists and parliamentarians, reluctant combatants drawn along by party enthusiasts, neutrals who tried to avoid commitment and side-changers who moved between parties.

There would have been no civil war without the creation of a party around the king and it is allegiance to the royalist party that first requires explanation. The royalist party was not principally composed of defenders of arbitrary royal government and long-established ministers and servants of the crown. Crucial to the formation of a viable party was the support of political moderates, such as Culpepper, Hyde and Falkland, who revered the ancient constitution and defended the rule of law with as much enthusiasm as their parliamentarian counterparts. They had been among the principal critics of the abuses of the personal rule and the ministers responsible, and had supported the Long Parliament's initial reform programme. They believed in regular parliaments, taxation by consent and the abolition of prerogative courts. They were consistently maintaining their commitment to the rule of law when they later opposed parliament's innovatory measures, especially legislation by ordinance without the king's consent.

Most of these same royalists also believed in a Church governed by bishops, the form of worship laid down in the book of common prayer and the Church's traditional festivals and rituals, and they strongly resented the Scottish and other pressures towards further reformation. They shared in the general belief that popish recusants needed to be controlled but did not subscribe to the frightening scenario of England about to fall victim to a popish conspiracy unless urgent action were taken. They were arguably more alarmed by the emergence of sectaries, lay preaching and religious radicalism in general. While not defenders of a Laudian Church, some of the excesses that accompanied the removal of Laudian innovations from churches [ch. 3, pp. 88–9] confirmed them in their opposition to further religious change. By the summer of 1642 a considerable body of royalists were prepared to fight and die for their traditional national Church.

How far social and economic factors shaped party allegiance is a much more contentious question which revisionist historians tend to treat dismissively. It is true that there has been no convincing class-conflict analysis of the rival parties. Peers, gentry, merchants and the middle and lower ranks of society can be found in significant numbers, and with equivalent degrees of commitment, on both sides. However, local studies have concluded that, away from the south-east and eastern England, a much higher proportion of the landowning elite of peers and gentry became royalists than parliamentarians. In London too the elite ranks of the wealthy and traditionally powerful were especially fertile territory for royalism, although the party also had definite popular roots as well, and the same pattern may obtain in other cities and large towns. An attempt to relate party allegiance to agricultural regions (with royalism the pattern in settled arable regions and parliamentarianism in wood-pasture areas) has been only partially successful, with the obvious objection that the royalism of northern England and Wales fails to conform to this model. There is much more force in the argument that a 'moral panic' triggered by the fear of popular unrest and disorder, and a growing belief that traditional authority and privilege were being undermined, led large numbers of the elite to rally to the king as a symbol of order and orthodoxy. A marked increase in the number of agrarian riots in the early 1640s [ch. 3, pp. 92–4], large-scale demonstrations in the capital and popular pressures on parliament, disturbances in churches as Laudian innovations were reversed [ch. 3, pp. 87–9], attacks on well-born papists and malignants by their social inferiors [ch. 3, pp. 94–5], subversive pamphlets and sermons as censorship collapsed, and the activities of sectaries [ch. 3, pp. 90–1, 96–8] all combined to convince some royalists, understandably but mistakenly, that their world was about to be turned upside-down.

Most parliamentarians in 1642 were not supporters of a party that was intent on wresting power from the king and vesting it in parliament. They still hoped for an eventual political settlement that would retain all the essential features of the ancient constitution, including a crucial role for the monarchy. As yet no principled defence of resistance to a monarch who would not agree to such a settlement had been developed. Parliamentarians prepared to fight their king hiding behind the fiction that they were engaged in self-defence against royalist aggression (for which 'evil counsellors' rather than the king himself were responsible) or, in the doctrine of the king's two bodies, that they were upholding the authority of the king while fighting against his person.

However, the most dynamic element in parliamentarianism was the belief of some, yet by no means all, that they were engaged in a religious crusade to rescue England from popery and complete the work of reformation in the Church. Those who were most militant and energetic in their parliamentarianism were those who were most obsessed by the fear of popery and ready to share in Pym's belief that they were engaged in a struggle against a popish conspiracy with roots stretching into the court itself. They were highly susceptible to rumours of popish plots and the Irish rebellion confirmed their worst fears [ch. 3, pp. 79–84]. At the same time, and as part of a strategy to avoid a popish victory, they were also committed to godly reformation, to not only cleanse the Church of Laudianism but guarantee its Protestantism for all time through fundamental changes. Hence the godly network became a mainstay of the parliamentarian party, rallying personal and material support from like-minded individuals whenever it was needed. Ultimately, therefore, those responsible for the civil war were the religious militants on both sides, the godly parliamentarians and the 'Anglican' royalists.

Socially the parliamentarians, it has been argued, probably attracted more gentry of middle to lesser rank than the royalists, as well as more members of the professions (other than churchmen) and merchants, craftsmen, artisans and yeomen farmers. Independent small property-owners and inhabitants of industrial districts, such as the Derbyshire lead miners, appear to have been especially, but never exclusively, drawn towards parliamentarianism. Towns and cities have also been identified as places tending to give the parliamentarians much greater support. Gaining control of London was absolutely vital for parliament's war effort and this was accomplished by a slight shift in the social basis of City politics which brought to positions of power some men who, in normal times, would not have enjoyed it. London's shopkeepers, professionals and artisans, and especially those inspired by godly convictions, provided much of the local backbone for parliament's cause.

Furthermore, there is some evidence to support the view that there is a connection between militant parliamentarianism among London merchants and an interest in westward colonial expansion, encompassing North America and the West Indies and taking in Ireland too.

So far as rural society is concerned, at no stage did parliamentarian leaders seek to capitalise on rural unrest in the early 1640s to recruit a following among enclosure rioters and other aggrieved peasants. They may have been more prepared to listen to complaints about enclosures initially but their attitude to the riots themselves was always ambivalent, and eventually they were to come down on the side of the enclosers. Parliamentarian gentry may have been less prone to exaggerating the seriousness of this popular unrest than their royalist counterparts. They may perhaps have recognised it for what it was, a series of opportunistic attempts to right particular grievances rather than the start of a social revolution, or have been more afraid of papists and cavaliers than popular unrest. Some of the enclosure rioters themselves who fought in parliament's army may have been attracted less by an attachment to parliamentarianism as such than by dislike of royalist enclosers and the hope that it would lead to the recovery of their common lands [ch. 3, pp. 94].

Considerable emphasis has been placed by a number of historians on the extent of neutralism in 1642 as England reluctantly edged towards civil war. It is argued that localism, the attachment to local communities and giving local concerns priority over national ones, provided the basis for this neutralism. Resistance to the descent into war was very strong but, once it became likely, a particular locality might take steps to ensure that it was kept war-free by negotiating neutrality agreements between potential combatants [ch. 3, pp. 101–2]. And if they failed, individuals might try to keep out of the conflict themselves. However, very few were principled neutrals and even neutrals had party preferences when forced to decide between them. Occasionally neutrality negotiations were a tactical move by one side to gain time for a planned offensive while, in some parts of the country, if maintaining local peace was the priority it might best be served by joining the dominant side.

As has been argued, there was a large area of common ground between the parties on most issues, with the notable exception of religion in the case of militant party activists. Changing sides, therefore, was not such a radical step when perceptions of where the respective parties stood on key matters, or calculations of how best to serve personal ambitions, changed. Thus the initially parliamentarian fifth earl of Bedford and the initially royalist Sir Edward Dering [ch. 3, pp. 102–4] changed sides twice. Peers and gentry were in the position to make choices between parties, and change their minds subsequently if they so wished, but the same is not generally true at the lower end of the social spectrum. Both sides pressed men into service in their armies, extracted contributions and in many other ways dominated the lives of the inhabitants in the parts of the country they controlled. Large numbers of people probably found themselves becoming involuntary royalists and involuntary parliamentarians. This is not to argue that no one below the ranks of the governing elite ever made an informed choice between the sides and gave their chosen party sincere commitment. Some undoubtedly did so, especially those who either shared godly concerns or, on the contrary, found godly reformation repellent, and there are examples of side-changers at this social level too. But many more hated the conflict, came to loathe both parties and yearned for a return to normality.

WHAT IMPACT DID THE WAR HAVE?

Both sides raised armies and organised for a war that was far longer, and much more costly, than anticipated. The material and human costs of the war were exceptionally high and there was an accompanying proliferation of committees and their personnel to marshal all available resources. Reluctance to engage in armed conflict still remained strong and in the initial stages there were pressures in favour of an early agreement and return to peace. In those areas under parliamentarian control godly reformation could at last be implemented and the Scots finally achieved their goal of an official English adoption of Presbyterian church government and worship as the price of Scottish military assistance for the parliamentarians in the war. Control of parliament's fighting forces eventually fell into the hands of men prepared to defeat the royalist army outright, rather than use them to force the king to the negotiating table, with the creation of the New Model Army. But before that army could finally defeat the king, war-weariness in the countryside manifested itself in armed uprisings of clubmen determined to prevent further incursions into their localities by the armies of either side.

Both sides adopted similar methods to raise money for their armies. The initial loans and theoretically voluntary contributions soon gave way to regular weekly contributions based on individual assessments of property or income. Those refusing or neglecting to pay faced the distraint and sale of their goods, with military assistance where necessary, to meet their assessments [ch. 4, pp. 105–7]. A new and unpopular tax, the excise or sales tax on basic commodities, was introduced by the parliamentarians and subsequently copied by the royalists. Each side also sequestered opponents' estates allowing most of them to be recovered on payment of a substantial fine or 'composition'. The parliamentarians' administration of all these financial levies was more efficient and hence much heavier than that of the royalists. Nevertheless, the country as a whole bore an unprecedented financial burden. Other material costs included arms, provisions and accommodation for troops, and an almost insatiable demand for horses for the cavalry. The armies of both sides plundered [ch. 4, pp. 111–12] and exacted free quarters for its troops when driven by necessity, although the parliamentarians made

both sides weve drained

20

much more successful efforts to limit such abuses. The war disrupted trade as markets were cut off, trade embargoes with enemy territory were implemented, ships lay idle, there was a shortage of money and shops closed as tradesmen and apprentices went to war [ch. 4, pp. 126]. Yet for those who made articles of war or could provide provisions for armies there were profits to be had in the war years.

The human costs of war were similarly heavy. Estimates of the number of deaths in England and Wales as a direct result of war range from tens of thousands to closer to a hundred thousand. Added to which, it has been claimed that more soldiers died of war-related diseases than war itself. In percentage terms, the numbers of deaths in Scotland, and in Ireland especially, greatly exceeded those of England and Wales. Ireland's long war had the exceptional brutality of a conflict shaped by religion and culture, linked to a struggle for land and dominance, in which the stakes could not have been higher [ch. 4, pp. 123–5]. This picture contrasts with the experience in England and Wales where there were remarkably few atrocities and torture and rape were rare.

In England and Wales, personal liberty was an early casualty of the conflict as identified enemies and those refusing contributions to the war effort were imprisoned. After London had run out of space for its royalist prisoners, ships on the Thames were notoriously used to house them. Both sides conscripted foot soldiers, usually from the lower levels of society, who served without party commitment and with the greatest reluctance [ch. 4, pp. 113–14]. Consequently, there were continuous desertions and a chronic shortage of foot soldiers, a particularly severe problem for royalist forces but one also experienced by the opposing side.

For both sides the war effort meant a plethora of committees, committeemen and their agents stretching from the headquarters of their respective parties to the localities. These committees possessed intimidatory powers and could call on military support if required. The men who served on parliamentarian committees, or acted as their agents, in London and elsewhere were sometimes newly risen bureaucrats of lesser social rank and militant leanings. County committees came into conflict with more traditional wielders of local power [ch. 4, pp. 115–16] and there were problems too in relations between civil and military leaders. The powers and responsibilities of committees increased from the original function of providing for an army to include tax raising powers and, in parliament's case, the enforcing of religious reformation. Serving these committees were new agents including assessors and collectors of levies, excisemen, and sequestrators of enemy estates and (for parliamentarians) Church livings. The money, goods and estates which came into the hands of committees and their agents inevitably led to accusations of corruption which were sometimes well-founded [ch. 4, pp. 115, 117–18], but what is probably more noteworthy is the large numbers of bureaucrats who appear to have resisted temptation and

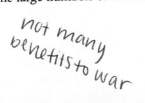
not many benefits to war

21

performed their duties conscientiously. This did not prevent the committees and their agents from becoming intensely unpopular. By 1646 parliament's committee for advance of money had become so hated in London that it was identified as one of the City's greatest grievances.

The urge towards peace and a negotiated end to conflict between the parties remained strong even after the outbreak of hostilities. A formidable peace campaign in London drew on a wide spectrum of support in 1642–3, from royalist sympathisers to the politically uncommitted who longed for a return to normality. Mass petitions to parliament were organised [ch. 4, pp. 118–19] and demonstrators lobbied at Westminster where they were accorded much more brutal official disapproval than the petitioners and demonstrators of 1641–2. Sharp divisions between the Houses over peace terms emerged in the summer of 1643 with the Lords backing a generous settlement with the king. By that stage, the new burdens and oppressions of a civil war, and the unsettling work of godly reformation, were being keenly felt and some public opinion was being accordingly transformed [ch. 4, pp. 119–21].

While the official stance of both sides was to search for a peaceful settlement, party leaders were working for an extension of the conflict by enlisting support from Charles's other two kingdoms. Charles concluded peace terms with the Irish at Kilkenny and by March 1644 large numbers of Irish troops had arrived in England and Wales to assist the king. Around the same time, the parliamentarians secured even more substantial military assistance from Scotland. Scottish intervention came at a price – the imposition of a religious uniformity modelled on the Scottish Church on England. The eventual outcome of negotiations between parliamentarian leaders and the Scots was the concession of a civil league (the military alliance with the Scots desired by the English) combined with a religious covenant (a pledge to secure religious unity insisted on by the Scots). The resultant 'solemn league and covenant' was to be sworn in both England and Scotland [ch. 4, pp. 128–31] and Scottish representatives were sent down to London to attend the Westminster assembly which had been convened to plan the future shape of the English Church. The Scots allied with their English supporters were to press for the adoption of a fully Presbyterian form of Church government, creed and liturgy.

English supporters of godly reformation had already been active in preparing the way for a fully reformed Church. The parish clergy were being systemically purged to remove not only religious dissidents from the new regime but political dissidents too [ch. 4, pp. 127]. By the end of the process, more than a quarter of the clergy had been ejected from their livings. Churches, cathedrals and medieval monuments with religious associations were being subjected to large-scale iconoclasm in areas of the country under parliamentarian control. Statues, inscriptions, stained glass and even the very crosses on church steeples experienced the iconoclast's hammer and chisel [ch. 4, pp. 127–8]. Organs were dismantled, fonts redesigned and relocated, and vestments and surplices dispensed with. Most of these changes were accomplished in an orderly fashion under the supervision of local officials and few dared protest at them.

It is generally agreed, however, that the attempt to impose a new Presbyterian order on the English Church was a dismal failure. The political will at the centre was lacking because parliament's preferences were Erastian, that is they were determined to keep ultimate control of the Church in their own (lay) hands. There was a lack of clerical personnel, there was no effective machinery of enforcement and there was little popular support for Presbyterianism. The new liturgy, the directory, was gravely defective and the insistence on a rigid vetting of communicants was resented. Only in London, Lancashire and Essex was anything approaching a full Presbyterian order established but its operation and survival was heavily dependent on the enthusiasm of individual ministers and leading laymen. Furthermore, the attempt to impose a coercive and comprehensive national Church, determined to suppress all religious dissent, exposed a major fault line running through the ranks of the godly. An influential godly minority, the Independents (or Congregationalists as they would later be known), believed in a non-coercive national Church in which each parish would be free to choose its own minister and exercise discipline over its congregation. Presbyterian hostility to these former godly allies led the Independents to ally with sectaries, members of gathered churches who would have no truck with a national Church, in a struggle to obtain religious toleration. Not only was the new Presbyterian order undermined by Independents and sectaries, supporters of a traditional 'Anglican' Church in some parishes also resisted its imposition.

Independents and sectaries were to find crucial allies in parliament's reorganised fighting force, the New Model Army. By autumn 1644 there was great dissatisfaction with the army leadership and a belief that they were not intent on defeating the king. The solution was to amalgamate the three existing armies to create the New Model Army which was purged of its old aristocratic leadership, provided with new officers and given more generous financial backing than parliament's previous armies. The new army developed a distinctive religious character which contributed greatly to its effectiveness as a fighting force. Four of its five generals, a high proportion of the lower ranking officers, and many of the rank and file shared in a godly religious fervour. Its troops gathered for frequent sermons from its chaplains, bible study was actively encouraged, days of fasting and humiliation became part of army routine and a harsh code of moral discipline was imposed on all [ch. 4, pp. 132–3]. Those who enthusiastically embraced this religious culture saw themselves as instruments of divine providence, and some believed that they were engaged in a fight against Antichrist to prepare the way for the second coming of Jesus Christ. The result was high morale, great courage in the face of the enemy and greater assurance than usual that God was directing his saints. However, there was a very wide distinction in this army between the horse and the foot. A high proportion of the latter were conscripts with little if any sense of commitment to the parliamentarian cause. They were drawn from the lowest ranks of society and like most pressed men were often ready to desert. They included former royalist soldiers as well as former clubmen attracted by regular pay.

Even a relatively well financed army such as the New Model Army would take free quarter and supplies when the need arose, although individual soldiers were punished harshly if they took from civilians without paying. By the latter stages of the conflict war-weariness was widespread and it manifested itself in some war-ravaged regions of England and Wales in the clubmen risings of 1645–6. The clubmen, as some historians have stressed, were the biggest mass movement of the entire period, dwarfing the better known later Leveller and Digger movements. By their very nature, they were not a homogeneous movement but they were essentially peasant movements with generally common concerns about the need to protect traditional rights and values in Church and state, and keep their local communities free from the depredations of armies [ch. 4, pp. 133–5]. There is some dispute among historians as to whether the clubmen were essentially armed neutrals intent on peace or whether some of them had hidden party leanings.

WHY WAS IT NOT POSSIBLE TO CONCLUDE A SETTLEMENT WITH THE KING AFTER THE WAR AND WHY DID REVOLUTION BECOME AN ALTERNATIVE POSSIBILITY?

It could be argued that a settlement with Charles proved impossible after the war for the simple reason that the king had no intention of concluding one, except on his own terms, thus making Charles's character once again of central significance. Certainly, the king's duplicity knew no bounds as he cynically tried to play on the divisions of his opponents and the second civil war fits into the well-established pattern of Charles attempting to gain by physical force what had been denied him by the political route. Yet if the victorious parliamentarians had not been divided among themselves, and there had not been divisions too among former covenanters in Scotland, Charles would have had no political scope for intrigue and no prospect of a counter-revolutionary restoration to power. Furthermore, the New Model Army soon became a key political player, insisting on having an input into any settlement made with the king, and was exposed to radical influences in the form of the Leveller movement which, for the first time, opened up the possibility of revolution.

By the time of the king's defeat in the first civil war, there is little doubt that the overwhelming urge in England was to return as swiftly as possible to normality. People longed to see an end to heavy taxation, the perceived tyranny of committees and their agents, and the great burden of an army that was no longer needed in England but might usefully be deployed in Ireland. During the last year or so of the civil war, political divisions had opened up in parliamentarian ranks. On the one hand, there were those labelled 'Presbyterians', the generally conservative followers of Essex who wanted a negotiated settlement with the king, were opposed to religious toleration, and were becoming increasingly alarmed at evidence of radicalism present in some parts of the New Model Army. These political Presbyterians also attracted support from the war-weary and disillusioned who yearned for peace. On the other hand, there were the Independents, those generally more susceptible to radical influences who pushed for an outright defeat of the royalists, favoured a loosely structured and non-coercive national Church and were committed supporters of the New Model Army. Political Independents drew a strong following from sectaries, anxious to secure religious toleration as the prospect loomed of a coercive Presbyterian Church, and from many of those determined that any future constitutional and political settlement made with the king should have sufficient safeguards to protect the freedoms that had been fought for. It is from the radical wing of Independency that the Leveller party was eventually to emerge.

It is important to note that, although religious labels have been applied to these two parties by some contemporaries and many historians since, it cannot always be assumed that the religious and political labels neatly match. Most religious Presbyterians probably supported political Presbyterianism and it is inherently unlikely, as turkeys voting for an early Christmas, that any religious Independents were political Presbyterians. Yet many, if not most, supporters of political Presbyterianism probably backed an exclusive Presbyterian Church because that was the only Church that was on offer which would provide the stability they craved rather than because of any deep-rooted Presbyterian convictions. A full-blooded Presbyterianism, under clerical control of the kind advocated by the Scots and their English clerical allies, probably appealed to only a limited number of political Presbyterians, most of whom were perhaps content enough with the lay-controlled Presbyterian Church that eventually emerged. Although all religious Independents were almost certainly political Independents too, that party also drew support from some prominent religious Presbyterians. Moreover, most leading political Independents could probably have lived with a lay-controlled Presbyterian Church provided that it tolerated godly diversity. This explains why some of them were to be found acting as elders and triers within the new Presbyterian order.

Explaining the politics of 1645–8 in 'party' terms can also be misleading. Consistent supporters of either party in the House of Commons, and probably in the governing body of the City of London too, were very much in the minority, while most MPs could be described as unaligned members voting for one or the other party as they judged appropriate. However, the strength of feeling in favour of reducing the heavy tax burden and reaching a swift settlement with the king, which could only be achieved by disbanding large numbers of the New Model Army, normally provided political Presbyterianism with a majority of support at Westminster and in the City. On a wider level, it might also acquire a temporary following among ever-hopeful royalists and exasperated neutrals. The Independent party, on the other hand, suffered from being too closely identified with the interests of the New Model Army, and ultimately came to rely on that army for protection and support. At the same time, some of its more radical supporters in London were denounced for endangering the peace process by such seditious gestures as attacking the king and even questioning the actual necessity for kingship.

Tensions between the parties, and a determination to neutralise the New Model Army, eventually led to a Presbyterian attempt to mount a counter-revolution in the capital in the summer of 1647. Political campaigning in the City of London in late 1646 had resulted in the election of a neo-royalist lord mayor and had further reduced the numbers of the beleaguered Independent minority on its governing body. The key Presbyterian objective was to gain control of all the capital's military resources and the Tower of London and then institute a thorough purge, replacing political enemies with friends. This was achieved in the summer of 1647 by the City resuming control over membership of its militia committee and extending City authority over the suburban militias as well. Furthermore, there were plenty of unemployed soldiers in the capital from the recently disbanded western brigade to join the militias in creating an alternative military force that could be used to face down the New Model if it refused to disband. There were moves too to engage forces in the north of England and possibly bring in Scottish military assistance. Yet the whole plan collapsed in the face of a united New Model Army that stood its ground and eventually occupied London after both Houses had been invaded and dictated to by a Presbyterian crowd on 26 July [ch. 5, pp. 142–3]. The precise nature and extent of the politicisation of the New Model Army has excited controversy among historians. Revisionists stress the soldiers' preoccupation with mate-rial and professional matters, such as arrears of pay, indemnity and conscription, and question the degree of tension existing between senior officers and the ranks, and the level of army support for the Levellers. The Leveller leaders themselves, it is argued, were extremely ambivalent about the army and there were similar reservations within the army about the Leveller programme. Doubt is even expressed as to whether the army repre-sentatives (the 'agitators') chosen in the spring of 1647 were actually elected by the ranks rather than being coopted by the officers. Given a sensitive handling of the army's grievances, no major problems would have arisen and there would have been no spectre of an imminent social revolution.

The New Model's most recent authority, however, has convincingly challenged much of this revisionist analysis. One surprising find is how well the army was paid in the months leading up to its becoming politically active, hence greatly reducing the significance of pay arrears in understanding the army's role in the upheavals of 1647. The army began its transformation into a revolutionary force because of the belief that parliament was out to divide and destroy it, and because of the deep resentment felt at attacks on its self-esteem by an ungrateful nation. The peculiar religious character of significant parts of the army, and the way it provided receptive territory for radical ideas and practices, largely shaped that transformation.

The immediate trigger of events was parliament's attempt to start disbanding the New Model, beginning with the foot which would be either recruited for Ireland or disbanded. At the same time, an attempt to replace Sir Thomas Fairfax as commander-in-chief with a Presbyterian officer failed in the Commons by only twelve votes. The following months saw the election of agitators by the rank and file of most regiments (possibly under officer supervision), the securing of the king's person by the army before its enemies could do so (almost certainly with the agreement of senior officers), a general rendezvous of the army at Newmarket, where it entered into a solemn engagement not to disband until its grievances had been redressed, and the formation of the General Council of the Army. The General Council was composed of two officers and two soldiers from the ranks from each regiment as well as the general staff, and thus had a guaranteed officer majority, yet at this stage there was a general harmony of purpose within the army. The machinations of the Presbyterians in parliament and the capital in the summer brought pressures from the agitators for a march on London and, partly to forestall that, the senior officers, after consultations with some radical peers, produced their own scheme for a political settlement known as the Heads of the Proposals. The latter were both the most radical and most generous terms that the king was to be offered but this did not prevent Charles from treating the army's negotiating team with rudeness bordering on contempt. Meanwhile, the invasion of the Houses on 26 July had led parliamentary Independents to flee to the army for protection and, shortly afterwards, it was the turn of Presbyterian leaders to flee as the army marched on London to return Independents to their seats at Westminster and occupied the capital [ch. 5, pp. 143–8]. By that stage, the Levellers were beginning to exert a sizeable influence on the army and its political direction.

The Leveller movement owed its original existence to the determination of a relatively few articulate and energetic spokesmen to champion the cause of freedom of conscience and draw especially on support from members of gathered churches, ranging from Independents to General Baptists. Freedom of conscience was always a core belief for the Levellers and much of their constitutional and political programme was designed to safeguard that freedom. Another core Leveller belief was that government derived its legitimacy from the people and that, with the king defeated and his regime discredited, power had devolved back upon the people who were now free to agree a fresh social contract placing themselves under a new and superior form of government. Practical Christianity, stressing the religious obligation to help the needy and vulnerable, was a further strong influence on Leveller thought. Despite the label applied to them by alarmed opponents, they were not aiming to level men's estates, still less to undermine private property. On the contrary, they put a premium on the ownership of property for the freedom it gave and wanted a society free of privilege, monopoly and restriction in which every man would have the opportunity to acquire property. The Leveller ideal, therefore, was of a property-owning democracy of free-born Englishmen enjoying freedom of conscience, equality for all before the law and other basic inalienable rights. They would be regularly engaged in returning MPs to frequent parliaments, in which they might occasionally serve themselves, and those parliaments would be free of any veto by king or Lords. They would also participate in elections for city and other local authorities and dutifully serve their turn in office. The connection linking great wealth with power and privilege would be broken and conditions created in which an increasing number of independent small property-owners would flourish.

Modern assessments of the Levellers and their historical significance point out that it was primarily an urban-based movement with a social and economic programme largely geared to urban concerns and that it failed to make any real impact in the countryside. Insufficient attention was paid to major agrarian problems such as enclosure and insecurity of land tenure in a society that was overwhelmingly rural. The Levellers' economic ideas have been described as deeply regressive, an attempt to turn back the clock to a world of independent small producers and block the development of an industrialised economy. There was also nothing in their programme for women. The Levellers were taking on virtually all the most entrenched and powerful vested interests, who could be expected to fight back, yet they never contemplated using violence to achieve their ends, settling instead for a strategy of 'moral force' rather than 'physical force'. Moreover, it is easy to exaggerate the numerical strength of the Levellers and their supporters, and their ability to influence events. They could draw on the support of thousands for some of their petitions and demonstrations and they did produce an impressive volume and novel quality of published material. But 1647 was the year of the Levellers' opportunity to deliver their programme by recruiting support in the New Model Army; the attempt failed and the opportunity never reoccurred.

Leveller attempts to dominate the army's political agenda met with some initial success. In September and October 1647 new representatives or agents, who were more radical and Leveller-inclined than the agitators chosen in the spring, emerged in about a dozen regiments. Some doubt has been expressed as to whether these new agents were actually elected as representatives by the ranks. Certainly they did not displace the existing agitators, and never gained recognition from the General Council of the Army, yet there are indications that some at least were mandated representatives. From some of these new agents and their Leveller friends came a long document, *The case of the army truly stated*, which crucially combined army grievances with the Levellers' constitutional programme. This document, along with the Levellers' blueprint for a new constitution, the 'Agreement of the people' [ch. 5, pp. 148–50], was tabled for discussion at a meeting of the General Council at Putney commencing on 28 October to which the Leveller leader, John Wildman, and another radical civilian had been invited. It was the question of the franchise in the first article of the Agreement that came to dominate discussion at Putney, with Commissary-General Henry Ireton attacking its implied advocacy of manhood suffrage. Ireton insisted that the franchise be restricted to property-owners and independent tradesmen, as was currently the case, and warned that manhood suffrage would result in the abolition of property. Colonel Thomas Rainsborough was the only senior officer to speak with the radicals at Putney and his motives may have been more personal than politically principled. Yet the debates demonstrated the remarkable extent to which the General Council was being won over to Leveller ideas and it was a recognition of this that prompted Cromwell, who was chairing the debates, and Ireton, his son-in-law, to bring them to a close and move to re-establish control over the army [ch. 5, pp. 150–7].

The crucial test of the senior officers' resolve to restore discipline and unity in the ranks came on 15 November at Corkbush Field near Ware in Hertfordshire [ch. 5, pp. 157–9]. This was the first of three rendezvous called by the officers instead of the general rendezvous the Levellers were hoping for to rally mass support for the Agreement. Whether an actual Leveller-inspired mutiny occurred in Corkbush Field has been disputed but the weight of evidence appears to confirm that that is what happened. Yet it was a somewhat limited, uncoordinated and uncertain kind of mutiny with Rainsborough failing to provide the vital leadership that was needed and civilian Levellers lurking in the shadows. Fairfax and Cromwell had little difficulty in restoring their authority and one of the 'ringleaders' was immediately executed before the regiment. There were no such problems at the other two rendezvous held very shortly afterwards. During the early months of 1648, nearly a half of the army were disbanded with senior officers taking the opportunity to purge the ranks of known radicals. At the same time, most regiments were being paid in full. The relatively brief period in which there was a real possibility that the New Model Army might become the vehicle for a Leveller-inspired revolution was finally over.

While these events were unfolding in the army, the king escaped from army custody to the Isle of Wight and royalist plotting commenced for a new war. An 'engagement' was concluded with the Scots whereby Charles agreed to confirm the covenant and introduce Presbyterianism in England for three years, in return for which Scottish military assistance was promised against the English parliament. There were also moves, ultimately unsuccessful ones, to enlist assistance from Ireland as well. At the same time, the royalists planned to capitalise on the widespread hostility felt in England and Wales at the continuing heavy taxation, free quarter, the intrusive county committees and central dictation from Westminster. The summer of 1648 witnessed a series of localised uprisings in England and Wales, a revolt of some of the fleet and an invasion by a Scottish army. A royalist counter-revolution in the capital was probably only prevented by the continuing fidelity of Philip Skippon as commander of its militia. The war lasted for only a few months until the New Model Army once again defeated parliament's foes.

WHY DID THE REVOLUTION TAKE THE FORM IT DID?

In the mid-winter of 1648–49 the New Model Army once again entered London, purged parliament of the majority of its members who still wished to negotiate a settlement with the king, secured a vote in favour of setting up a court to try the king and presided over Charles's execution. A political revolution took place in which the institution of monarchy was abolished along with the House of Lords, and England became in effect, if not in name, a republic. A large measure of freedom of conscience was conceded and the legal obligation to attend the parish church was removed. Nevertheless, the political revolution was not accompanied by a social and economic revolution in England. Any hope of progress in that direction was doomed to disappointment as the army's senior officers and their civilian supporters brought the revolution to a halt and dealt ruthlessly with opponents. Many of the godly had become sadly disillusioned by this stage but those who ardently believed that Christ's second coming was imminent could still prepare optimistically for God's transformation of the world. A tiny minority of men, on the other hand, believed that God was calling for the transformation of the world now by human action and began establishing communes organised on the basis of social and economic equality. Meanwhile, a social revolution of a temporary nature in Scotland, and of a permanent nature in Ireland, was brought about by direct English intervention.

Many officers and soldiers in the New Model Army probably believed that God had brought them victory in the first civil war, and had done so again in the second, and this was a belief shared by many of the army's civilian supporters too. In refusing to recognise God's judgement in the first war, so the reasoning went, the king had committed an outrage against God and, in Old Testament terms, had become a 'man of blood' who had once again shed the blood of his saints. God now cried out for judgement on this king and it was the army's duty, as his chosen instrument, to bring Charles to justice. The army leadership, Cromwell included, appear to have come to this conclusion at a prayer meeting held in Windsor Castle as the second civil war was beginning [ch. 6, pp. 167–8]. Yet following through the logic of such a conviction, Charles's trial and execution, was not easy and even at a very late stage army leaders were prepared to send negotiators to the king.

The vital impetus for the trial and execution of the king came from army leaders and a small minority of members of parliament. Perhaps as many as 90 per cent of MPs were opposed to this course of action and certainly a comfortable majority of them were intent on continuing the search for a political settlement with Charles towards the end of 1648. Faced with this situation, the army's options were a forcible dissolution or a purge of the parliament, and its parliamentary allies persuaded it to settle for a purge. In rapid succession, the army once again occupied the capital, a small committee of officers and MPs drew up a list of eighty or ninety MPs for arrest and, on 6 December, troops under the command of Colonel Thomas Pride stationed on all approaches to both Houses arrested over forty MPs as they came to take their seats [ch. 6, pp. 168–9]. Many more MPs stayed away that day or were prevented from entering the chamber or withdrew in protest. As a result, about three-fifths of MPs were removed leaving only fifty or sixty MPs in the House. After lengthy secret discussions with senior officers, those MPs voted for the setting up of a high court of justice to try the king on the charge of treason and levying war against his people. When the Lords rejected this measure, the Commons passed a series of resolutions declaring themselves the supreme representative of the people and law-maker, and proceeded to pass the measure as an act. Charles's trial was in effect a show-trial whose outcome had been predetermined and his legally sound refusal to recognise the court advertised the fact. Only fifty-nine regicides signed the king's death warrant although another ten were present and assented when sentence was given. The execution of the king had been made possible by a military coup and show-trial probably supported by no more than a tiny minority of the political nation.

The removal of the king and the sidelining of the House of Lords was followed by the early abolition of both institutions. Yet the new regime was reluctant to call itself a 'republic', with all its possible radical associations, and settled instead for the more familiar description of a 'commonwealth', a term expressing the idea of a whole nation dedicated to the pursuit of the welfare of all [ch. 6, pp. 169–72]. There has been a tendency to emphasise the conservative nature of England's political revolution. It has been argued that action was taken to prevent further radical change being imposed on the country by radicals such as the Levellers. The retention of the 'rump' of a purged Commons to draft the constitutional changes was symptomatic of the conservative need felt to legitimise those changes through familiar

King Charles = Crucial

31

forms. Few of those who enjoyed power after 1649 wanted to follow the path to further change. Apart from the experiment with a Nominated Assembly, the dominant trend was in a conservative, restorative direction, with the possibility of Cromwell becoming king and the return to a bicameral legis-lature natural outcomes. Only in the religious sphere, with the end of compulsory church attendance and a large measure of religious toleration, was further radical ferment possible for a minority of the nation.

The main prospect of a revolution that would have combined radical constitutional changes with fundamental shifts in the relationship between political, social and economic power lay with the Levellers. Yet how close the Levellers came to decisively influencing events in 1648–9, or whether in reality they were a spent force after 1647, is open to debate. Certainly in the autumn of 1648 Ireton, with Cromwell's backing, began making friendly approaches towards the Levellers while the latter in turn felt it expedient to highlight the army's main grievances in the petition of 11 September. Both joint and separate Leveller and officer consultations on a possible constitu-tional settlement resulted in a second Leveller Agreement (with important concessions to conservative opinion on the franchise) and an officers' Agreement. Leveller influences also manifested themselves again among the soldiers, who were falling seriously behind with their pay in the second half of 1648, and there was a reappearance of agitators in two regiments. However, past experiences had made Lilburne extremely distrustful of the army; he and other Levellers (there was no unanimity on this) opposed the whole idea of trying the king until agreement had been reached on the constitution and a new representative assembly had been chosen. In retrospect, Lilburne and others were to see the whole sequence of events from Pride's purge onwards as a subterfuge to exchange one kind of tyranny for another, thereby locking Englishmen in 'new chains'. Vitriolic Leveller attacks on senior army officers eventually led to the imprisonment of Lilburne and three other leading Levellers in March 1649 on a charge of treason. Yet although there were demonstrations in the capital calling for their release, civilian support for the Levellers was very much on the wane. Many of the gathered Church members, in particular, who had supported the Leveller movement when it was championing religious toleration deserted it, and even turned on it with hostility, once toleration had been conceded by the new regime.

The biggest immediate challenge to the new regime, however, came from developments within the army after a fresh attempt had been made to send troops over to Ireland. In May soldiers in three regiments in southern England mutinied, freed themselves of their officers and began marching across country hoping that other men would join them. Historians differ as to whether or not these troops were Leveller-inspired. The mutineers made no public reference to the third and final Agreement of 1 May 1649 and Lilburne not only denied any involvement with them but attacked them for not declaring for the Agreement and trying to negotiate with Fairfax. On

*freedom
searchers*

the other hand, they had probably been influenced by Leveller activity in the ranks over the previous weeks and their defeat at Burford [ch. 6, pp. 173–4] was celebrated as the end of a Leveller conspiracy. The mutinies of 1649 ironically proved the reliability of the vast majority of the army who were prepared to crush the mutinies and execute mutineers. If the Levellers had been a serious potential threat to the new regime before the mutinies, they were certainly no longer one after them.

For those inspired by millenarian expectations, the political revolution was open to another interpretation. Fifth Monarchists believed that recent events pointed to the imminent second coming of Jesus Christ and his thousand-year rule over his saints on earth. The execution of King Charles had made way for King Jesus and it was up to the godly to peacefully prepare for this transformation which would be brought about by divine intervention. There preparations involved placing power in the hands of the godly thus making the Fifth Monarchists essentially an elitist movement [ch. 6, pp. 174–6]. However, it had distinctly subversive characteristics not least of which was the belief that the godly were drawn from all social ranks and their future society would be egalitarian. Their advocacy of law reforms, the abolition of tithes, lower rents, relief for the poor and the end of monopolies and feudal tenures meant that they shared much common ground with the Levellers. They also appealed to the same social strata of small traders, artisans and apprentices, and drew support largely from towns and the army.

A religiously inspired vision of a non-elitist and strictly egalitarian kind led the Diggers to set up experiments in communal living on St George's Hill, in Surrey, and in approximately nine other locations, mainly in the home counties and midlands. The Diggers advocated the collective cultivation of waste or common lands thereby returning the earth to its original purpose before the Fall as a common treasury for mankind. For them the rise of private property, and the resultant division into rich and poor, was the entry of sin into the world and the basis on which tyranny and oppression had been structured ever since [ch. 6, pp. 176–80]. Whereas the Levellers were largely an urban-based movement aimed at men of modest economic independence, the Diggers addressed the great mass of the rural poor, cottagers and landless labourers. Violence played no part in their strategy; the property of the rich was not to be attacked directly and expropriated (such a call would have brought the Diggers' immediate suppression) but they were to be persuaded by example to divest themselves of their wealth. The Diggers never developed a mass following, attracting at the most a few hundred followers, whereas Leveller supporters at their peak were numbered in their thousands. Their programme ran directly counter to an established tradition of seeking to protect common rights, and brought the Diggers into conflict not only with local landowners and clergy but the very poor whose cause they espoused. Digger communities were constantly harassed and by the summer of 1650 they had all been abandoned. Their actual impact on

*Diggers
vs
Levellers*

contemporaries had been minimal and it is perhaps more in the realm of the history of ideas that their lasting significance is to be measured.

Although the English revolution developed no further than the political phase, the same is not true for Scotland and Ireland, both of which experienced a social revolution too. Scotland was forcibly brought into union with England and exchanged its legislative independence for a token representation at Westminster. The power of the Scottish nobility was systematically undermined by massive forfeitures of land, the granting of security of tenure on easily manageable terms to all tenants and the abolition of all the feudal relationships. Nevertheless, the social revolution in Scotland did not survive the Restoration which restored the Scottish elite to their earlier dominance. There was to be no such reversal in the case of Ireland. After the reconquest of Ireland at huge expense in 1649–52, large numbers of Catholic landowners were transplanted to the western province of Connacht, and starvation and plague brought on by the scorched-earth policy of the English army cleared great swathes of Ireland of its population. Over half of the land of Ireland was transferred into the hands of English settlers, composed of those who had invested in the reconquest and soldiers and civilian creditors of the army who had been paid in Irish land. A permanent basis was laid for a Protestant ascendancy in Ireland based on the vanquishing of its traditional native Irish and old English elites, and the economic, social and political dominance of a new class of largely English Protestant settlers.

1

THE COLLAPSE OF
CHARLES I'S GOVERNMENT

SHIP MONEY

Thomas Knyvett on Hampden's ship money case, 1637

Thomas Knyvett (1596–1658), a Norfolk squire who was often in London
attending to legal matters, held a regular correspondence with his wife in
which he frequently commented on public affairs of the day. In this letter he
shows how much interest was aroused by John Hampden's legal challenge to
ship money. A cultured man of later moderate royalist inclinations, he had
unsuccessfully tried to attend a session of the trial which took place in a
packed courtroom.
Source: Thomas Knyvett of Ashwellthorpe, Norfolk, to his wife, 11 November
1637, *The Knyvett Letters, 1620–44*, ed. B. Schofield (London, 1949), p. 91.

The business now talked on in town is all about the question of the ship
money. The king is pleased to give way to those subjects that refuses to pay,
whereof Mr John Hampden is one, to have their counsel to argue the case in
point of law in the exchequer chamber before all the judges, and Mr St John
hath already argued for the subject very boldly and bravely. Yesterday was the
first on the king's part. I cannot relate any particulars because I heard it not.
Although I was up by peep of the day to that purpose, I was so far from getting
into the room that I could not get near the door by 2 or 3 yards, the crowd was
so great. . . .

Resistance to payment in Middlesex, 1639

By 1639, with contributions also being levied for payment of the army to meet
the Scots, resistance to the payment of ship money had become widespread.
Sheriffs were charged with the duty of raising ship money and those refusing
to pay faced the distraint of goods up to the value of their assessment. This
official record of resistance to distraints in Harrow and surrounding parishes
in Middlesex indicates the strength of the defiance to the levy.
Source: Public Record Office (PRO), state papers, domestic 16/427/19.

4 August 1639

Middlesex. Robert Markes, clerk to the undersheriff of Middlesex, and William Caninge, a bailiff, being authorised by warrant from the high sheriff of the county of Middlesex for the levying of money arrears for his majesty's service of shipping within the parish of Harrow upon the Hill and other parishes within the hundred of Gore were much abused in the execution of their office by several persons in many particulars as calling them thieves, rogues, assaulting them, throwing scalding water upon them, rescuing distresses taken, threatening suits against them in case they brought not the distresses to them back again and saying that they came progging and prowling up and down the country to cheat them by whose examples many men are encouraged to oppose the said service; many affirming they are to be borne out by some particular persons though they oppose.

The names of such [as] were most obstinate against the service being distrained;

Distress taken. Mrs Miller of Pinner being distrained and a piece of cloth now in custody; more was brought to them by one Mr Hatch. She would question them for felony.

Distress was taken. Robert Wayland of Pinner being distrained for ship money his servant rescued the distress; whose name the officers could not enquire yet know him again if they see him.

Distress Rescue. John Edlyn of Pinner Marsh being distrained and a horse in custody: the said William Caninge, the bailiff, was much beaten by the servant of the said Edlyn and the horse rescued away: Edlyn having had notice to pay the money the night before yet refused and bade them take their course.

Distress was taken free. Richard Owen being demanded the money charged upon him refused to pay, and then opposed the bailiff, William Caninge, in distraining; threatening them and saying he would try a suit therein.

Distress. The wife of John Bugberd of Stanmore Parva did shut the door against the bailiff and hurt one of them.

Distress. The wife of Thomas Russell of Stanmore Parva did call the officers rogues and railed upon them saying they came to prog and prowl the country.

A Distress. The wife of George Platt of Hendon did assault Robert Markes with a knife drawn and had undoubtedly hurt him had he not run back, a distress being taken.

John Norwood of Stanmore, gentleman, and a freeholder in Middlesex being assessed refused to pay alleging he hath made over his goods before the assessment, yet resideth in his house; the officers being fearful to distrain.

Robert Markes and William Caninge do believe and in some places have discovered that the women and servants were instigated by their husbands and masters and sent by them.

All the persons aforesaid being distrained the said officers were threatened if they brought not the distress back again to them and many threaten the collectors for keeping the distresses.

When the inhabitants there do perceive that any come to distrain they forthwith shut the doors against them and they or their servants cry thieves at which the other neighbours take notice and shut their doors.

There hath been about forty distre~
most of them refusing ~~   ~~without distresses saying they can but pay at last and that there is no for it.

> Robert Markes
> the mark of William Caninge

LAUDIANISM

A survey of nonconformity in London, 1637

The 1637 visitation of the London diocese exposed several ministers who were still not entirely conformable to the Laudian Church in matters such as wearing surplices when conducting worship, performing the whole of the set liturgy and requiring communicants to kneel at the rails to receive the sacrament. The ministers concerned were quickly forced to come into line or face suspension and ultimately be deprived of their livings. Not all communion tables had yet been converted into altars but the process was to be completed by the end of the decade. There was concern also about factious prayers and the need to ensure that churches were respected as holy places and not used for secular purposes.
Source: PRO, state papers, domestic 16/371/39 information of divers abuses in the City of London, [November 6?] 1637.

That divers curates have subcurates (and those scarce licensed) by which themselves avoid the practise of conformity.
[*Margin*]: lecturer of St Margaret's, Fish Street, Mr Simpson, Mr Hughes, etc.
That some preachers take great liberty to pray before and after sermons,

loosely and factiously, as for the conversion of the queen, for a neighbour minister in persecution, etc.

[*Margin*]: Mr Walker of St John the Evangelist,[1] Mr Burton's curate, etc. St Matthew's, Friday Street.[2]

[*Interlined*]: Mr Fountaine Mr Burton's curate is faulty.

That the companies[3] when they are to dine with the lord mayor or sheriffs, used to meet at some neighbouring churches, there to put on and off their gowns and cloaks.

That the wards on St Thomas his day[4] in many parishes meet in the church to make their outcries and brabbles about the choice of their officers, notwithstanding some order given by my lord treasurer[5] to the contrary.

That the pews in churches are so made that men do as much sit as kneel at prayers, which by taking away the lower ledge on which the knees do rest would be well remedied.

That boys put on their hats in sermon time which in their masters' shops they do not at any time.

That the sacrament of baptism is generally administered not after the 2nd lesson but after the sermon in the afternoon.

That the holy communion is given to many in their pews (and those so made in some churches that those who are in them cannot receive it on their knees) and that in some churches where there is a decent rail to come to.

[*Margin*]: Blackfriars

That priests and people suffer many inconveniences for want of an appointed hour for funerals.

St Stephen's, Coleman Street. Mr Goodwin[6] upon Easter day last gave the communion to divers strangers sitting.
Testis Hicks apparitor.[7]

Allhallows by the Wall. Mr Genoa (on the 3rd and 4th Sundays in May last) read prayers in a cloak.

Allhallows Staining. Mr Byfield (on the 4 Sunday in May) had prayers read without surplice, without litany, commandments, epistle or gospel.

St Martin's, Ironmonger Lane. Mr Simmonds on the last Sunday in May had no surplice worn nor litany read. At the repairing of his church a new gallery is set up, and the communion table pent up with pews about it.

Christ Church. Mr Finch hath a lecture in his church on Sunday mornings (to which they come from all parts) which is maintained by collections at the church door, one crying, pray remember the minister.

At Mercer's chapel. Prayers were read in a cloak, and ended after the first lesson on Shrove Sunday last, and on February 26 without a surplice, and the prayers for king, queen, etc. omitted, and lessons read out of a bible of the old translation.

[*Margin*]: Mr Cowdal

The sermons (out of Lent) are of late erection and draw many people to them which therefore leave their own churches thin and naked.

We have enquired after Mr Lawson of Allhallows, Bread Street, and find his church one of my lord grace his peculiars which come not to this visitation.

Mr Palmer, vicar of St Bride's in Fleet Street, at morning prayer at 7 of the clock doth often omit the prayer for the right reverend fathers the bishops and the rest of the clergy. And he reads divine service at that hour sometimes without the surplice in his gown, and sometimes without either surplice or gown in his cloak.

Many of the parish clerks in London do complain that albeit his majesty hath been graciously pleased in their late charter to grant them power to receive and gather their clerks' wages or duties themselves and to prohibit all others upon pain of his high displeasure, yet many of them are opposed and not suffered so to do.

There are many communion tables in several churches of the City of London that are not railed in, and some of them are placed in the middle of the chancel when as they may be placed more conveniently at the east end thereof.

[Endorsed]: Information of divers abuses in the City of London.

An official record of factionalism in a London parish, c. 1640

Laudian-inspired changes to the interiors of churches in the 1630s could divide parishioners into rival factions. Allhallows Barking followed the example of other London churches by 'beautifying' its church and converting its communion table into an altar. These changes were made with the general approval of the parish elite but they brought protests to the bishop of London from local zealots. Dr Ducke, the bishop's chancellor, was sent into the parish to restore harmony and had managed to find a compromise solution by 1640. However, after the convening of the Long Parliament, some militants were to saw the wooden angels off the church's altar rails and carry them before the Commons as an example of popish innovations. The vicar, Edward Layfield, a nephew of Archbishop Laud's, was also to be denounced for ceremonialism by the same faction and eventually to be removed from the living. This passage details the earlier efforts of Dr Ducke to arrive at a peaceful settlement in the parish.
Source: Greater London Record Office, consistory court of London DL/C/344, ff. 68–9 vicar-general's book.

18 January 1640 Order for the taking down of pictures over the font in the church of Allhallows Barking London.

Whereas some of the parishioners of the parish of Allhallows Barking London lately exhibited a petition unto the right honourable and right reverend father in God William [Juxon] lord bishop of London setting forth that of late years the said parish church hath been repaired and beautified and a new font erected and the communion table placed and railed about according to the laws, canons and customs of the Church of England and that over the font is set or placed certain carved images, the picture of the Holy Ghost, and a cross. And that also the communion table is removed out of its ancient and accustomed place, and certain images placed on the rail that standeth round about it, which images they desire may be taken down, and the communion table set in the place where it formerly stood. And whereas the said lord bishop of London being employed in his majesty's weighty affairs referred the consideration of the said petition unto the right worshipful Arthur Ducke, Doctor of the Laws, his chancellor[8], who for the due examination of the complaint made in the petition repaired to the said parish church and viewed it in the particulars complained of calling to him the right worshipful Edward Layfield, Doctor in Divinity, vicar of the said church, some of the vestrymen together with some of the complainants, but could not at that time settle and reconcile the differences between them concerning the said things complained of and afterwards at several times the said parties with others both of the vestry and of the complainants meeting before him he treated with them to agree this business and to reduce the parish to peace and after divers meetings finding the difference to continue the said Mr chancellor sent for the greater part of the vestry and a sufficient number of the complainants and upon examination found most of the vestry approved and liked of all the particulars complained of in the said petition, and the complainants held and retained their dislike of all the said particulars according to the tenor and effect of the petition but at that time before their departure some of the vestry for and in the name of the parish and some of the complainants of the more moderate of them proposed by way of mediation that some of the things complained of might be removed and some continue as they are viz. that the pictures over the canopy of the font and also the pictures on the rails about the communion table might be removed, which proposition they hoped (as they then said) would give contentment to all sides and procure the peace and quiet of the whole parish, upon the hearing of which overture or proposal the said Mr chancellor then ordered that Dr Layfield should appoint a vestry meeting to be held the next day, and against that time the vestrymen should make enquiry of the opinions of the parishioners, and that some of the principal complainants should in the meantime enquire the opinions of the rest of their party and complainants and that in the said vestry meeting declaration by both parties should be made what their desires or opinions were respectively concerning the proposed mediation aforesaid, and it was then further ordered that the said meeting ended the same day both parties should repair to him and declare whether both sides would yield to the way of accord and moderation proposed by themselves as aforesaid. After this meeting appointed as aforesaid on the day of the date of this order appeared personally before the said Mr chancellor the said Dr Layfield, the greatest part of the vestrymen and a sufficient number of complainants and divers other parishioners, of whom the said chancellor required or demanded what they had agreed on in the last vestry and what the opinion of the parishioners on both sides was concerning the proposal made at their last meeting before him, to which some of the vestry on the behalf of the parishioners of that party and the complainants on the behalf and in the name of the parishioners complainants of their party made reply, that it was agreed and consented on both sides that the pictures over the canopy and the pictures round about the rails of the communion table should be taken down and did now again express and declare their joint consent and willingness thereunto, and made it their humble suit to Mr chancellor to interpose his order and decree accordingly, and on both sides submitted to his sentence and determination therein and promised they would rest satisfied and abide by his order and on both sides they further declared that this being done as then desired they would be quiet and not further pursue the other complaints mentioned in the petition. Whereupon Mr chancellor well weighing the premises and being studious to preserve and continue the peace and quiet of the parish ordered and decreed that all the said pictures about and on the canopy of the said font should be taken down and that the pictures upon the rail of the communion table should likewise be taken down and that in the four corners of the said canopy in the room or place where the said pictures at the corners stood should be set up in wainscot[9] work either globes or pilasters[10] or some other work for ornament as by workmen skilful in that art shall be advised, which order being declared both parties willingly submitted thereunto and promised to rest quiet and contented therewith and also not further to prosecute the other complaints recited in the petition, in fine the said chancellor [ad]monished the churchwardens then present to see this said order put in execution together with the advice of the said Dr Layfield and some of the principal of the vestrymen and to certify of the performance thereof before the feast of the annunciation of our blessed lady the Virgin[11] next coming. . . .

A printed sheet of verse against bishops, 1639

Despite theoretically tight controls in the 1630s, some subversive literature was printed on illicit underground presses or was smuggled in from continental Europe. These lines of satirical verse about bishops, which were apparently circulating around the eastern boundaries of the City of London, were a foretaste of the deluge of anti-episcopal propaganda that followed the collapse of censorship after 1640. The part played by Laudian bishops in implementing religious changes and silencing opposition had earned them widespread resentment, and the writer takes pleasure in the fact that arrogant, popish prelates have been humbled by the Scots and hopes that the English will shortly follow their example.
Source: PRO, state papers, domestic 16/538/140.

O yes, o yes, I do cry, the bishops' bridles will you buy

Since bishops first began to ride

in state, so near the crown,
they have been aye puffed up with pride,
and rode with great renown:
but GOD hath pulled these prelates down,
in spite of Spain and pope;
so shall their next eclipse be soon
in England seen I hope . . .

Since they their horse and harness sold,
come buy their bridles here,
that afterwards it may be told,
who bought their riding-gear.
For this hath been a fatal year,
for prelates in this part,
then let these Romish rogues retire,
and seek some other art . . .

But now brave England be thou bent,
to banish all that brood,
and make your Lambeth lad repent,
that never yet did good;
but shamefully hath sought the blood
of sakeless[12] saints of GOD,
relieve your Lincoln[13], better loved,
and set him safe abroad.

And as for Ireland's odious name,
that hath endured so long,
their tyranny shall end with shame,
albeit their state be strong;
for GOD will sure revenge their wrong,
their villany so vile,
the heaven hath heard their sorrowing song,
and sighing all this while.

So let the devil go bishop them,
as he hath done before,
for never man shall worship them
in any kingdom more:
for Scotland that they crossed so sore,
shall now with gladness sing,
and bless him did our state restore,
that was our gracious king.

[Endorsed]: Ellis Rothwell servant to Sir Bevis Thelwall received this from

John Naylor, a tailor in the Minories[14], and the said Naylor received it from Nathaniel Deacon a Hackney man in Goodman's yard in the Minories.

Archbishop Laud's account of the attack on Lambeth Palace, 1640

William Laud (1573–1645) had become a special target of hatred by 1640 when he shared the blame for the dissolution of the Short Parliament. These extracts from his diary records the attack on Lambeth Palace by hundreds of Londoners on 11 May and the riotous rescue from Southwark prisons a few days later of suspects awaiting trial for the Lambeth attack. Forewarned of the rioters' approach, Laud had in fact left by river for Whitehall. The riots were subsequently classified as rebellious and one of those convicted suffered a traitor's death.
Source: 'The history of the troubles and trial of . . . William Laud', *The Works of the Most Reverend Father in God, William Laud*, ed. J. Bliss, 4 vols (Oxford, 1853) iii, 234–6.

May 9 and 11 [1640]. Saturday, a paper posted upon the Old Exchange[15], animating prentices to sack my house upon the Monday following, early . . .

May 11. Monday night, at midnight my house at Lambeth was beset with 500 of these rascal routers. I had notice, and strengthened the house as well as I could; and God be thanked, I had no harm; they continued there full two hours. Since I have fortified my house as well as I can; and hope all may be safe. But yet libels are continually set up in all places of note in the city.

May 11. My deliverance was great; God make me thankful for it.

May 21. Thursday, one of the chief being taken, was condemned at Southwark, and hanged and quartered on Saturday morning following (May 23).

May 15. But before this, some of these mutinous people came in the day-time, and brake the White Lion Prison, and let loose their fellows, both out of that prison and the King's Bench, and the other prisoners also out of the White Lion . . .

Comment on Laud and the Lambeth attack by a Berkshire husbandman, 1640

The attack on Lambeth Palace and Laud's alleged popery became principal topics of conversation in London and adjacent counties. Francis Windebank, as secretary of state, would have been expected to gather any seditious comments, rumours or reports for possible action by the privy council. This record of the interrogation of a Berkshire husbandman by a local JP illustrates

Figure 1 The attack on Lambeth Palace, 11 May 1640

the way in which news and rumours about what was happening in the capital could travel across the country.
Source: information provided by John Fettiplace to Secretary Windebank, PRO, state papers, domestic 16/461/46II.

Examination of William Horne of South Fawley [Berkshire], husbandman, taken before John Fettiplace, esquire, one of his majesty's justices of the peace for this county the 26th day of July anno domini 1640.

This examinant saith that he never saw Thomas Webb [a clothier from Devizes, Wiltshire] before the five and twentieth day of this instant July and that as he was going from Kingstone [Bagpuize], he overtook him that day some half a mile from Wantage, and bid him good even, and then the said Thomas Webb asked him when there came any soldiers that way, who answered that none came of late that way, but some came the last week by Hungerford. Then this examinant asked the said Thomas Webb what price wool was at in their country, who answered that it was worth 18s. or 19s. a tod: and that if this world did hold he thought it would come to a mark. And then this examinant asked Thomas Webb what news was in their country and he answered none. And then the said Thomas Webb asked this examinant what news was in their country, and he answered that he had heard that the apprentices did rise in London and would have destroyed the bishop. And further this examinant being asked, whether that he did not tell the said Thomas Webb that it would be a pitiful time, saith that he spake no such thing unto him. And further this examinant being asked whether he did not tell Thomas Webb, that

Bishop Laud was the cause of the raising of all this army and that the king was ruled by him: he answered that he told him no such thing. And further this examinant being demanded by Thomas Webb what bishop, Bishop Laud was, answered that he thought he was lord of Canterbury. And further this examinant saith that being demanded by Thomas Webb what the reason was why the apprentices did rise in London, answered that there was a noise in the country that it was thought it was because my lord of Canterbury was turned papist. And further this examinant saith that he never said that it was well known that my lord was a papist, and further saith not.

William Horne

SCOTLAND

Walter Balcanquall, A large declaration, *1639*

The Edinburgh prayer book riots of 23 July 1637 were well-organised demonstrations, disguised as spontaneous eruptions, against the new form of service. The week's notice given that the prayer book would be used in Edinburgh gave its opponents time to prepare protests. The most spectacular riot was in St Giles's in the presence of privy councillors, bishops, judges and civic dignitaries. A Scottish divine, Walter Balcanquall (1586?–1645), dean of Durham and steadfast royalist, wrote this account of the riots, which was published in the king's name.
Source: W. Balcanquall, *A large declaration concerning the late tumults in Scotland, from their first originals* (London, 1639), pp. 23–5.

On the twenty third day of July 1637, being Sunday, according to the public warning given the Sunday before, the service book was begun to be read in Edinburgh in Saint Giles's church, commonly called the great church; where were present (as usually they are) many of our council, both the archbishops and divers other bishops, the lords of the sessions, the magistrates of Edinburgh, and a very great auditory of all sorts of people. Amongst this great multitude there appeared no sign of trouble: but, no sooner was the book opened by the dean of Edinburgh, but a number of the meaner sort, who used to keep places for the better sort, most of them women, with clapping of their hands, cursings, and outcries, raised such a barbarous hubbub in that sacred place, that not any one could either hear or be heard: the bishop of Edinburgh, who was to preach, stepped into the pulpit, which is immediately above the place where the dean was to read, intending to appease the tumult, by putting them in mind that the place, in which they were, was holy ground, and by entreating them to desist from that fearful and horrible profanation of it: but he was entertained with as much irreverence as the dean, and with more violence; in so much, that if a stool, aimed to be thrown at him, had not by the

45

providence of God been diverted by the hand of one present, the life of that reverend bishop, in that holy place, and in the pulpit, had been endangered, if not lost: the archbishop of Saint Andrews lord chancellor, and divers others offering to appease the multitude, were entertained with such bitter curses and imprecations, as they not being able to prevail with the people, the provost, bailiffs, and divers others of the council of that city were forced to come down from the gallery in which they do usually sit, and with much ado, in a very great tumult and confusion, thrust out of the church these disorderly people, making fast the church doors: after all which, the dean devoutly read service, assisted by our councillors, bishops, and many other persons of quality there present: yet the outcries, rapping at the church doors, throwing of stones at the church windows by the tumultuous multitude without, was so great as the bailiffs of the city were once more put to forsake their places, and use their best endeavours for the appeasing of the rage and fury of those who were without. Service being ended, the bishop preached, after which the congregation was dismissed: the bishop of Edinburgh retiring himself to a lodging distant not many places from the church, was so environed with a multitude of the meaner sort of people, cursing and crowding him, that he was near being trod to death; and in all probability had been so, if he had not recovered the stairs of his lodging, which he no sooner began to go up, but he was so pulled by the sleeve of his gown by some of that rude rout, that he had like to have tumbled backward down the stairs, to the endangering of his life, yet with much ado getting up the stairs he found the door, at which he should have entered, shut against him, and so being put to a stand, he had certainly been oppressed with the press and violence of that rabble, if the earl of Wemyss from his next lodging, seeing the bishop's life in danger, had not sent his servants to rescue him, who got the bishop almost breathless into his lodging . . .

The Scottish national covenant, 1638

The national covenant was in response to the king's threat to treat organised resistance to his religious policy in Scotland as treasonable. It was drafted by Alexander Henderson and Archibald Johnston of Wariston with advice from several ministers and revised by three leading opposition figures. Its starting point is a renewal of the confession of faith signed by James VI in 1581, which upheld true religion and opposed popery and superstition. Concessions were made in the wording of the covenant to satisfy moderate opinion and there is no outright condemnation of episcopacy. It attracted mass subscriptions in most parts of Scotland and bound its signatories to each other as well as to God in mutual support of each other.
Source: J. Rushworth, *Historical Collections*, 8 vols, (London, 1721), ii, 734–41.

The confession of faith of the Kirk of Scotland, subscribed at first by the king's majesty and his household in the year of God 1580; thereafter by persons of all ranks in the year 1581, by ordinance of the lords of the secret council, and acts of the general assembly; subscribed again by all sorts of persons, in the year 1590, by a new ordinance of council, at the desire of the general assembly; with a general band[16] for maintenance of the true religion, and the king's person, and now subscribed in the year 1638, by us noblemen, barons, gentlemen, burgesses, ministers, and commons under subscribing; together with our resolution and promises for the causes after specified, to maintain the said true religion, and the king's majesty, according to the confession aforesaid, and acts of parliament; the tenure whereof here followeth.

We all, and every one of us under written, do protest, that after long and due examination of our own consciences in matters of true and false religion, are now thoroughly resolved of the truth, by the word and spirit of God; and therefore we believe . . . that this only is the true Christian faith and religion, pleasing God, and bringing salvation to man, which now is by the mercy of God revealed to the world by the preaching of the blessed evangel.[17] And received, believed, and defended by many and sundry notable kirks and realms, but chiefly by the Kirk of Scotland, the king's majesty, and three estates of this realm, as God's eternal truth, and only ground of our salvation; as more particularly is expressed in the confession of our faith, established and publicly confirmed by sundry acts of parliament; and now of a long time hath been openly professed by the king's majesty, and whole body of this realm, both in burgh and land . . . and therefore we abhor and detest all contrary religion and doctrine, but chiefly all kinds of papistry in general and particular heads, even as they are now damned and confuted by the Word of God, and

Figure 2 The Edinburgh prayer book riots of 23 July 1637

Kirk of Scotland. But in special, we detest and refute the usurped authority of that Roman Antichrist upon the scriptures of God, upon the kirk, the civil magistrate and consciences of men. . . . And seeing that many are stirred up by Satan, and that Roman Antichrist, to promise, swear, subscribe, and for a time use the holy sacraments in the kirk, deceitfully against their own consciences, minding thereby, first under the external cloak of religion, to corrupt and subvert secretly God's true religion within the kirk; and afterwards, when time may serve, to become open enemies and persecuters of the same, under vain hope of the pope's dispensation, devised against the Word of God, to his great confusion, and their double condemnation in the day of the Lord Jesus.

We are therefore willing to take away all suspicion of hypocrisy, and of such double dealing with God and his kirk, protest and call the searcher of all hearts for witness, that our minds and hearts do fully agree with this our confession, promise, oath, and subscription: so that we are not moved for any worldly respect, but are persuaded only in our consciences, through the knowledge and love of God's true religion, printed in our hearts by the Holy Spirit, as we shall answer to him in the day when the secrets of all hearts shall be disclosed. And because we perceive that the quietness and stability of our religion and kirk doth depend upon the safety and good behaviour of the king's majesty, as upon a comfortable instrument of God's mercy granted to this country for the maintenance of his kirk, and ministration of justice among us, we protest and promise with our hearts under the same oath, hand-writ, and pains, that we shall defend his person and authority, with our goods, bodies, and lives, in the defence of Christ his evangel, liberties of our country, ministration of justice, and punishment of iniquity, against all enemies within this realm, or without, as we desire our God to be a strong and merciful defender to us in the day of our death, and coming of our Lord Jesus Christ; to whom, with the Father and the Holy Spirit, be all honour and glory eternally.

. . . And therefore for the preservation of the said true religion, laws and liberties of this kingdom, it is statute . . . that all kings and princes at their coronation and reception of their princely authority, shall make their faithful promise by their solemn oath in the presence of the Eternal God, that during the whole time of their lives they shall serve the same Eternal God to the utmost of their power, according as he hath required in his most holy Word, contained in the old and new testaments, and according to the same Word shall maintain the true religion of Christ Jesus, the preaching of his holy Word, the due and right ministration of the sacraments now received and preached within this realm (according to the confession of faith immediately preceding); and shall abolish and gain-stand all false religion contrary to the same; and shall rule the people committed to their charge according to the will and commandment of God revealed in his foresaid Word, and according to the lowable laws and constitutions received in this realm, no ways repugnant to the said will of the Eternal God; and shall procure, to the utmost of their power, to the kirk of God, and whole Christian people, true and perfect peace in all time coming: and that they shall be careful to root out of their empire, all heretics and enemies to the true worship of God, who shall be convicted by the true kirk of God of the foresaid crimes. Which was also observed by his majesty at his coronation in Edinburgh 1638, as may be seen in the order of the coronation.

In obedience to the commands of God, conform to the practice of the godly in former times, and according to the laudable example of our worthy and religious progenitors, and of many yet living amongst us, which was warranted also by act of council, commanding a general band to be made and subscribed by his majesty's subjects of all ranks, for two causes: one was, for defending the true religion, as it was then reformed . . . which had been for many years with a blessing from heaven preached and professed in this kirk and kingdom, as God's undoubted truth, grounded only upon his written Word: the other cause was for maintaining the king's majesty, his person and estate; the true worship of God and the king's authority being so straightly joined, as that they had the same friends and common enemies, and did stand and fall together. And finally being convinced in our minds, and confessing with our mouths, that the present and succeeding generations in this land are bound to keep the foresaid national oath and subscription inviolable,

We noblemen, barons, gentlemen, burgesses, ministers, and commons under subscribing . . . do hereby profess, and before God, his angels, and world solemnly declare, that with our whole hearts we agree and resolve all the days of our life constantly to adhere unto, and to defend the foresaid true religion, and forbearing the practice of all innovations already introduced in the matters of the worship of God, or approbation of the corruptions of the public government of the kirk, or civil places and powers of kirkmen, till they be tried and allowed in free assemblies, and in parliaments, to labour by all means lawful to recover the purity and liberty of the gospel, as it was established and professed before the aforesaid innovations: and because after due examination we plainly perceive, and undoubtedly believe, that the innovations and evils . . . have no warrant of the Word of God, are contrary to the articles of the aforesaid confessions, to the intention and meaning of the blessed reformers of religion in this land, to . . . acts of parliament, and do sensibly tend to the re-establishing of the popish religion and tyranny, and to the subversion and ruin of the true reformed religion, and of our liberties, laws and estates . . . and therefore from the knowledge and conscience of our duty to God, to our king and country . . . we promise and swear by the great name of the Lord our God, to continue in the profession and obedience of the aforesaid religion; that we shall defend the same, and resist all these contrary errors and corruptions, according to our vocation, and to the utmost of that power that God hath put into our hands all the days of our life. And in like manner with the same heart we declare before God and men, that we have no intention or desire to attempt anything that may turn to the dishonour of God or the diminution of the king's greatness and authority; but on the contrary we promise and swear, that we shall to the utmost of our power, with our means and lives, stand to the defence of our dread sovereign the king's majesty, his person and authority, in the defence and preservation of the aforesaid true religion, liberties and laws of the kingdom; as also to the mutual defence and assistance, every one of us of another, in the same cause of maintaining the true religion, and his majesty's authority, with our best counsels, our bodies, means and whole power, against all sorts of persons whatsoever. So that whatsoever shall be done to the least of us for that cause, shall be taken as done to us all in general, and to every one of us in particular. . . . Neither do we fear the foul aspersions of *rebellion, combination*, or what else our adversaries from their craft and malice would put upon us, seeing what we do is so well warranted, and ariseth from an unfeigned desire to maintain the true worship of God, the majesty of our king, and the peace of the kingdom, for the common happiness of ourselves and posterity. . . . And that this our union and conjunction may be observed without violation, we call the living God, the searcher of our hearts, to witness, who knoweth this to be our sincere desire, and unfeigned resolution, as we shall answer to Jesus Christ in the great day, and under the pain of God's everlasting wrath, and of infamy, and of loss of all honour and respect in this world: most humbly beseeching the Lord to strengthen us by his Holy Spirit for this end, and to bless our desires and proceedings with a happy success, that religion and righteousness may flourish in the land, to the glory of God, the honour of our king, and peace and comfort of us all.

In witness whereof we have subscribed with our hands all the premises, etc.

A London tailor voices support for the Scots, 1640

Scottish propaganda, which had been circulating widely in England through the godly network, included the claim that the Scots were fighting for religion and to help the English complete their religious reformation. Such a message would have an obvious appeal to godly Londoners such as the individual below who had been engaged in conversation with a fellow tailor about the presence of the Scots army in the north of England.
Source: PRO, state papers, domestic 16/468/89.

The information of James Davis of St Saviour's [Southwark], tailor, taken before Daniel Featley, D.D., the 29th of September 1640.

He saith that this last night one Steven Williams being in his company spoke these words; that the Scots army which were now in the north were honest men, and that if they were all here at London they would find that as many would take their parts as would take the king's and more he saith not.

The examination of Steven Williams.

He confesseth that he spoke these words that there were in London a great many of religious men, which if the Scots were here would take their parts rather than the king's, for which words speaking he is heartily sorry.

THE SHORT PARLIAMENT

Sir Thomas Peyton on its proceedings and dissolution, 1640

Sir Thomas Peyton (1613–84), a Kent baronet, made the following observations on proceedings in the Short Parliament and its dissolution in two letters to his brother-in-law, Henry Oxinden, dated 20 April and 6 May 1640. Peyton had failed to secure election as an MP to this parliament but he was to serve as MP for Sandwich in the Long Parliament. A leading moderate figure in Kent, he eventually became a royalist. In the first letter, Pym's famous speech to the Commons on 17 April and Saye's clash with Archbishop Laud in the Lords the previous day are regarded as particularly noteworthy. Already there are rumours in the capital that the parliament will be dissolved and the second letter recounts the dissolution on 5 May.
Source: D. Gardiner (ed.), *The Oxinden Letters, 1607–42* (London, 1933), pp. 162–4, 173–4.

20 April 1640

. . . One fault was observed to be committed in the Lower House by one Mr [Harbottle] Grimston, who first spake in the House and jumped upon the grievances of our state untimely and too early, which speech was endeavoured to be qualified by Sir Benjamin Rudyerd; yet feared not Sir Francis Seymour to say as much again and compare our affairs to the bondage of Israelites in Egypt, with whose speech the session ended for that day. Yesterday [17 April] one Mr [Francis] Rous, whether out of some daunt at the assembly, or zeal to his cause, or abundance of matter, made a good but a confused speech, declaring the grievances of state. Upon whose conclusion presently arose Mr [John] Pym, an ancient and stout man of the parliament, that ever zealously affected the good of his country, who as yet only made the full complaint of the Commons, for he left not anything untouched, ship-money, forests, knighthood, recusants, monopolies, the present inclination of our church to popery, and more than my memory can suggest to me, and in the close desired the Lower House to move the Upper in an humble request that they would be pleased to join with them in a petition to the king for redress of all those grievances. But though I am in Friday [17 April], yet let me go back a little day and tell you a remarkable passage in the Upper House on Thursday: my lord of Canterbury moved that the House might be adjourned since a week, because the bishops having occasion to be present at the convocation could not at such times be there. My Lord Saye [and Sele] answered that it was never known that the House was adjourned for the bishops, and if the bishops had those occasions they might attend them, and the Lords could sit and go forward with any business without them. Then my lord keeper moved that it might be his humble request to the Lords that the House might be adjourned till Saturday, this day, by reason he found himself at some ill ease, which was condescended unto, and my Lord Saye again replied and requested that the record might be made that at my lord keeper's suit the House was adjourned.. . . .

And first upon Saturday [18 April] they [i.e. the Commons] did little, because they could not agree where to begin their grievances, but in the end elected a committee which is to prepare and prefer the business to the House.

And these smart proceedings do cause a murmur about the town that the parliament will dissolve, but we hope not: however wonderful things are about to be brought forth. On Monday [20 April] they cast bones at one another all the day, for so Sir Peter Heyman's phrase was, which was I think contradicting one another's opinions . . .

6 May 1640

. . . I have not good news to send you. . . . The [king's] words in effect were that he never with greater reluctation did deliver his mind unto them and the grief he had conceived at the ill success of this parliament would hardly suffer him to speak at all. The Lords he thanked for their respects and readiness to do him all good services, and were it not for some tumultuous and popular spirits he might have had as good respects from the House of Commons, and therefore would not blame all for the faults of some particular refractions: for the grievances so much inculcated among them, he did assure them for that of religion first, he would preserve it in its purity and truth, and have as tender a care of the church as can be required of any Christian prince: for monopolies and other grievances, his subjects should see that he would redress them as well as they themselves would have done or could desire. And so leaving the royal pleasure to be delivered by the lord keeper, who only said 'it is his majesty's pleasure this parliament be dissolved'. The Commons left the House full of heaviness; and so was this great council dissolved, because it was so long a resolving. And now some say we are where we were, but I think we are worse; for what grievances so ever the subjects thought themselves molested with, and therefore would resist them, this striving with the king could be thought but the act of private men, till now it is in parliament made the act of the third estate;[18] and there I think the king suffers in the honour of his government among neighbouring princes, who may privately rejoice to see distractions breed in so flourishing a kingdom, of which the whole world grew jealous daily but now will perhaps lay aside those fears, when it is discovered at what disagreement he is with his own people. . . .

PROVINCIAL GENTRY

Sir Henry Slingsby's Diary, *1638–40*

Sir Henry Slingsby (1602–58), a wealthy Yorkshire baronet, like many of the provincial gentry found himself reluctantly being drawn into the conflict, eventually ending up on the royalist side. These extracts from his diary reveal his scruples about the Laudian insistence on bowing towards the altar and suspicions about the way the Scottish covenanters were using religion to justify their actions. Gentry resentment in Yorkshire at the financial and other burdens of the bishops' wars is made plain. He was returned as MP for Knaresborough in both the 1640 elections yet with some difficulty in the case of the Long Parliament election. Arriving at Westminster shortly after the opening of the Long Parliament, he senses the feeling of great hope in the air at the prospect of a reforming parliament. He was to be beheaded on Tower Hill in 1658 for plotting to bring in Charles II.
Source: D. Parsons (ed.), *The Diary of Sir Henry Slingsby of Scriven, Bart.* (London, 1836), pp. 7–8, 10–12, 14, 31–2, 48–51, 56–65.

The 19th of December [1638] I came acquainted with Mr Timothy Thurscross a prebend of York. . . . He is a man of most holy life, only he is conformable to the church discipline that now is used and to those late imposed ceremonies of bowing and adoring towards the altar.

When I asked him his opinion concerning this or that, I thought it came too near idolatry to adore a place with rich cloths and other furniture and to command to use towards it bodily worship: to which he answered that his bowing was not to the altar but to God especially in that place; which gesture he said was frequently used in primitive times, and every one may do as he is persuaded in mind. . . .

The 3rd of January [1639] (out of curiosity to see the spectacle of our public death) I went to Bramham moor to see the training of our light horse, for which service I myself had sent 2 horses, by commandment from the deputy lieutenants and Sir Jacob Astley who is lately come down with special commission from the king to train and exercise them. These are strange, strange spectacles to this nation in this age, that have lived thus long peaceably, without noise of shot or drum and after we have stood neutrals and in peace when all the world besides hath been in arms and wasted with it; it is I say a thing most horrible that we should engage ourself in a war one with another, and with our own venom gnaw and consume ourself. . . . Our fear proceeds from the Scots who at this time are become most warlike, being exercised in the Swedish and German wars. . . . The cause of their grievance as they pretend is matter of religion; a fair pretext if the design be answerable to the cause, or that the cause be taken upon good ground: for what is more usual than to make religion a pretence and cloak for wickedness. . . . The Scots do mainly stand in defence of the government of their church by the presbytery, and admit not of any bishops and therefore do now seek to expell out of the church those whom our king in his time hath established, fearing lest he might by degrees introduce a new form in their church; and that which make them the more fear it was that now of late he enjoined them to accept a form of public prayer and administering the sacrament somewhat differing from our book of common prayer, which they have refused to accept.

. . . I desire not employments at these times; it is for those that will purchase it at any rates . . . where to do evil is common, to do nothing is in a manner commendable. Yet I happened to be in some employment though it were but short. My lord deputy of Ireland[19] sent his letters unto my lord mayor of York and to myself as deputy lieutenants. My lord mayor had a commission, but I had no other but his lordship's letters; by which I sat to assist my lord mayor in the taking the view of arms, the which I did perform most diligently, a thing not usual with me who does little affect business: therefore as I entered upon it by virtue of my lord deputy's letters directed to my lord mayor and myself, after 2 months service I gave it over, being left out by the vice-president in a general summons to all the deputy lieutenants.

. . . It was at this time [April 1639] the king lay at York at his going into Scotland with an army, and there remained until he had drawn down such foot companies of pressed soldiers and troops of horse as he intended to take with him: on Wednesday in Easter week, the king's majesty went to Selby, to view his troops that lay there; it was an extraordinary preparation that was made for this war, wherein the greatest part of the nobility and gentry of this kingdom was personally engaged, every one coming according to his ability completely furnished with horse, some more some less. The king's letters to the nobility did engage them according as they did: offer they brought, some 10, some 20, some more. I am charged with 2 light horse within the West Riding according to my estate there, and I took 2 light horse with me to serve the king in this journey. I did design them for my lord of Holland's troop, and had billet for them at my lord's quarters where his troop lay at Twizel; my lord had the use of my cousin [Sir William] Selby's house, and there kept a very noble house and gave great entertainments to many of the commanders that frequented to him; at this place having the freedom of my lord's house and a chamber to myself by my cousin Selby's means, I did continue as one of my lord's troops till a peace was concluded between the king and the lords of the covenant in Scotland. . . .

The 13th of April anno 1640 began the court of parliament to sit which was so unfortunate that it lasted but 3 weeks without having anything done to content either king or country. The House of Commons sat to advise how to have their grievances redressed, and the king by my lord keeper,[20] whom he had lately created baron, did signify to both the Houses the great need he had of supplies to maintain his wars against his rebellious subjects of Scotland; this held the House of Commons in debate whether they should not represent unto the king their grievances, and to obtain a redress thereof, before their giving of subsidy, or that they should supply the king first and take his word for the latter, which he did largely promise by my lord keeper, that he would reform all their just grievances. These they had drawn into 3 principal heads. That is 1st grievances concerning matter of religion. 2ndly property of goods. 3rdly privilege of parliament. But chiefly they insist upon that of ship money, which the House had voted to be absolutely against law, if the king had not suddenly dissolved the house of parliament. Upon the breaking of the parliament there was a search made in the trunks and pockets of some parliament men, yea of some of [the] Lords, to discover what letters they could find, but nothing was found: and after that, my brother [Henry] Bellasis the knight of our shire, and Sir John Hotham, were committed to the Fleet for their undutiful speeches to the king at council board, as they served them for not answering directly what it was they spoke in parliament at such a time in answer to such and such. I was chosen a burgess of Knaresborough at this parliament: which I obtained with much ado through the diligence of my man Thomas Richardson, to whom I committed the whole carriage of it, and went not down myself to be at the election, which gave my competitors Sir Richard Hutton and Henry Benson the more advantage against me: but my man's care prevented their subtle plots. . . .

The 28th of July [1640], being the assize week, I went to York, where the gentlemen of the county intended to meet to consult together of an answer to return the king, who had sent to desire that his soldiers that lay billeted in the county might be maintained by the county for 14 days: hereupon they petitioned and pleaded their inability, and hoped the king would lay no such burdens upon them considering they so willingly and cheerfully had served him the last year, in which service and other militant expenses they had expended a £100,000. But not withstanding the county must do it, and the king promises to repay it back again, so that the county shall be no loser by it. After this the king being at York, sends to speak with all the gentlemen and the substance of that he spoke was to assure them the money should be paid, and likewise to know of them how soon they could raise the train bands, for he intended to lead them and be their general. The gentlemen met again and petitioned the king and desired leave to petition him, for my lord deputy [the earl of Strafford] that now is grown a stranger to his county, though heretofore a patriot, seem to quarrel at them that they had not addressed his petition to him; and moreover they petitioned his majesty that he would be pleased to advance 14 days pay beforehand, otherwise they could not get them to stir; but the king was so far from giving, as he expected the county should pay the train bands themselves, and wished them to meet together and our lord president the lord deputy to consider how the money might be raised. The gentlemen had drawn another petition, but the king would not receive it, being advertised of it by my lord deputy, who was desired to prefer it at our meeting in the common hall: the lord deputy seemed utterly to dislike that part of our petition, where we desired the king would call a parliament; seeing he knew that he intended it, and uncivil to anticipate him in point of time. . . . The 1st of September I set forward to Hull with my wife and children . . . and from thence to Worlaby . . . the reason of my wife's remove thither was her own safety, after the news was brought of the Scots taking Newcastle, and repelling the king's forces, which he sent to stop their passage at Newburn . . . it is strange to see how the ways are pestered with carriages of all manner of preparations for war; 30 pieces of ordnance I met coming from Hull, and abundance of waggons, with all things belonging to powder, shot, and match, tents, pikes, spades, and shovels. It was then too late to march with their train of artillery, for before they could get to Newcastle the Scots had possessed themselves of it; and now the whole county of Northumberland and bishopric of Durham are compelled to pay contribution money to Leslie[21] the Scots' general: £300 a day they demanded of the county of Northumberland, and £350 of the bishopric of Durham: their proportion for victualling the army after their demands, is 30 thousands weight of bread a day, 10 tun of beer a day, 6000 weight of cheese, £50 worth of beef, and £24 worth of mutton by the day. We come not yet in Yorkshire into contribution with the Scots, for they have not yet invaded us; but notwithstanding we feel the burden of the war as well as our neighbours, by those regiments of foot and horse that are quartered amongst us and about us, and the train bands. . . . The charge this year hath been so great to this county, by impositions and taxes laid upon it, and by that waste which is made by the soldiers that are billeted here, that men are at a stand what course to take, or how to dispose of themselves. . . . all is lost, if war continue amongst us; one year's continuance shall make a greater desolation than 20 years shall recover. . . .

The 24 of September [1640] the king and the lords met together in the great hall at the dean's house to consult what answer to give the Scottish petition, and how the king might have a supply of monies to maintain his armies in the meantime, whilst things were in debate: and it was concluded upon the first day that commissioners should be appointed to the number of 16 lords and earls, and the place to be at Ripon, to meet such commissioners as the Scottish lords at Newcastle shall appoint . . . and for a supply of monies a letter was sent by my lord chamberlain Lord Goring and my lord privy seal unto the City of London, in the name of all the lords, to borrow £200,000; and but £50,000 was granted. . . . After much delay, and messages sent to and fro, in 3 weeks time the parley broke up, our English lords having condescended to the demands of the Scots, and £25,000 a month for 2 months granted to the Scots to maintain their army about Newcastle, till all things were agreed on in our English parliament. My lord of Holland[22] kept his table at Ripon for all the lords, and the Scots commissioners sometime were invited by him, who kept a correspondence with one another. . . . The 13 of October I went to the election of burgesses of Knaresborough with intention to stand, and coming thither, I found Sir Richard Hutton and Henry Benson to be competitors with me; when it came to polling I carried it, but with some difficulty, and Henry Benson. Sir Richard Hutton laboured all he could to carry it by the industry of his father's man Moore who dwells in the town, and I likewise by the diligence of my man Thomas Richardson who took great pains to bring the burgesses together whom he knew would give their votes for me, he himself being one. There is an ill custom at these elections to bestow wine in all the town, which cost me £16 at the least and many a man a broken pate. . . .

The 2nd of November I took my journey to London to be at the parliament, and came thither 2 days after it had begun. Great expectance there is of a happy parliament where the subject may have a total redress of all his grievances: and here they apply them to question all delinquents, all projectors, and monopolizers, such as levied ship money, and such judges as gave it for law. All innovators either in church or state: and as chief actors therein, they fell upon my lord of Canterbury and Strafford[23] and accused them of high treason; they fear not the dissolving of parliament, for the Scots are at Newcastle with an army fortified and they second our accusation against those 2 great persons; and money must be found to satisfy the Scots in their demands, which would not be found till the parliament had passed certain bills; as namely, that bill for the preventing the untimely dissolving of parliament, and another for triennial parliaments, and for the taking away the high commission and star chamber courts, with many other of public and private concernments.

The Scots would not away till they had such articles granted as was exhibited to the parliament for the better establishing a firm peace between the 2 nations. This proved a business of great difficulty not easily effected. . . .

DISAFFECTED PEERS

Petition of twelve peers for the summoning of a new parliament, 1640

This petition was the work of a group of disaffected peers and their leading followers. It was drawn up at a meeting in Bedford House (Westminster) attended by, among others, Bedford, Essex, Warwick, Saye and Brooke as well as Pym and Hampden. It was said to have been written by Pym and St John but it was left to peers actually to sign the petition. Of the twelve signatories, only one (Hertford) later became a royalist, Bedford died in May 1641 and the rest became parliamentarians. Along with their Commons allies they played key roles in the politics of the early 1640s.
Source: S. R. Gardiner, *The Constitutional Documents of the Puritan Revolution, 1625–1660*, 3rd edn (Oxford, 1906), pp. 134–6.

To the king's most excellent majesty.

The humble petition of your majesty's most loyal and obedient subjects, whose names are here underwritten in behalf of themselves and divers others.

Most gracious sovereign,

The sense of that duty and service which we owe to your sacred majesty, and our earnest affection to the good and welfare of this your realm of England, have moved us in all humility to beseech your royal majesty to give us leave to offer unto your princely wisdom the apprehension which we and other your faithful subjects have conceived of the great distempers and dangers now threatening the church and state and your royal person, and the fittest means by which they may be removed and prevented.

The evils and dangers whereof your majesty may be pleased to take notice are these:

That your majesty's sacred person is exposed to hazard and danger in the present expedition against the Scottish army, and by occasion of this war your revenue is much wasted, your subjects burdened with coat-and-conduct money, billeting of soldiers, and other military charges, and divers rapines and disorders committed in several parts in this your realm, by the soldiers raised for that service, and your whole kingdom become full of fear and discontents.

The sundry innovations in matters of religion, the oath and canons lately imposed upon the clergy and other your majesty's subjects.

The great increase of popery, and employing of popish recusants, and others ill-affected to the religion by law established in places of power and trust, especially in commanding of men and arms both in the field and in sundry counties of this your realm, whereas by the laws they are not permitted to have arms in their own houses.

The great mischiefs which may fall upon this kingdom if the intentions which have been credibly reported, of bringing in Irish and foreign forces, shall take effect.

The urging of ship-money, and the prosecution of some sheriffs in the star chamber for not levying of it.

The heavy charges of merchandise to the discouragement of trade, the multitude of monopolies, and other patents, whereby the commodities and manufactures of the kingdom are much burthened, to the great and universal grievance of your people.

The great grief of your subjects by the long intermission of parliaments, in the late and former dissolving of such as have been called, without the hoped effects which otherwise they might have procured.

For remedy whereof, and prevention of the dangers that may ensue to your royal person and to the whole state, they do in all humility and faithfulness beseech your most excellent majesty that you would be pleased to summon a parliament within some short and convenient time, whereby the causes of these and other great grievances which your people lie under may be taken away, and the authors and counsellors of them may be there brought to such legal trial and condign punishment as the nature of the several offences shall require, and that the present war may be composed by your Majesty's wisdom without bloodshed, in such manner as may conduce to the honour and safety of your majesty's person, the comforts of your people, and the uniting of both your realms against the common enemies of the reformed religion. And your majesty's petitioners shall ever pray, etc.

[Signed by]: Rutland, Bolingbroke, Bedford, Mulgrave, Hertford, Say and Sele, Essex, Brooke, Exeter, Mandeville, Warwick, Howard (of Escrick).

2

THE LONG PARLIAMENT

MEMBERS OF PARLIAMENT

The election of Middlesex and London MPs, 1640

In both these elections, as soon as the result had been declared petitions containing statements of the constituents' grievances were handed up to the platform for presentation to parliament by their newly elected MPs. As in the previous Short Parliament elections, London chose leading court critics as MPs. The court-backed City of London's recorder, who would generally expect to be an MP, was once again humiliatingly rejected.
Source: British Library, Additional Ms. 11045, f. 128.

When the county of Middlesex had made choice of their knights to send to the parliament, after the sheriff had declared them, the country people having a petition ready presented it to their knights requiring them to deliver it to the House of Commons, to whom it was directed, in this petition are set down their present grievances of all sorts, one being against the subordinate officers of the ecclesiastical courts for excess of fees. The last week, the City of London made choice of their knights and burgesses, the very same they chose for the last parliament. The sheriff of London having declared them, forthwith a petition was given by the multitude to the sheriff to be by him delivered over to the knights for the parliament, some of the people cried out to have this petition read out, but the major part by far cried down that motion, saying, they would not have their grievances published but in parliament, so to avoid the censure of libelling, much ado there was, before this could be over-ruled, but the sheriffs putting it to the question in the hall, it was concluded, it should not be read, but in parliament, where many of them would appear to prove all true set down in that petition: certain it is, that very many of those people gave their voices against the reading of that petition that knew nothing what was in it.

27 October 1640

The exclusion of monopolists, 1641

The House of Commons had ultimate authority when it came to adjudicating on disputed elections and deciding who should be expelled from the House. In the early days of the new parliament, it was decided that all monopolists should be declared unfit to sit in the House and that fresh elections should be held in their constituencies.
Source: *Commons' Journals* (1641), ii, 70–1.

Die Jovis,[1] 21 Jan[uary] 1641.

Mr Peard reports from the committee for monopolists, these four cases ensuing:
And, upon his report it was

Resolved, upon the question, that Mr William Sandys is within the order made against monopolists; and not fit, nor ought to sit as a member in the House, this parliament: and that a warrant issue forth, under Mr Speaker's hand, to the clerk of the crown, for a new writ for electing of another to serve for the town of Evesham in Com. Wigorn',[2] in his stead.

Resolved, upon the question, that Sir John Jacob is a monopolist, and projector in the business of tobacco, and within the order against monopolists; and ought not to sit as a member in the House, this parliament: and that a warrant issue forth . . . for a new writ for electing of another to serve in his stead, this parliament, for the town of Rye in Sussex.

Resolved, upon the question, that Mr Thomas Webb is interested in the project and monopoly concerning the sealing of bone-lace, and within the order of this House made against monopolists; and ought not to sit as a member in this House, this parliament: and that a warrant issue forth . . . for a new writ for electing of another to serve in his stead, this parliament.

Resolved, upon the question, that Mr Edmund Wyndham is a monopolist and projector, and within the order made against monopolists; and ought not to sit as a member in this House, this parliament: and that a warrant issue forth . . . for a new writ for electing of another burgess to serve in his stead, this parliament, for Bridgewater in the county of Somerset.

PETITIONS

The presentation of the first London root and branch petition, 1640

The first London root and branch petition was ready for presentation to the Commons on 11 December 1640. A remarkably radical document, it had been extensively canvassed in the City and had attracted an impressive number of signatures. The manner in which the petition was delivered, involving large crowds of supporters descending on Westminster, set a pattern that was followed by other petitioners in the early 1640s.
Source: British Library, Additional Ms. 11045, f. 135.

The same morning a petition was brought by the citizens of London subscribed by fifteen thousand hands in a schedule annexed to the petition. It is said two of the aldermen accompanied with two or three of the City captains delivered it, but there were thousands of the citizens at Westminster at the same time to look after this business that the hall and places thereabouts was thronged again. The petition was read in the House, it was much to this purpose against innovations of the clergy in point of ceremonies, concerning bowing at the name of Jesus at the altar, against coming up to the rails to receive the sacrament, they require the [communion] table to be set again in the midst of the chancel, they require they may be no more enjoined to receive the sacrament kneeling, and some other old ceremonies they would have abolished, they complain also against the high commission and the bishops' courts in their dioceses, and against the insolency of the clergy of late years, which they cannot undergo, and they allege the clergy to have been the causes of the divisions of the two kingdoms of England and Scotland, they therefore desire episcopacy may be absolutely taken away root and branches, and that they are afraid, the Scots will never remove hence, till episcopacy be utterly destroyed. The Commons have appointed a committee to debate upon these particulars and require that only half a dozen citizens may prosecute this petition, and that they forbear hereafter to come in such multitudes. Concerning the names to this petition the House ordered the roll should not be read, but sealed up by two seals, and to be kept by Mr Speaker, and not by the clerk of the House, till the House shall call for it. It is said there are petitions of the same kind come and coming from several parts of the kingdom, but then the clergy say again that they can procure ten hands for the continuing of episcopal government for every one hand that subscribes against it. . . .

15 December 1640

The remonstrance and petition of the county of Huntingdon, 1642

In 1641–2 petitions in defence of a Church governed by bishops and worship conducted according to the book of common prayer circulated in over half of the English counties. These petitions were usually careful to disown Laudianism and were not calling for a return to the religious policies of the 1630s. They drew upon widespread anxieties about the spread of religious radicalism and a genuine affection for the traditions of the national Church. Source: Thomason Tracts, E. 131/5.

To the right honourable the Lords and Commons assembled in parliament:

We humbly show, that whereas many attempts have been practised, and divers petitions from several counties, and other places within this kingdom, framed and penned in a close and subtle manner, to import more than is at first discernible by any ordinary eye, or that was imparted to those who signed the

Figure 3 London citizens portrayed as rejecting bishops, 1642

same, have been carried about to most places against the present form and frame of church government, and divine service, or common prayers, and the hands of many persons of ordinary quality solicited to the same with pretence to be presented to this honourable assembly in parliament, and under colour of removing some innovations lately crept into the Church, and worship of God, and reforming some abuses in the ecclesiastical courts, which we conceiving and fearing not so much to aim at the taking away of the said innovations, and reformation of abuses, as tending to an absolute innovation of church government, and subversion of that order and form of divine service which hath happily continued amongst us ever since the reformation of religion. Out of a tender and zealous regard hereunto, we have thought it our duty not only to disavow all such petitions, but also to manifest our public affections, and desires to continue the form of divine service, and common prayers, and the present government of the Church, as the same have been continued since the first reformation, and stand so established by the laws and statutes of this kingdom.

For when we consider that the form of divine service expressed and contained in the book of common prayer, was with great care, piety, and sincerity revised and reduced from all former corruptions and Romish superstitions, by those holy and selected instruments of the reformation of religion within this Church, and was by them restored to its first purity, according as it was instituted and practised in primitive times, standeth confirmed, established, and enjoined by act of parliament, and royal injunctions, and hath ever since had the general approbation of the godly, and a public use and continuance within this Church. And that bishops were instituted, and have had their being and continuance ever since the first planting of Christian religion amongst us, and the rest of the Christian world, that they were the lights and glorious lamps of God's Church, that so many of them sowed the seeds of Christian religion in their bloods, which they willingly poured out therefore . . . and that their government hath been so ancient, so long approved, and so often established by the laws and statutes of this kingdom, and as yet nothing in their doctrine (generally taught) dissonant from the Word of God, or the articles established by law, and that most of them are of singular learning and piety. In this case to call the form of divine service and common prayers erroneous, popish, superstitious, idolatrous and blasphemous, and to call the government by bishops, a perpetual vassalage, and intolerable bondage, and at the first step, and before the parties concerned be heard, to pray the present removal of them, or the utter dissolution and extirpation of them, their courts, and their officers, as antichristian and diabolical, we cannot conceive to savour or relish of piety, justice, or charity, nor can we join with them herein, but rather humbly pray a reformation of the abuses, and punishment of the offenders, but not the ruin or abolition of the innocent.

Now on the contrary, when we consider the tenor of such writings, as in the name of petitions are spread amongst the common people, the contents of many printed pamphlets swarming at London, and over all counties, the sermons preached publicly in pulpits, and other private places, and the bitter invectives divulged, and commonly spoken by many disaffected persons, all of them showing an extreme averseness and dislike of the present government of the Church, and divine service, or common prayers, dangerously exciting a disobedience to the established form of government and church service, their several intimations of the desire of the power of the keys, and that their congregations may be independent, and may execute ecclesiastical censure within themselves, whereby many sects and several and contrary opinions will soon grow and arise, whereby great divisions and horrible factions will soon ensue thereupon, to the breach of that union, which is the sacred band and preservation of the common peace of Church and state: their peremptory desires and bold assuming to themselves the liberty of conscience to introduce into the Church whatsoever they affect, and to refuse and oppose all things which themselves shall dislike, and what they dislike must not only to themselves but also to all others be scandalous and burthensome, and must be cried out upon, as great and unsupportable grievances, yea though the things in themselves be never so indifferent, of never so long continuance in use and practise, and never so much desired and affected of others, so that where three or four of them be in a parish, though five hundred others desires the use and continuance of things long used, all must be altered or taken away as scandals and grievances for these three or four, though to the offence of many others, and whatsoever they will have introduced, must be imposed upon all others, and must by all be admitted without scandal or offence, whereby multitudes of godly and well-affected people are in some things deprived or abridged of what they desire and take comfort in, and have had a long and lawful use and practise of, and other things imposed upon them against their wills and liking, as if no account were to be made of them, or no liberty of conscience were left unto them: which bold attempts of some few to arrogate to themselves, and to exercise over all others, what high presumption is it? And how great a tyranny may it prove over the minds and consciences of men? The great increase of late of schismatics and sectaries, and of persons not only separating and sequestering themselves from the public assembly at common prayers and divine service, but also opposing and tumultuously interrupting others in the performance thereof in the public congregation, the frequent and many conventicles held amongst them, and their often meetings at all public conventions of assizes, sessions, fairs, markets, and other public assemblies, their earnest labouring to solicit and draw the people to them, and the general correspondence held amongst them to advance their ends herein. Of these things we cannot but take notice, and must needs express our just fears, that their desires and endeavours are to work some great change and mutation in the present state of the church government, and in the form of the public worship of God, and divine service, and common prayers.

noticing the change

Of the common grievances of the kingdom, we as others, have been and are sensible, and do profess that we have just cause with joy and comfort to remember, and with thankfulness to acknowledge the pious care which is already taken for the suppressing of the growth of popery, the better supply of able and painful ministers,[3] and the removing of all innovation, and we doubt not but in your great wisdoms you will regulate the rigour and exorbitancy of the ecclesiastical courts to suit with the temper of our common laws, and the nature and condition of freemen: and we hope and humbly pray, that the present form of church government and of church service, and common prayers now established by the statutes of this kingdom shall be settled, and that all such as shall oppose themselves against the same or shall do or speak anything in derogation or depraving of the said divine service or book of common prayer may without any further toleration or connivance undergo the pains, punishment, and forfeitures due therefore; and that such care shall be taken for placing of orthodox and peaceable men, lecturers in all places, whose doctrine may tend rather to sound instruction and edification than lead to schism and faction; all which we humbly submit to your great judgements, and shall pray to God to assist and direct you from above with His heavenly wisdom, to guide and bring all your consultations to happy conclusions.

trying to prevent a divide

London citizens on the causes of the decay of trade, 1641

The political crisis in the early 1640s had an adverse impact on the economy as business confidence collapsed and credit became unattainable. This in turn added to political pressures as some of those most affected petitioned for an urgent remedying of the nation's grievances so that political stability might return and with it economic recovery.

Source: J. Thirsk and J. P. Cooper (eds.), *Seventeenth-century Economic Documents* (Oxford, 1972), pp. 40–1.

The humble petition of divers citizens of London.

Sheweth that whereas there hath been a great decay of trade in this kingdom and great scarcity of money thereby ever since the first motions in the kingdom of Scotland, but more especially since the most unhappy breach of the pacification, whereby this state, being looked upon by foreign nations as in an unsettled condition, it hath been a cause that such strangers who were wont to furnish great sums of money at use have called in and remitted those monies by exchange into foreign parts. And such of our own nation as were wont to be lenders have called in their monies and stand in expectation of what the issue of things may be. Commodities also brought in find no usual vent but at great loss, which, if it shall continue still, will hinder exportation also by reason of the high exchange abroad, whereby there is as great loss as by goods imported. Such among us as have monies owing in Scotland cannot yet receive them by reason of their great disability through their troubles since the last breach. Ireland is so impoverished by the great oppressions that lately exercised there that such debts as have been owing there are still for the most part detained; and by our general fears and distractions the inland trade of this kingdom is so far decayed that country tradesmen cannot pay their debts in London as formerly and many of them have been ruined. . . .

And whereas at the first sitting of this present parliament we hoped that we should soon have our grievances removed and the incendiaries of the kingdoms and oppressors of our liberties speedily, condignly, and exemplarily punished and all things so perfectly settled that security might appear and a free and full trade return as before; yet after five months' sitting of the parliament we see no man's person condignly punished, no man's estate confiscate, the earl of Strafford himself used with usual favour, though a man charged by all the three kingdoms, and whose life and our safety are, as we conceive, incompatible, which cannot but be a great encouragement to the rest of the great incendiaries, and other offenders highly guilty. Subsidies are granted, monies still required, but our grievances remain; the laws continue still unexecuted; papists still armed, some of the most active of them still resident at court; the Irish popish army not yet disbanded, though all these often humbly and earnestly by both houses of parliament desired; the great affairs of the Church sticking in debate and not yet determined. . . .

Which considerations we present to this most honourable assembly as the true grounds of the decay of trade, the scarcity of money, and the increase of our fears, not expecting that the Scottish army should be willing to depart, or

66

if they should depart, that we shall be in any better condition, till justice be executed upon the notorious offenders, a perfect peace concluded by parliament between the kingdoms, and thereby security given to our fears. All which we most humbly pray and hope we shall in the end receive no less from this most honourable assembly as those from whom under God we expect our peace; and for His blessings upon you and presence with you in this great work shall ever pray.

A petition of London gentlewomen and tradesmen's wives, 1642

Women petitioned parliament on their own for the first time in early 1642 in defiance of the dependent and deferential status assigned to them by law and society. In the petition below of February 1642 the women felt obliged to justify their action and to emphasise that they were not claiming equality with men. The religious radicalism of the petitioners' demands and the fact that these demands were coming from women added to conservative fears that order and authority were being undermined.
Source: Thomason Tracts, E. 134/17.

To the honourable knights, citizens and burgesses of the House of Commons assembled in parliament.

The most humble petition of the gentlewomen, tradesmen's wives, and many others of the female sex, inhabitants of the City of London, and suburbs thereof.

With lowest submission showing, that we also with all thankful humility acknowledging the unwearied pains, care and great charge, besides hazard of health and life, which you the noble worthies of their honourable renowned assembly have undergone, for the safety of both Church and commonwealth, for a long time already past . . . yet notwithstanding that many worthy deeds have been done by you, great danger and fear do still attend us, and will, as long as popish lords and superstitious bishops are suffered to have their voice in the House of Peers, and that accursed and abominable idol of the Mass suffered in the kingdom, and that arch-enemy of our prosperity and reformation[4] lieth in the Tower, yet not receiving his deserved punishment. . . .

And whereas we, whose hearts have joined cheerfully with all those petitions which have been exhibited unto you in behalf of the purity of religion, and the liberty of our husbands' persons and estates, recounting ourselves to have an interest in the common privileges with them, do with the same confidence assure ourselves to find the same gracious acceptance with you, for easing of those grievances, which in regard of our frail condition, do more nearly concern us, and do deeply terrify our souls: our domestical dangers with which this kingdom is so much distracted, especially growing on us from those treacherous and wicked attempts already are such, as we find ourselves to have as deep a share as any other.

We cannot but tremble at the very thoughts of the horrid and hideous facts which modesty forbids us now to name, occasioned by the bloody wars in Germany,[5] his majesty's late northern army, how often did it affright our hearts, whilst their violence began to break out so furiously upon the persons of those, whose husbands or parents were not able to rescue: we wish we had no cause to speak of those insolencies, and savage usage and unheard of rapes, exercised upon our sex in Ireland, and have we not just cause to fear they will prove the forerunners of our ruin, except Almighty God by the wisdom and care of this parliament be pleased to succour us, our husbands and children . . . our present fears are, that unless the blood-thirsty faction of the papists and prelates be hindered in their designs, ourselves here in England as well as they in Ireland, shall be exposed to that misery which is more intolerable than that which is already past, as namely to the rage not of men alone, but of devils incarnate, (as we may so say) besides the thraldom of our souls and consciences in matters concerning GOD, which of all things are most dear unto us.

. . . and we humbly beseech . . . you would move his majesty with our humble requests, that he would be graciously pleased . . . to purge both the court and kingdom of that great idolatrous service of the Mass, which is toler-ated in the queen's court, this sin (as we conceive) is able to draw down a greater curse upon the whole kingdom, than all your noble and pious endeav-ours can prevent, . . . to subdue the papists and their abettors, and by taking away the power of the prelates, whose government by long and woeful experi-ence we have found to be against the liberty of our conscience and the freedom of the gospel, and the sincere profession and practise thereof, then shall our fears be removed, and we may expect that GOD will power down his blessings in abundance both upon his majesty, and upon this honourable assembly, and upon the whole land.

. . . It may be thought strange, and unbeseeming our sex to show ourselves by way of petition to this honourable assembly: but the matter being rightly considered, of the right and interest we have in the common and public cause of the Church, it will, as we conceive (under correction) be found a duty commanded and required. . . .

On which grounds we are emboldened to present our humble petition unto this honourable assembly, not weighing the reproaches which may and are by many cast upon us, who (not well weighing the premises) scoff and deride our good intent. We do it not out of any self conceit, or pride of heart, as seeking to equal ourselves with men, either in authority or wisdom: but according to our places to discharge that duty we owe to God, and the cause of the Church, as far as lyeth in us, following herein the example of the men, which have gone in this duty before us.

PARLIAMENTARY PROCEEDINGS

Lord Digby's speech in the Commons to the bill for triennial parliaments,
1641

This was one of a number of Commons speeches which were subsequently printed for circulation despite some reservations about the propriety of divulging what was said in the House to the general public. George Digby (1612–77), the eldest son of the first earl of Bristol, was one of the MPs for Dorset in the Long Parliament until June 1641, when he was called up to the Lords. His speech made on 19 January 1641 reflected a general recognition of the need for regular parliaments which Digby, a future leading royalist, could share at this time with future parliamentarians.
Source: *The Speeches of the Lord Digby in the High Court of Parliament,* Thomason Tracts E. 196/6.

Mr Speaker, I rise not now with an intent to speak to the frame and structure of this bill, nor much by way of answer to objections that may be made; I hope there will be no occasion of that, but that we shall concur all unanimously in what concerneth all so universally. Only Sir, by way of preparation to the end that we may not be discouraged in this great work by difficulties that may appear in the way of it, I shall deliver unto you my apprehensions in general of the vast importance and necessity that we should go through with it. The result of my sense is in short this. That unless for the frequent convening of parliaments there be some such course settled, as may not be eluded; neither the people can be prosperous and secure, nor the king himself solidly happy. I take this to be the *unum necessarium*:[6] let us procure this, and all our other desires will effect themselves: if this bill miscarry, I shall have left me no public hopes, and once passed, I shall be freed of all public fears. The essentialness, sir, of frequent parliaments to the happiness of this kingdom, might be inferred unto you, by the reason of contraries, from the woeful experience which former times have had of the mischievous effects of any long intermission of them. . . . 'Tis true, sir, wicked ministers have been the proximate causes of our miseries, but the want of parliaments the primary, the efficient cause. Ill ministers have made ill times, but that, sir, hath made ill ministers. . . .

Let his majesty hear our complaint never so compassionately. Let him purge away our grievances never so efficaciously. Let him punish and dispell ill ministers never so exemplarily. Let him make choice of good ones never so exactly. If there be not a way settled to preserve and keep them good; the mischiefs and they will grow again like Sampson's locks, and pull down the house upon our heads. Believe it, Mr Speaker, they will. It hath been a maxim among the wisest legislators, that whosoever means to settle good laws, must proceed in them, with a sinister opinion of all mankind; and suppose that whosoever is not wicked, it is for want only of the opportunity. It is that opportunity of being ill, Mr Speaker, that we must take away, if ever we mean to be happy, which can never be done, but by the frequency of parliaments. No state can wisely be confident of any public minister's continuing good, longer than the rod is over him. . . .

The people of England, sir, cannot open their ears, their hearts, their mouths, nor their purses, to his majesty, but in parliament. We can neither hear him, nor complain, nor acknowledge, nor give, but there. This bill, sir, is the sole key that can open the way to a frequency of those reciprocal endearments, which must make and perpetuate the happiness of the king and kingdom. Let no man object any derogation from the king's prerogative by it. We do but present the bill, 'tis to be made a law by him, his honour, his power, will be as conspicuous, in commanding at once that parliament shall assemble every third year, as in commanding a parliament to be called this or that year: there is more of majesty in ordaining primary and universal causes, than in the actuating particularly of subordinate effects. I doubt not but that glorious King Edward the third, when he made those laws for the yearly calling of parliament, did it with a right sense of his dignity and honour. The truth is, sir, the kings of England are never in their glory, in their splendour, in their majestic sovereignty, but in parliaments. . . . The king out of parliament hath a limited, a circumscribed jurisdiction. But waited on by his parliament, no monarch of the east is so absolute in dispelling grievances. Mr Speaker, in chasing ill ministers, we do but dissipate clouds that may gather again, but in voting this bill, we shall contribute, as much as in us lies to the perpetuating our sun, our sovereign, in his vestical in his noon day lustre.

Sir Simonds D'Ewes's Journal, 1641

D'Ewes (1602–50) was a distinguished antiquarian and constitutional historian who as MP for Sudbury (Suffolk) kept a journal of proceedings in the Long Parliament. His journal is the most important private record of debates and events in the Commons kept by an MP in the seventeenth century and it is extensively drawn on by historians. An active contributor himself to debates in the House, he rarely missed an opportunity to display his knowledge and learning, often at great length. This extract from his journal shows the divisive potential of the issue of episcopacy and includes an early intervention by Oliver Cromwell.
Source: W. Notestein (ed.), The Journal of Sir Simonds D'Ewes: From the Beginning of the Long Parliament to the Opening of the Trial of the Earl of Strafford (New Haven, 1923), pp. 339–42.

9 February 1641

Then after some short motions for our returning to the matter of religion, Alderman Penington stood up and justified the London petition[7] to have been warranted by the hands of men of worth and known integrity. And if there were any mean men's hands to it, yet if they were honest men, there was no reason but their hands should be received. And for the delivery of it, himself was one of them who received it from persons of quality and worth. It was done without tumult, and then upon a word after they that came with the petition though many in number departed quietly. There was no course used to rake up hands, for he said he might boldly say, if that course had been taken instead of 15000 they might have had fifteen times fifteen thousand.

Some after this called to have Gloucester and Hertford petitions read against episcopacy: others to go on to the business of the day, where we left yesternight, which at last prevailed. But then we fell into a new dispute what question should be put: and some would have the question of episcopacy put. Sir John Strangeways rose up and spake on their behalf: saying, if we made a parity in the church we must at last come to a parity in the commonwealth. And that the bishops were one of the three estates of the kingdom and had voice in parliament. Mr Cromwell stood up next and said, he knew no reason of those suppositions and inferences which the gentleman had made that last spake; upon this divers interrupted him and called him to the bar. Mr Pym and Mr Holles thereupon spake to the orders of the House that if the gentleman had said anything that might offend, he might explain himself in his place.

I also spake to the orders of the House; and showed that I had been often ready to speak against the frequent calling men to the bar in this House upon trivial occasions. For to call a member to the bar here is the highest and most supreme censure we can exercise within these walls. For it is a rending away a part of our body; because if once a member amongst us is placed at yonder bar (then I looked towards it) he ceaseth to be a member. I could not better compare it then to excommunication which was anciently accounted the supreme censure of the church, and was greatly feared; but being abused upon every trivial occasion is now grown contemptible. And so will this supreme censure of this House, of calling to the bar if we make a common practice of it. . . . I therefore moved that if any man hereafter should without just cause call another to the bar, that he might be well fined.

So after I had spoken Mr Cromwell went on: and said he did not understand why the gentleman that last spake should make an inference of parity from the church to the commonwealth: nor that there was any necessity of the great revenues of bishops. He was more convinced touching the irregularity of bishops than ever before, because like the Roman hierarchy, they would not endure to have their condition come to a trial.

Then after some motions of little moment, Sir Francis Seymour stood up and desired to have it put to the question whether we should refer episcopacy or not to be considered of by the committee, to which we intended to refer the London petition. The Lord Falkland and Sir John Culpepper spake severally that they desired that the business should be referred to a committee, but that the same committee might have no power to meddle with episcopacy.

I moved, that I was sorry to see the question of episcopacy or not episcopacy at all debated. . . . I desired therefore we might for the present lay aside the dispute of episcopacy or referring it; but refer the London petition as it stood to a select committee.

After I had spoken, many moved the matter of episcopacy might be left out of the reference of the said petition, and others moved it might not at all be mentioned; but the petition be generally referred only. And when we were likely to have fallen into a long debate about what question we should put, the Speaker stood up, and desired leave to speak; he said he desired to divert the question, and seeing now what the general sense of the House was, he had drawn an order which he conceived would settle this business, and so he read it being almost verbatim as followeth for some words were afterwards added to it.

It is this day ordered that this House doth refer to the consideration of a select committee, that part of the ministers' remonstrance which hath been read and the petition of the inhabitants in and about the City of London; and all other petitions of the like nature; which have been read in this House, reserving to itself the consideration of the main point of episcopacy when this House shall think fit.

And yet this order did not pass without the dissent of many; so as it was at last put to the question; before it was allowed. This being past and ratified then we fell upon a new debate; to what committee this matter should be referred: and at last it was agreed that it should be referred to the committee of four and twenty.

A bishop's diary, 1641

Several MPs kept diaries of proceedings in the Commons while the passage below is from the only known diary of debates in the Lords during the Long Parliament and the diary as a whole only covers a one-year period: January 1641 to January 1642. It is an anonymous document whose most likely author is the Laudian bishop of Rochester, John Warner (1581–1666). This extract is concerned with proceedings in the Lords against Strafford, 3 to 4 May 1641, and the accompanying mass lobbying of the Upper House, a design to seize control of the Tower of London and the taking of the Protestation. One of the demonstrators demanding justice on Strafford was the future Leveller leader, John Lilburne, who was questioned at the bar of the House for treasonable words.
Source: British Library, Harleian Ms. 6424 'Diary of a Bishop 1641', ff. 58–9.

3 May

This day in the morning multitudes of the City came to the Lords' House pressing them for justice, complaining that their trade was lost, and they undone, no man would pay or part with money, till they saw justice done upon the Lord Strafford, the other incendiaries and great offenders. The Lords gave their answer that they would do them justice with all expedition; but the people continued and increased in greater number to the afternoon, in which interim it was delivered to the king and witnessed that some had said, 'If they had not justice tomorrow, they would either take the king or my Lord Strafford.' Upon this the king gave warrant to the lieutenant of the Tower to put in one Captain Billingsley with 100 men for the securing of the ammunition. This afternoon the Londoners petition that they have heard of this captain and 100 men put into the Tower and thence are suspicious that it is for some plot to do the City mischief and to make an escape for the Lord Strafford therefore desire the Lord Strafford, other incendiaries and offenders may speedily have justice, and that none may be put in to defend the Tower, but those of the nine hamlets.[8] The Lords answered them that the Lord Newport, lieutenant of the ordnance, shall be sent this night to look to his charge at the Tower. The Lord Strafford shall have justice in the first place, that none but the nine hamlets shall be there suffered to ward or defend.

4 May

The earl of Bristol, Bath and [Lord] Saville wished that the tumults of the people might be removed and pacified, or else they might be deemed to condemn him for fear of force, or else if they acquit him to be in danger of their own persons. The issue hereof was, that some of the ministers and best of the City of London should be called in and acquainted with what we had done, viz. that this day we had made the Protestation which anon follows and that tomorrow the bill against the Lord Strafford should be voted, and thereupon they should persuade the people to keep at home, but neither of these ministers nor better sort of citizens being there, the thing was left undone, and notwithstanding the trial, the voting of the bill is to proceed tomorrow.

One Lilburne,[9] a late servant of Mr Prynne, was brought into the House, against whom one Mr Andrews, a barrister, and Mr Littleton, a servant of the king's, did upon oath affirm, that yesterday the 3rd of this May, the said Lilburne said unto them, 'This day there are but 7,000 come to crave judgement against the Lord Strafford, without weapons, but tomorrow there will be 40 or 50,000 in arms who if they cannot have the Lord Strafford they will have the king's person.' This Lilburne notwithstanding without admonition or being called into the House, is utterly and freely discharged. The Lords have a conference with the Commons to desire them to pacify the tumults of the people, that thereby the dignity and freedom of the House may be preserved, and they to go to a clear voting but the Commons all this day gave no answer to it.

ARMY PLOTS

Parliamentary investigation of the first army plot, 1641

There were two separate bouts of plotting in the spring and summer respectively of 1641 centring on the use of the English army in the north to overawe

The Earle of Strafford for treasonable practises beheaded on the Tower-hill

Figure 4 The execution of the earl of Strafford on Tower Hill, 12 May 1641

parliament. The revelations about the first of these plots in the Commons on 3 May caused great anger and dismay, and both the Protestation and the act against dissolving the present parliament without its own consent were reactions to it. Later parliamentary investigations into the plot, from which the following extract is derived, helped to establish Charles's record for perfidy which the discovery of a second plot in the summer only served to confirm.

Source: J. Rushworth, *Historical Collections*, 8 vols (London, 1721), viii, pp. 746–8.

This plot consisted of three heads; the first was, the design upon the Tower; the second, to engage the army; the third, to bring in foreign forces. For the Tower, it appeared to be thus, Captain Billingsley, being examined upon oath, confessed, that he was acquainted with Sir John Suckling. . . . That this deponent having notice to meet at the privy lodgings at Whitehall, did there receive orders to get 100 men to serve in the Tower under him, and if he did fail, he should answer it with his life: and afterwards meeting with Sir John Suckling, and acquainting him therewith, he told him he would furnish him with the said number. Sir William Balfour lieutenant of the Tower being examined, said that he had a command to receive Captain Billingsley with 100 men into the Tower, who should be under his command. That the earl of Strafford, at that time expostulating with him about his escape, told him he would attempt nothing in that kind without his privity, and that he should have the king's warrant for his indemnity, and that the warrant should be to command him to remove the said earl of Strafford from the Tower to some other castle, and he would then take his opportunity to escape . . .

The plot concerning the army, was thus:

Colonel [Sir George] Goring, upon his examination in the House of Commons, did confess that Sir John Suckling was the first person that ever made any overture unto him concerning the army's marching towards London; afterwards being in the queen's lodgings, he met with Mr H. P.[10] which was about the beginning or middle of Lent last, and Mr P. told him, there was a consultation of officers to be had, concerning the good of the army and desired him to go along with him to his chamber, where the meeting was to be; there were present in the same meeting, Commissary Willmott, Colonel Ashburnham, Captain Pollard, Sir John Berkeley, Daniel O'Neill, Mr Jermyn, and himself. That Mr P. said, there were propositions to be made, which were of great concernment, and that it was necessary there should be an oath of secrecy taken, before anything was propounded. . . . He further said, that the whole number there met, were of opinion, that the army should not march towards London, 'till a declaration had been first sent up to the parliament. . . . That shortly after, there was another meeting of the same persons, and in the same place in Mr Percy's chamber, where there were propositions of another nature, desperate and impious on the one hand, and foolish on the other. . . . For how could the army, lodged in several quarters, unpaid, and at such a distance, march on a sudden to London, and surprise what they had in design? . . . Being again examined upon his oath, before the committee of Lords and Commons, and pressed more particularly to answer questions not before proposed unto him; he did confess, that meeting with Mr Jermyn in the queen's drawing-chamber, her majesty came and told him, the king would speak with him; and meeting with his majesty, he told him, he was minded to set his army in a good posture, being advised thereto by the earl of Bristol (as he said); and his majesty then commanded him to join with Mr Percy, and some others, in that business.

As for the designs from beyond seas, the committee did make report to the House, that it was cleared unto them, that Jermyn endeavoured to have got possession of Portsmouth; that the king of France had drawn down great forces to the sea-side; that the governor of Calais had examined some Englishmen, whether the earl of Strafford's head was off yet? And this was, in point of time, the 1st of May . . . and Sir Philip Cartwright governor of Guernsey wrote letters also, which came in great haste, that he understood the French had a design upon that island, or some part of England. It also appeared to the committee, by divers of the letters which were opened coming from beyond sea, that they expected the earl of Strafford there . . . and in some of those letters, there was advice to the cardinal,[11] to bestir himself betimes, to interrupt the height of the proceedings here in England. . . .

THE FIVE MEMBERS

D'Ewes's Journal, 1642

D'Ewes's account of the king's attempt to seize five of his principal opponents in the Commons on 4 January 1642 is one of the most dramatic and
memorable. The failure of this attempted coup, and the mass protests he
experienced in the City of London the next day when he went in pursuit of the
five members, persuaded Charles to abandon his capital. At the same time,
the king's willingness yet again to resort to physical force set parliament on
the road that was to lead to the militia ordinance.
Source: W. H. Coates (ed.), *The Journal of Sir Simonds D'Ewes: From the First
Recess of the Long Parliament to the Withdrawal of King Charles from London*
(Yale, 1942), pp. 381–3.

4 January 1642

About 3 of the clock we had notice that his majesty was coming from
Whitehall to Westminster with a great company of armed men but it proved
otherwise in the issue that they were only some of the officers who served in
his majesty's late army and some other loose persons to the number of about
some [2 or 300 *crossed out*] 400.

Mr Pym and the other 4 members of our House who stood accused by his
majesty's attorney of high treason knowing that his majesty was coming to the
House of Commons did withdraw out of it. The House leaving it to their own
liberty whether they would withdraw or stay within, and it was a pretty
whiles before Mr Strode could be persuaded to it. His majesty came into the
House with Charles Prince Elector Palatine[12] with him a little after three of
the clock in the afternoon, who all stood up and uncovered our heads and the
Speaker stood up just before his chair. His majesty as he came up along the
House came for the most part of the way uncovered also bowing to either side
of the House and we all bowed again towards him and so he went to the
Speaker's chair on the left hand of it coming up close by the place where I sat
between the south end of the clerk's table and me; he first spake to the Speaker
saying 'Mr Speaker I must for a time make bold with your chair' . . . when he
asked for Mr Pym whether he were present or not and when there followed a
general silence that nobody would answer him he then asked for Mr Holles
whether he were present and when nobody answered him he pressed the
Speaker to tell him who kneeling down did very wisely desire his majesty to
pardon him saying that he could neither see nor speak but by command of the
House to which the king answered 'well well tis no matter I think my eyes are
as good as anothers' and then he looked round about the House a pretty whiles
to see if he could espie any of them. . . .

After he had ended his speech he went out of the House in a more discontented and angry passion than he came in, going out again between myself and

the south end of the clerk's table and the Prince Elector after him: as soon as he was gone and the doors were shut the Speaker asked us if he should make report of his majesty's speech but Sir John Hotham said we had all heard it and there needed no report of it to be made and others cried to adjourn till tomorrow at one of the clock in the afternoon, upon which in the issue we agreed and so the Speaker having adjourned the House till that hour we rose about half an hour after 3 of the clock in the afternoon little imagining for the present at least a greater part of us the extreme danger we had escaped through God's wonderful providence.

For the design was to have taken out of our House by force and violence the said five members if we had refused to have delivered them up peaceably and willingly which for the preservation of the privileges of our House we must have refused. And in the taking of them away, they were to have set upon us all if we had resisted in an hostile manner. It is very true that the plot was so contrived as that the king should have withdrawn out of the House and passed through the lobby or little room next without it before the massacre should have begun upon a watchword by him to have been given upon his passing through them: but tis most likely that those ruffians being about 80 in number who were gotten into the said lobby being armed all of them with swords and some of them with pistols, ready charged were so thirsty after innocent blood as they would scarce have stayed the watchword if those members had been there but would have begun their violence as soon as they had understood of our denial, to the hazard of the persons of the king and the Prince Elector as well as of us. For one of them understanding a little before the king came out that those five gentlemen were absent. 'Zounds' said he, 'they are gone and now we are never the better for our coming.'

The Countie of Buckingham cometh to London the very same day of the Lords & Comons so quarded, with their Petition to the Parl: Carrying the Protestation on their staves on horseback, and the Counties of Essex, Hertford, Barkshire, Surrey, & others, followed them in like maner, shortly after

Figure 5 Petitioners from Buckinghamshire ride into London on 11 January 1642 to support their MP, John Hampden, one of the 'five members'.

3

CHOOSING SIDES

IRELAND

An alleged proclamation of the Irish rebels, 1641

Events in Ireland became a major item of news after reports of the uprisings in Ulster reached England. Tracts describing with a mixture of fact and fiction the motives of the rebels and the progress of the rebellion streamed from the presses in 1641–2. From an English and Scottish perspective, the Irish were engaged in a Catholic crusade against Protestantism and the following document, which was printed for circulation in England, purports to be a proclamation issued by the head of the Catholic friars in Ireland to rally the faithful to arms.

Source: *Joyful news from Ireland . . . also the copy of a proclamation set forth by the rebels* (London, 1641), Thomason Tracts E. 177/9.

Upon the 30th day of October, being Saturday, did certain of the rebels in Ireland remove out of Armagh privately into the City of Dublin, but the day before a proclamation was set forth by the chief of the rebels to this effect.

The proclamation set forth by the rebels:

Patrick O'Neill, chief commander of the Catholic friars in Ireland, doth publish and declare, that Irish Catholics are a nation not conquered, nor ought they to live under the laws that of late have been enacted: they ought to have a free use of their religion, without interruption, which they had now cause to fear would be restrained, if not utterly taken away: therefore we which are constant friends to the Catholic faith, proclaim to all our loving brethren, that it is high time to stir, since it is of so great a consequence, therefore all that wish well to the Catholic faith let them now betake them to their arms, and come now and assist us who are now in the field to defend the religion with our swords, which hath been established in this kingdom by our worthy ancestors: and hereby we shall put honour upon our religion, and make our names famous throughout the Christian world; and if any of the Catholic religion shall refuse to assist us in this our just defence, let them know they will be kept under like slaves, and draw upon them a curse from all the Catholics in the world, and the curse of us priests, and friars, and soldiers. Given at the council held the 29th of October in the county of Monaghan.

The forged royal commission of 1641

Whether or not Charles can justifiably be charged with complicity in the Irish rebellion, there were people in England who were ready to believe that he was guilty. Those who believed in the full popish conspiracy thesis would be particularly predisposed to this conviction. The publication by Phelim O'Neill at Newry of a royal commission (which was almost certainly a forgery) endorsing the rebels' actions was particularly damaging to the king.
Source: R. Dunlop, 'The forged commission of 1641', *The English Historical Review*, ii, 1887, pp. 529–30.

Charles, by the grace of God, king of England, Scotland, France, and Ireland, defender of the faith, etc. to all Catholic subjects within the kingdom of Ireland, greeting: know ye, that we, for the safeguard and preservation of our person, have been enforced to make our abode and residence in the kingdom of Scotland for a long season,[1] occasioned by reason of the obstinate and disobedient carriage of the parliament of England against us; that hath not only presumed to take upon them the government and disposition of those princely rights and prerogatives, that have justly descended upon us and our predecessors, being kings and queens of the said kingdom for many hundred years past, but also have possessed themselves of the whole strength of the said kingdom, in appointing governors, commanders, and officers in all places therein, at their own will and pleasure without our consent, whereby we are deprived of our sovereignty and are left naked without defence. And forasmuch as we are in ourselves very sensible that these storms blow aloft and are very likely to be carried by the vehemence of the Protestant party of the kingdom of Ireland, and endanger our regal power and authority there also; know ye, that we, reposing much care and trust in your duty and obedience, which we have for many years past found, do hereby give unto you full power and authority to assemble and meet together with all the speed and diligence that business of so great a consequence doth require, and to advise and consult together by sufficient and discreet numbers at all times, days, and places, which you shall in your judgement hold most convenient, and most for the ordering, settling, and effecting the great work [illegible] and directed to you in our letters, and to use all politic means and ways possible to possess yourselves for [illegible] and safety of all the forts, castles, and places of strength and defence within the kingdom, except the places, persons, and estates of our loyal and loving subjects the Scots; also to arrest and seize the goods, estates, and persons of all the English Protestants, within the said kingdom to our use. And in your care and speedy performance of this our will and pleasure we shall rely on your wonted duty and allegiance to us, which we shall accept and reward in due time. Witness ourself at Edinburgh this 1st day of October in the seventeenth year of our reign.[2]

[The following proclamation was said to have accompanied the publication of the commission at Newry on 4 November]

Phelim O'Neill, Rory Maguire. To all Catholics of the Roman party, both English and Irish, in the kingdom of Ireland we wish all happiness, freedom of conscience, and victory over the English heretics, who for a long time have tyrannised over our bodies and usurped by extortion our estates. Be it hereby made known unto you all, our friends and countrymen, that the king's most excellent majesty for many great and urgent causes him thereunto moving, imposing trust and confidence in our fidelity, hath signified unto us, by his commission under the great seal of Scotland, bearing date at Edinburgh, the 1st day of this instant October 1641, and also by letters under his sign manual, bearing date with the said commission, of divers great and heinous affronts that the English Protestants, especially the English parliament, have published against his royal prerogative, and also against his Catholic friends, within the kingdom of England, the copy of which commission we herewith send unto you, to be published with all speed in all parts of this kingdom that you may be assured of our sufficient warrant and authority therein.

Worse and worse news from Ireland, *1641*

Many of the published tracts dealing with the early stages of the rebellion contain graphic descriptions of atrocities supposedly inflicted by the Irish on English Protestant settlers. Accounts of barbarities committed on women and children, mass murders of civilians and desecration of the dead, such as that contained in the tract below, conform to patterns of atrocity propaganda encountered at other stages in history. Clearly atrocities were committed but tracts like this one were not attempts at objective reporting and readers would be only too prepared to believe the worst.
Source: Thomason Tracts, E. 180/15.

A copy of a letter read in the House of Parliament, the 14 of this instant month of December 1641:

All I can tell you is the miserable estate we continue under, for the rebels daily increase in men and munitions in all parts except the province of Munster, exercising all manner of cruelties, and striving who can be most barbarously exquisite in tormenting the poor Protestants, wheresoever they come, cutting off the privy members, ears, fingers, and hands, plucking out their eyes, boiling the heads of little children before their mothers' faces, and then ripping up their mothers' bowels, stripping women naked, and standing by

Figure 6 Alleged Irish atrocities in the early stages of the rebellion of 1641

them being naked, whilst they are in travail, killing the children as soon as they are born, and ripping up their mothers' bellies, as soon as they are delivered; driving men, women, and children, by hundreds together upon bridges, and from thence cast them down into rivers, such as drowned not, they knock their brains out with poles, or shoot them with muskets, that endeavour to escape by swimming out; ravishing wives before their husbands' faces, and virgins before their parents' faces, after they have abused their bodies, making them renounce their religion, and then marry them to the basest of their fellows.

Oh that the Lord, who hath moved the kingdoms of England and Scotland, to send relief to those afflicted Protestants, would likewise stir them to effect their undertaking, with all possible expedition, lest it be too late.

Some of the persons particularly mentioned to have suffered, who are known unto you, are, Master German, minister of Brides, his body mangled, and his members cut off, Master Fullerton minister of Lughall, Simon Hastings his ears cut off, Master Blandry minister, hanged, his flesh pulled off from his bones, in the presence of his wife, in small pieces, he being hanged two days before her, in the place where she is now prisoner. Abraham James of Newtown, in the diocese of Clogher, cut in pieces, and it is reported that the bishop of Clogher is turned to the rebels, thus moving pardon in presuming to trouble you at this time in your public employment, do with humble remembrance of his best respects to you, and your virtuous lady, remain, your servant to command, Thomas Partington. 27 November 1641.

This letter was read in the House of Commons, upon the 14 day of this month, and also read again before the Lords, at a committee of both Houses, and humbly prayed to have the same entered in the journals of both Houses. The said House of Commons likewise desired the Lords to join with them, to petition his majesty, to take off the reprieve from the seven condemned priests,[3] and that they might be forthwith executed according to their judgement, and the law.

Joseph Lister's Autobiography

The nonconformist autobiographer, Joseph Lister (1627–1709), vividly recalls his experience as an adolescent of an episode in the West Riding of Yorkshire triggered by news that Irish rebels had landed in England and were already in the neighbourhood. The belief that the English were about to experience the kind of Irish atrocities they had recently read or heard tell of led to panic. Ironically, the 'Irish rebels' were Protestant refugees from Ireland.
Source: T. Wright (ed.), *The Autobiography of Joseph Lister, of Bradford in Yorkshire* (London, 1862), pp. 6–8.

About this time (in the year 1641) did the rebellion in Ireland break out, and many thousand Protestants of all ages, sexes, and degrees, were put to death, with great inhumanity and cruelty; and great fear came upon the Protestants in England, these villains giving it out, that what they had done there was by the king's commission, and that in a little time the English Protestants (or heretics as they called them) should drink of the same cup; and it was verily believed by many, it would be so, if God should suffer it; and O what fears and tears, cries and prayers, night and day, was there then in many places, and in my dear mother's house, in particular! I was then about twelve or thirteen years of age, and though I was afraid to be killed, yet was I weary of so much fasting and praying, and longed to see those nights and days over. I remember one public fast day (for godly ministers appointed many, and kept them in their respective places;) Mr Wales kept many at Pudsey, it was two miles from Bradford, and thither my pious mother and all the family went constantly upon these days . . . that day I say, which I am speaking of, I think about three o'clock in the afternoon, a certain man that I remember well, – (his name was John Sugden) – came and stood up in the chapel door, and cried out with a lamentable voice, 'Friends', said he, 'we are all as good as dead men, for the Irish rebels are coming; they are come as far as Rochdale, and Littleborough, and the Batings, and will be at Halifax and Bradford shortly'; he came, he said, out of pity and good will, to give us this notice. And having given this alarm, away he ran towards Bradford again, where the same report was spread about. Upon which the congregation was all in confusion, some ran out, others wept, others fell to talking to friends, and the Irish massacre being but lately acted, and all circumstances put together, the people's hearts failed them with fear; so that the Reverend Mr Wales desired the congregation to compose them-selves as well as they could, while he put himself and them into the hands of Almighty God by prayer, and so he did, and so dismissed us. But O what a sad and sorrowful going home had we that evening, for we must needs go to Bradford, and knew not but incarnate devils and death would be there before us, and meet us there. What sad and strange conjectures, or rather conclu-sions, will surprise and fear make! Methinks I shall never forget this time.

Well we got home, and found friends and neighbours in our case, and expecting the cut-throats coming. But at last some few horsemen were prevailed with to go to Halifax, to know how the case stood. They went with a great deal of fear, but found matters better when they came there, it proving only to be some Protestants that were escaping out of Ireland for their lives into England; and this news we received with great joy, and spent the residue of that night in praises and thanksgivings to God. And I well remember what sad discourses I heard about this time, the papists being desperate, bloody men; and those that were put into offices and places of trust were such as would serve the king and his design. . . .

PAPISTS

Accounts of a popish scare, 1641

English Catholics were believed to be plotting to overthrow Protestantism and introduce popery and tyranny and, as a bulwark against the latter, parliament could expect to be the target of such plots. There were two anti-popish panics in May 1641 both prompted by rumours that parliament had finally fallen prey to the papists. Just how easily such a rumour could arise and spread is illustrated by the following reports on the first panic of 5 May.
Sources: D. Laing (ed.), *The Letters and Journals of Robert Baillie*, 3 vols (Edinburgh, 1841–2), i, 352; British Library, Additional Ms. 19398, f. 130.

Robert Baillie to the presbytery of Irvine, 7 May 1641:

Wednesday [5 May] a sudden bruit ran through the City that the papists had set the House of Commons on fire and had beset it with arms: in a clap all the City is in alarum; shops close; a world of people runs down to Westminster. When they come, they find the report all utterly groundless. The matter was, about 10 a.m. some coming out of the House of Commons had said there was hot work and a great fire within; which being mistaken, put the rash and foolish alarm abroad. . . .

Thomas Dillingham to his father at Barnwell in Northamptonshire, 6 May 1641:

[5 May] This day, there came an old woman into Blackfriars and told them that the parliament house was on fire and also a note to my lord mayor and the aldermen to the same purpose which made great tumult and so at Blackfriars the people ran up and down as if they had been wild the minister stood still a good while asking 'What was the matter?' at the last after much stir the minister fell to his sermon again, and divers fellows ran down with swords as fast as they could to the parliament house, but there was no such thing. The House of Commons came down to them and desired them to depart and so they did. . . .

A discovery of a horrible and bloody treason and conspiracy, *1641*

This is the most famous of the supposedly popish plots aimed directly at parliament. Prominent members of both Houses were to be murdered as they left for home in the evening and in the ensuing tumult there were to be Catholic uprisings in five English counties and in Wales. Coming as it did so shortly after news of the risings in Ireland, the 'discovery' of the plot by a young London tailor made particular impact.
Source: Thomason Tracts E. 176/12.

Treason discovered: or an ample and real relation of a late horrible plot and conspiracy against the Protestants of England, in general and the citizens of London in particular.

Being intended to murder divers of the nobility and many others of the honourable House of Commons in parliament, taken by confession, and examined by the parliament, the 15 of November 1641 being Monday.

The information of Thomas Beale, a tailor living in Whitecross Street in Goodman Warner's house, delivered in parliament on Monday and Tuesday November 15, 16, 1641.

On the Sabbath day last the said young man, late at night passing through Moorfields[4] near the City of London did overhear certain fellows talking and whispering together about their intended plot and machinations, the one of them saying that he had received 40 shillings in hand to murder divers persons eminent in the house of parliament, which he would shortly accomplish, and another of them also made report that he had also received a larger sum to do the like enterprise upon some great persons of the higher house, which pretended plot of theirs, they verily expected should have taken effect on Thursday night following, had not the providence of Almighty God miraculously prevented the bloody designs of those cruel and merciless papists: for it happened that those miscreant traitors espying the said young man in the dark, and fearing by him to be discovered made at him with their weapons and grievously wounded him, intending to deprive him of his sweet life, which they had effected, had not the divine providence of God prevented in his good time by his escaping from them.

In which conference of theirs he also overheard them to whisper about some great plots or treacheries in Wales now intended against England, and that the next shires adjoining Raglan Castle were lately come in with all their forces to the assistance of the earl of Worcester.[5]

And the said young man coming before the parliament house, really and truly did relate the said former passages with great modesty and honest confidence, moreover alleging that they intended the murder of many protestant lords, with many other gentlemen such as Mr Pym and the like, and that the papists in Wales intended to seize into their hands all the strongholds of Cheshire and Lancashire with the adjacent parts, and that in that hurly-burly and combustion the plot was so laid and contrived, that by the papists at the same instant, the City of London should have been surprised, and all the Protestants' throats cut. Upon which relation the Houses of Parliament sat very late on Monday night last, and the lords and others of both Houses were conducted to their lodgings and houses by most of the trained bands in Middlesex the same night.

On the morrow very early, both Houses met, where upon serious deliberation, it was immediately concluded that the house of the said earl of Worcester situated in the Strand in the liberties of Westminster, should be by strong watch guarded both by land and water, and that strict search should be made

Popiſh Recuſants diſarmed, for the greate ſecuri: ty of the kingdome

Figure 7 English Catholics disarmed as a security measure in 1641–2

in the said house for the apprehending of the persons of Father Andrewes and Father Jones in the house of the Lord Herbert, son and heir to the foresaid lord of Worcester and divers other suspicious persons, supposed to be confederated in that wicked and most diabolical design, who are thought also to be lurking in the said house, which search was accordingly performed the same day about eleven a clock in the fore-noon.

The said Father Jones escaped out of a back door into the Savoy, and Father Andrewes was taken in the French ordinary over against the Lord Herbert's house and is now in custody.

There are divers warrants gone out to the lord mayor of the City of London, for the apprehending of divers other suspicious persons.

RELIGIOUS RADICALISM

Depositions before the Lords about a disrupted communion service, 1641

The violent disruption of the Sunday communion in St Olave, Southwark, on 6 June 1641, by an over-zealous minority drawn from the lower reaches of society caused particular offence. An appeal against the violence to the House of Lords resulted in deliberately severe sentences being meted out to those at the centre of the incident. Such an incident was a relatively unusual occurrence despite royalist anxieties about the prospect of religious and political anarchy.
Source: House of Lords record office, Braye Ms. 19, 17 June 1641.

The parishioners [of] St Olave in Southwark called in, and the petition of Mr [Oliver] Whitby the curate and the petition of that parish read.

Mr Whitby the curate deposed, that Sunday sevennight in the receiving [of the] sacrament some persons as Hugh Evans, Robert Wainman, John Moore, George Bonace did disturb him in administering the sacrament.

Hugh Evans, John Moore laid hands on him, and thrusting him about the church, forced him to give them the communion sitting, when he had the bread in his hand.

Wainman and Bonace cried out of the gallery, 'Why do you suffer Baal's priest[6] to give you the communion and serve you so? Kick him out of the church; kneel to a pope, hang him. Baal's priest get you home and crum your porridge with your bread.'

Robert Wainman said for himself, that the minister made trouble himself, and he called to the people to speak and stand in God's cause. . . .

Hugh Evans, said he sat down to receive the sacrament and desired [the] minister to give him the sacrament, who refused, then he took him by the gown.

John Moore, said he sat down by [the] communion table and desired the minister to give him the sacrament, but he denied it.

A petition about the violent demolition of altar rails, 1641

The demolition of altar rails in St Thomas the Apostle, London, on 11 June 1641 immediately followed on from a meeting of parishioners in the church to take the Protestation, and disagreement between rival parish factions over the matter of the rails. The actual work of destruction was done by some local youths but not without encouragement from some more senior parish zealots. The rector and his supporters complained to the Lords and a fine was imposed on one of the chief zealots but no order was given to restore the rails.
Source: House of Lords record office, main papers, 30 June 1641 petition of the parson, churchwardens, and inhabitants of the parish of St Thomas the Apostle to the House of Lords.

That on the eleventh day of this instant June, your petitioners with divers other inhabitants of the said parish repaired to their parish church, by order from the lord mayor of the City of London, for the taking of the Protestation, lately made by the House of Commons now assembled in parliament, where one John Blackwell the king's majesty's grocer having made the same Protestation, in the audience of the people that were present, uttered these, or the like speeches (viz.) 'Gentlemen, we have here made a protestation before Almighty God against all popery and popish innovations, and these rails (laying his hand upon the rails about the communion table) are popish innovations, and therefore it is fit they be pulled down, and shall be pulled down.' Upon which words many being as ill-affected as the said Blackwell, consulted to pull them down. The table neither standing altarwise, nor at the east end of the chancel, but in the usual place where it hath stood, time beyond the memory of man being only railed about for decency, and the people not pressed to come up to the same, at the time of the administration of the sacrament.

And that after they and your petitioners had made the Protestation and all gone (except those that were confederates with the said Blackwell, and some few of your petitioners) the said Blackwell and one Francis Webb, having incensed many factious people, with scandalous and reproachful words against petitioners, for their conformity to the order and decency of the church, they, or some of their complices having striken the churchwardens and threatened others, Thomas Calley, Michael Robinson, Zacheus Iles, George Tye, John Roberts, and many others whose names your petitioners cannot yet learn, with great insolence pulled down the rails aforesaid, and having broken them in pieces carried them to the church door (saying they were formerly a sin offering, but now they would make them a burnt offering, and that Dagon[7] being now down, they would burn him, with divers other irreverent speeches) they having provided chips and other materials aforehand, set them on fire, and burnt them to ashes. And further one of them said, that if the parson came to read service in a surplice, they would burn him and the surplice with the rails.

D'Ewes's account of the censure of a churchwarden for iconoclasm, 1641

The Commons order of 8 September 1641, requiring churchwardens to remove railed altars and level chancels, and purge their churches of offensive symbols and images generally appears to have led to orderly, staged changes depending on the state of local opinion. However, it gave a green light to some zealots, such as the junior churchwarden of St Mary Woolchurch in London, to commence thorough purges of all remnants of popery from their churches. Funeral monuments, which would generally have been associated with the leading families of a parish, had been specifically excluded from any purges.
Source: Coates (ed.), *The Journal of Sir Simonds D'Ewes*, pp. 6–7.

October 16 Saturday, 1641. At the committee [for the recess].

There was a petition read from one [Michael] Herring one of the church-wardens of Woolchurch in London in which he showed that in obedience to the order of the House of Commons of the 8 September last past for the removing of idolatrous pictures he had taken up divers brass inscriptions which tended to idolatry: and defaced some statues on tombs which were in the posture of praying and the like, and desired direction how he should raise to defray the charge with other particulars to the same effect. I desired after Mr Pym had read the petition that all might withdraw: and so all strangers[8] did.
Then I spake in effect following. That this man's indiscretion had brought a

great scandal upon the House of Commons as if we meant to deface all antiquities. That when we had prepared a statute to pass to this end and purpose for the removing of all offensive pictures yet we had specially provided that no tombs should be meddled withall: for though the words *orate pro anima*, or pray for the soul etc. were left on the tomb yet that might rather serve for a monument of the miserable ignorance of those times than give any just offence to such as were judicious as Constantine[9] preserved some of the heathen idols, for a monument of shame to such as had adored them. I conceived the man who had done this, to be an honest man and to have done it with a good intention, and therefore I would wish we might have the tombs again repaired and the matters so compounded as he might come into no further danger for this, his indiscreet act.

Others spake after me and at last the said Mr Herring and divers others of the parish were called in, and we declared openly our disapproving of his indiscreet act, and so advised them to agree the matter amongst themselves, and that the brass might be again laid on upon the tombs: and so they departed.

Lords proceedings against a baptist congregation, 1641

The calling of the Long Parliament meant a virtual end to the coercion of Protestant consciences and some radical sects seized the opportunity to gather together and organise. The Southwark congregation below was one of seven separatist churches discovered in the London area in 1640–2. Although the king intervened to recommend that the Lords take severe action against this particular congregation, especially in view of some of the seditious opinions held by them, they escaped with nothing more than a stern warning of future severity if they remained obdurate.
Source: *Lords' Journals*, iv, 133–4.

Saturday, 16 January 1641. Anabaptists recommended to the justice of this House by his majesty.

The lord privy seal, by command from his majesty, presented to the House a paper, which was lately delivered to his majesty, which he commended to the justice and care of the House to consider of. The contents of the paper was read, *in haec verba*:[10]

Decimo tertio die Januarii, 1641.[11]

Edmund Chillenden, Nicholas Tyne, John Webb, Richard Sturges, Thomas Gunn, John Ellis, with at least 60 people more. They were all taken on Sunday last, in the afternoon, in the time of divine service, by the constables and churchwardens of St Saviour's [Southwark], in the house of Richard Sturges; where they said they met to teach and edify one another in Christ.

Their tenets.

1   They being brought before Sir John Lenthall, he demanded why they would not go and resort to their parish church, according to the law of 35 Elizabeth.[12] They answered, that the law of 35 Elizabeth was not a true law, for that it was made by the bishops; and that they would not obey it.

2   That they would not go to their parish churches: that those churches were not true churches; and that there was no true church but where the faithful met.

3   That the king could not make a perfect law, for that he was not a perfect man.

4   That they ought not to obey him but in civil things.

5   That some of them threatened the churchwardens and constables, that they had not yet answered for this day's work.

JOHN LENTHALL.	THOMAS BUTLER, churchwarden.
THOMAS TEMPLE.	JOHN LUNTLEY.

Hereupon it was ordered, that Sir John Lenthall do take care that the aforesaid persons shall be forthcoming, and appear before this House on Monday morning next; and likewise that he cause the constable, the churchwardens, and whosoever else can testify anything in the business, to attend the same time here.

Die Lunae, videlicet, 18 die Januarii [1641].[13]

The lord privy seal, earl marshall, and lord chamberlain gave the House thanks from his majesty, for the course they had taken concerning the sectaries.

And Edmund Chillenden [and the others], being brought by order of this House, were called severally in, all of them denying the material things which they were charged with. Hereupon Sir John Lenthall, Thomas Temple, Thomas Butler, and John Luntley were sworn; and upon their oath, did justify that what was contained and subscribed by them, in the paper delivered, was true.

Thereupon the House did order, that the said sectaries should receive for this time an admonition from this House, that they shall hereafter repair to their several parish churches, to hear divine service, and to give obedience thereunto, according to the acts of parliament of this realm; to that purpose the order was read unto them, made by this House the 16th of January 1641;[14] and to be told that, if hereafter they do not observe these commands, they shall be severely punished, according to the law.

RIOTS AND DISORDERS

Accounts by JPs of fenland riots, 1641, and a retrospective view of fenland politics, 1646

Fens, along with forests, were the scene of some of the most serious outbreaks of rural unrest in the pre-civil war period. The riots themselves were part of a well-established tradition of periodically attacking unpopular enclosures of common land and had little, if any, wider political or social content. But some anxious observers linked these riots with the tumults in the capital and incidents elsewhere and saw them as evidence that social order was being threatened. So far as the fenmen themselves were concerned, there was a natural inclination to side with parliament in the civil war given that the king had enthusiastically backed fenland drainage and enclosure. However, as the words of the Lincolnshire husbandman (below) indicate, party allegiance for some fenmen could be entirely opportunistic.
Sources: PRO, SP 16/484/8; House of Lords record office, main papers, 10 February 1646, affidavit of Robert Palmer of Epworth, Lincolnshire, husbandman.

Certificate of Sir Thomas Bishop, William Cony and Rutland Snoden, Lincolnshire JPs, to the House of Commons, 6 September 1641.

To the honourable House of knights, citizens and burgesses in this present parliament assembled.

Whereas upon the petition of Humphrey Walrond, esquire, and others to this honourable House concerning the riotous assemblies and forcible entries made by the commoners within the West and North Fens in the county of Lincoln, the justices of the peace of the said county by order of this House of the thirteenth of August last were required to employ their best endeavours for suppressing the said force and all riotous and tumultuous assemblies that might arise upon like occasions. We whose names are hereunto subscribed justices of the peace in the said county in obedience to the said order and upon the request of the said Mr Walrond and Robert Webster, gentleman, respectively upon the several days hereafter mentioned repaired to the said fens where we found as followeth.

On Friday the seven and twentieth day of August, William Cony and Rutland Snoden, esquires, justices of the peace within the said county at the request of Robert Webster, gentleman, did repair to the said fens to the lands of the said Mr Webster where we found great multitudes that day assembled in his said lands who committed great waste and destruction there, of wheat and other grain and behaved themselves furiously and outrageously contrary to the peace not regarding our commands in his majesty's name for keeping the peace, but utterly contemning the same threatening further mischiefs by beating and wounding those that opposed them, some of which we then committed to the gaol of Lincoln.

[Signed by]: William Cony Rutland Snoden

On Monday being the thirtieth day of August last most of the justices of the said county being then gone to the assizes at Lincoln great numbers of people both men and women to the number of 200 persons or thereabouts forcibly entered upon a certain parcel of land in Mr Walrond's possession containing about one hundred acres beating and wounding his servants and though they were in his majesty's name commanded by Sir Thomas Bishop, knight, one of his majesty's justices within the said county to keep the peace, and that proclamation for their departure was made by the said Sir Thomas Bishop who only remained in those parts during the time of the assizes, yet they did not wholly depart from the said ground, but there continued and carried from thence a great quantity of Mr Walrond's wheat in their carts to a very great value. And on the day following being Tuesday last a great number of men and women assembled themselves together in great multitudes and by force and strong hand carried from off the lands of George Kirke, esquire,[15] great quantities of wheat and other grain belonging to his tenants notwithstanding they were then required to desist and depart from the same by the said Sir Thomas Bishop.

[Signed by]: Sir Thomas Bishop

We whose names are hereunder subscribed do further certify that Michael Broughton of Boston in the county of Lincoln, yeoman, being sworn by us on the sixth day of September 1641 deposed as followeth, that is to say, that on the thirtieth day of August last, Nicholas Gardiner of Sibsey in the county aforesaid and James Finch of Sibsey aforesaid with others being on the lands of the said Mr Walrond in the said fens and from thence cutting and carrying away his corn the said Finch demanded of the said Gardiner whether or no they should carry away certain shocks of wheat formerly cut by and then standing upon the said lands of the said Mr Walrond the said Gardiner answered thereunto, 'Yes, yes, we will have it all and what we cannot carry away we will burn and the house too before we sleep.' William Daniel of Fotheringhay in the county of Northampton, yeoman, on the day abovesaid deposed likewise to the same effect as abovesaid and further deposed that the said Gardiner and others present with him at the time abovesaid did say, 'If we do not take away all the corn (meaning the said Mr Walrond's corn which then they were carrying) I would some of us might kill or be killed', and further deposed that other principal instigators and leaders of the said rioters to the number of about 40 did then threaten in like manner as abovesaid. And we do humbly conceive that unless some speedy course be taken by order from this honourable House for appeasing these riotous and tumultuous proceedings, there is just cause to fear further and greater mischiefs and a more evil consequence will ensue hereupon to the disturbing of his majesty's peace, the evil examples of his majesty's subjects and the endangering of a rebellion. All which we humbly certify and submit to the grave and judicious consideration of this honourable assembly. Dated under our hands the sixth day of September: anno domini: 1641.

[Signed by]: Sir Thomas Bishop, William Cony and Rutland Snoden

Affidavit of Robert Palmer of Epworth, husbandman, 10 February 1646:
... That he hath very often heard divers of the inhabitants of the Isle of Axholme ... say and affirm in their private discourse, that they would never have taken arms for the parliament, but that they intended thereby to have the power in their hand to destroy the draining and improvement and lay all waste again to their common.

Arthur Wilson's account of anti-popish riots against the Countess Rivers, 1642

One of the most spectacular outbursts of anti-popery rioting in 1642 was that directed at the Countess Rivers, a leading Catholic landowner and a lady of the bedchamber to the queen. Lady Rivers appealed for help to the earl of Warwick who sent his steward, Arthur Wilson (1595–1652), to rescue her. In his autobiography Wilson, who was also an historian and dramatist, recounts his experience of that mission and the strength of grassroots anti-popery which even parliament's friends had difficulty dealing with.
Source: Arthur Wilson, *Observations of God's Providence, in the Tract of my Life*, in F. Peck, *Desiderata Curiosa* (London, 1735), ii, lib. XII, pp. 23–4.

The twentieth of August, 1642, the king having left the parliament, and thereby a loose rein being put into the mouth of the unruly multitude, many thousands swarmed to the pulling down of Long Melford House, a gallant seat belonging to the countess of Rivers;[16] and to the endangering of her person; she being a recusant, they made that their pretence, but spoil and plunder was their aim. This fury was not only in the rabble, but many of the better sort behaved themselves as if there had been a dissolution of all government; no man could remain in his own house without fear, nor be abroad with safety.

A gentleman came posting from the countess of Rivers to crave the protection of lord's family. My lord the earl of Warwick[17] was then at sea, being lord high admiral for the parliament. My Lord Rich was at Oxford, with the king. Mr Charles Rich, hunting the stag at Rochford. So I was commanded to take some few men and a coach with six horses, to fetch the Lady Rivers to Leighs. Which I hastened to do, not dreaming of any danger by the way; though I might hap'ly meet some there.

With difficulty I passed through the little villages of Essex. . . . And, but that they had some knowledge both of me and the coach, I had not passed with safety. My design and pretence was to go for Bury; but to stay in some place near Long Melford; to find out where the Lady Rivers was.

When I came to Sudbury in Suffolk, within three miles of Long Melford, not a man appeared 'till we were within the chain. And then they began to run to their weapons, and before we could get to the market place, the streets swarmed with people. I came out of the coach, as soon as they took the horses by the heads, and desired, that I might speak with the mayor, or some of the magistrates; to know the cause of this tumult: for we had offended no body. The mouth cried out, this coach belongs to the Lady Rivers; and they are going to her. (And indeed the gentleman, who came along with me, was known by some of the town). And some, who pretended to be more wise and knowing than the rest, said, that I was the Lord Rivers. And they swarmed about me, and were so kind as to lay hold on me. But I calmly entreated those many hundreds which encircled me, to hear me speak; which before they had not patience to do, the confusion and noise was so great. I told them, I was steward to the earl of Warwick, a lover of his country, and now in the parliament's employment. That I was going to Bury, about business of his. And that I had letters in my pockets (if they would let any of the magistrates see them) which would make me appear to be a friend and an honest man. This said, the mouth cried out, 'Letters, letters!' The tops of the trees, and all the windows, were thronged with people, who cried the same.

At last the mayor came crowding in with his officers; and I showed him my letters (which indeed I had received a little before from my lord, and, fearing the worst, thought the bringing of them might be an advantage to my passage). The mayor's wisdom said, he knew not my lord's hand; it might be, and it might be not. And away he went, not knowing what to do with me, nor I to say to them. But I found they had an itching desire after the coach horses (the town being to set out horses for the parliament's service) and therefore they were the willinger to believe nothing, 'till Mr Man, the town-clerk (whose father was my lord's servant) saw me at a distance, and came crowding in to be assured, having once seen me, as he said, at Leighs. He told the mayor and the people, I was the earl of Warwick's steward: and his assurance got some credit with them. And so the great cloud vanished.

But I could go no further to succour the Lady Rivers. For I heard, from all hands, there was so great a confusion at Melford, that no man appeared like a gentleman, but was made a prey to that ravenous crew. So my lady's gentleman, Mr Man and myself took horse (leaving the coach at Sudbury) and went a bye-way to Sir Robert Crane's, a little nearer Melford, to listen after the countess. Sir Robert told us, that she had in her own person escaped to Bury; and so was gone to London. But he was forced to retain a trained band in his house (although he was a parliament man) to secure himself from the fury of that rabble; who threatened him, for being assistant to her escape. So monstrous is the beast when it holds the bridle in the teeth. . . .

PRESS AND PULPIT

The Stationers' Company's report on unlicensed printing to the Lords, 1641

The collapse of censorship and the growing circulation of unlicensed publications, often of a subversive nature, prompted action by the Lords. Investigations conducted for the Lords by the Stationers' Company, the chief agency for controlling the printing press, exposed a radical underground of printers and booksellers. Several of the individuals noted below were to later gain prominence as publishers, and sometimes authors too, of Leveller and other radical writings.
Source: House of Lords record office, main papers, 4 March 1641 list of unlicensed books and pamphlets with names of printers.

1.   Bernard Alsop printed several unlawful books, as Bacon's *Consideration of the Church, Privilege of parliament in England, Prerogative of parliaments, England's joy for banishing of priests, The black box of Rome.*
The copies of these books he had from Mr Sheeres, and Vavasor, bookbinders, who undertook to save them harmless.

2.   Matthew Symons confesseth, that he did join Mr [Thomas] Paine in the printing of a book called *The historical narration of that memorable parliament that wrought wonders.*

3.   Nicholas Vavasor confessed he sold one book, called *Smart's sermons*, the copy he had from [Richard] Albon, and it was printed by Alsop and [Thomas] Fawcett.

4.   Whiticar affirmed that he found in [Henry] Walker's house at the least 100 pamphlets, called *The lord of Canterbury's dream.* And these were printed at Fawcett's house.
The said Walker confessed he did disperse pamphlets called *The prelates' pride*, and verses made of the Lord Finch, and of Bishop Wren, and these he told us he made himself.
He dispersed likewise one book called *Prelacy's misery.* The printers of these books were Fawcett and Symons.

5.   Robert Harper confessed he printed *My lord of Strafford's charge.* The copy of which he had of one Ralph Mabb, who with Benson his partner sold them.

6.   Richard Lownes confesseth that he sold *The articles against the bishop of Canterbury* and *The articles against the Lord Finch.*
These were printed by Thomas Harper, who had the copy of them from Lownes.

7.   John Hammond confesseth he sold a book called *The dream or news from hell.* It was printed by Fawcett and Alsop, who had the copy from Pecham, a minister.

8.   Thomas Bates confesseth he sold a book called *The dream or news from hell*, which book he had from [Giles] Calvert, a bookbinder, who confessed it

was printed by Fawcett. But being asked from whence he had the copy, told us, he had it from one of the City, but refused to tell his name.

9.   Paine confessed he printed *Rome's echo*, the copy he had of one Bates, a bookbinder.

10. John Dawson printed *The orders for the committee made by the House of Commons*. The copy he had from one Henry [mistakenly referred to as 'Edward'] Overton, a bookseller, who promised the said Dawson to bring him an allowance from the House of Commons, but did not.

11. Upon search made in Beale's house, [Stephen] Buckley being his

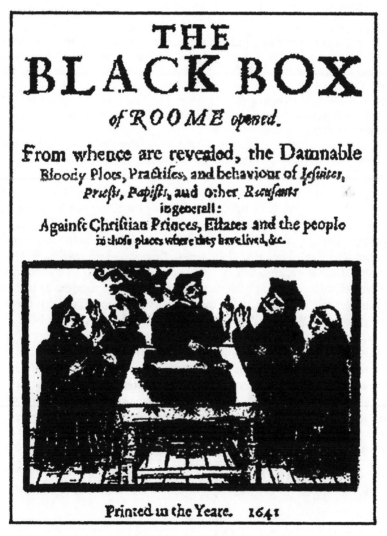

Figure 8 One of the subversive pamphlets reported by the Stationers' Company in March 1641

partner, there were found divers printed copies of the Scots' declaration that came but last.

12. Richard Lownes affirmed that John Wells of Moorfields did print *The answer to my lord of Canterbury's book against Fisher* and that he received £80 by those books. And that he likewise printed *The answer to the Commons*.

There was one Wells and Buckley being sent for by the committee refused to come, and they desire that they may be sent for by order of this House.

Clarendon's History *on the collapse of controls over press and pulpit*

The mass media of the period were the printing press and the pulpit which prior to 1640 had been subjected to theoretically stringent controls. Looking back on events, the moderate royalist and great contemporary historian of the period Edward Hyde (1609–74), who was created first earl of Clarendon after the Restoration, attached considerable importance to the collapse of these controls in creating the circumstances that eventually led to war. Prompt action taken by the senior authorities at the time, he believed, would have averted the conflict.
Source: E. Hyde, earl of Clarendon, *The History of the Rebellion and Civil Wars in England*, ed. W. D. Macray, 6 vols (Oxford, 1888), i, 269–70.

And from this time[18] the license of preaching and printing increased to that degree that all pulpits were freely delivered to the schismatical and silenced preachers, who till then had lurked in corners or lived in New England; and the presses [were] at liberty for the publishing of the most invective, seditious, and scurrilous pamphlets that their wit and malice could invent. Whilst the ministers of the state, and judges of the law, like men in an ecstasy, surprised and amazed with several apparitions, had no speech or motion; as if, having committed such an excess of jurisdiction, as men upon great surfeits are enjoined for a time to eat nothing, they had been prescribed to exercise no jurisdiction at all. Whereas, without doubt, if either the privy council, or the judges and the king's learned counsel, had assumed the courage to have questioned the preaching, or the printing, or the seditious riots upon the triumph of these three scandalous men, before the uninterruption and security had confirmed the people in all three, it had been no hard matter to have destroyed those seeds and pulled up those plants, which, neglected, grew up and prospered to a full harvest of rebellion and treason. . . .

CONTROL OF THE MILITIA

The militia ordinance, 1642

Parliament's militia ordinance of 5 March 1642 broke new ground in that a measure passed by both Houses that had not received the royal assent was presented as having the force of law. The ordinance took control of the appointment of lord lieutenants, who commanded the militia in England and Wales, out of royal hands and vested it in parliament instead. It was put into effect in a little over half the English counties, and some of the initial local confrontations between rival parties arose from attempts by parliamentarians to implement this ordinance and royalist rival efforts to execute their commission of array.

Source: C. H. Firth and R. S. Rait (eds), *Acts and Ordinances of the Interregnum*, 1642–60, 2 vols (London, 1911), i, 1–5.

An ordinance of the Lords and Commons in parliament, for the safety and defence of the kingdom of England, and dominium of Wales.

Whereas there hath been of late a most dangerous and desperate design upon the House of Commons, which we have just cause to believe to be an effect of the bloody counsels of papists and other ill-affected persons, who have already raised a rebellion in the kingdom of Ireland, and, by reason of many discoveries, we cannot but fear they will proceed not only to stir up the like rebellion and insurrections in the kingdom of England, but also to back them with forces from abroad; for the safety, thereof, of his majesty's person, the parliament, and kingdom, in this time of imminent danger, it is ordained by the Lords and Commons now in parliament assembled that Henry earl of Holland shall be lieutenant of the county of Berkshire [the lieutenants for each county and place named] and severally and respectively have power to assemble and call together all and singular his majesty's subjects, within the said several and respective counties and places, as well within liberties as without, that are meet and fit for the wars; and them to train, exercise, and put in readiness; and them, after their abilities and faculties, well and sufficiently, from time to time, to cause to be arrayed and weaponed, and to take the muster of them in places most fit for that purpose. And the aforesaid Henry earl of Holland [and the other named lieutenants] shall severally and respectively have power, within the several and respective counties and places aforesaid, to nominate and appoint such persons of quality as to them shall seem meet, to be their deputy lieutenants, to be approved of by both Houses of Parliament. . . . And the aforesaid Henry earl of Holland [and the others] shall have power to make colonels and captains, and other officers, and to remove them out of their places, and make others from time to time, as they shall think fit for that purpose. And [they], their deputy or deputies, in their absence, or by their command, shall have power to lead, conduct, and employ the persons aforesaid, arrayed and weaponed, for the suppression of all rebellions, insurrections, and invasions, that may happen within the several and respective counties and place; and shall have further power and authority to lead, conduct, and employ the persons aforesaid, arrayed and weaponed, as well within their said several and respective counties and places as within any other part of this realm of England, or dominium of Wales, for the suppression of all rebellions, insurrections and invasions that may happen, according as they from time to time shall receive directions from the Lords and Commons assembled in parliament. . . .

Thomas Knyvett's dilemma over the ordinance, 1642

The implementation of the militia ordinance put a political moderate like Thomas Knyvett in a quandary. Having reluctantly accepted his former militia command again under the new ordinance, shortly afterwards he was faced with a royal declaration condemning it. He resolved to lie low but was eventually to join the royalist camp.
Source: *The Knyvett Letters, 1620–44*, ed. B. Schofield (London, 1949), pp. 102–3.

Thomas Knyvett to his wife, 18 May 1642.

Oh sweet heart, I am now in a great straight what to do. Walking this other morning at Westminster, Sir John Potts,[19] with Commissary Muttford, saluted me with a commission from the Lord of Warwick,[20] to take upon me (by virtue of an ordinance of parliament) my company and command again. I was surprised what to do, whether to take or refuse. 'Twas no place to dispute, so I took it and desired some time to advise upon it. I had not received this many hours, but I met with a declaration point blank against it by the king. This distraction made me to advise with some understanding men what condition I stand in, which is no other than a great many men of quality do. What further commands we shall receive to put this ordinance in execution, if they run in a way that trenches upon my obedience against the king, I shall do according to my conscience, and this is the resolution of all honest men that I can speak with. In the meantime I hold it good wisdom and security to keep my company as close to me as I can in these dangerous times, and to stay out of the way of my new masters till these first musterings be over. . . .

The commission of array in Worcestershire, 1642

The king unwisely sought to raise forces by reviving a medieval instrument, the commission of array. It lacked statutory authority, was open to serious misinterpretation and was generally unpopular. In only a quarter of English counties was the commission put into effect and attempts to execute it elsewhere were thwarted.
Source: J. W. Willis Bund (ed.), 'Diary of Henry Townsend of Elmley Lovett, 1640–1663', *The Worcestershire Historical Society*, 1920, ii, p. 66.

The copy of the commissioners of array to the high constable for to send to the petty constables throughout the county of Worcester.

We his majesty's commissioners of array for the county of Worcester whose names are subscribed send greeting.

Whereas the king's majesty by his commission under the great seal of England bearing date at Beverley the 23rd day of July last past in the eighteenth year of his majesty's reign[21] have authorised us amongst others in the said commission named to array, train and muster the inhabitants of this county in these times of distraction according to the tenor of the said commission and instructions sent to us from his majesty under his hand. These are therefore to will and require you forthwith upon receipt hereof you issue forth your warrant to all the petty constables within your limits and division thereby requiring them to give warning to all the trained and freehold and clergy bands within their constablewick both horse and foot that are charged with arms to come and appear before us or any three or more of us upon the twelfth day of August next being Friday in the morning by nine of the clock, at and in the great meadow called Pitchcroft near the City of Worcester completely armed and arrayed, and you are to take notice yourself and give warning to the petty constables that neither you nor they nor any of the said trained band horse or foot fail of their appearance upon pain of such penalties as shall fall thereon.

And further we do require you and every of you to signify unto all such as are well affected to this service that so many as will voluntarily come in at the day and place appointed with their arms or otherwise shall be well received and perform an acceptable service to their king and country. Dated at Talbot in Sidbury, the first day of August in the 18th year of the reign of our sovereign lord Charles[22] by the grace of God king of England Scotland France and Ireland defender of the faith etc.

NEUTRALS AND SIDE-CHANGERS

A Cheshire neutrality agreement, 1642

Reluctance to be drawn into the war was strong enough in some counties for the local leadership to take the initiative in appealing for an immediate peace or even to conclude formal neutrality agreements between the contending parties. One such agreement reached in Cheshire on 23 December 1642 aimed to prevent any further preparations for war within the county and to reverse those already made. It also hoped to preserve peace by making a united stand against outside belligerents. All these agreements eventually failed but in the short term they helped to slow down the spread of armed conflict.
Source: J. S. Morrill, *The Revolt of the Provinces: Conservatives and Radicals in the English Civil War, 1630–50* (London, 1976), pp. 160–1.

An agreement made the day above at Bunbury, in the county of Chester, for a pacification and settling of the peace of that county by us whose names are subscribed, authorised hereunto by the lords and gentlemen nominated commissioners of array and deputy lieutenants of the said county.

1. It is agreed that there be an absolute cessation of arms from henceforth within this county, and no arms taken up to offend one another but by consent of the king and both Houses of Parliament, unless it be to resist forces brought into the county.

2. That all but 200 of either side shall be disbanded tomorrow, being Saturday, and on Monday all the rest on both sides, both horse and foot, shall be disbanded.

3. That all prisoners, on both sides, shall be enlarged. . . .

4. That the fortifications of . . . any town in Cheshire, lately made by either party, be presently demolished.

5. That all goods and arms taken on both sides now remaining in the county in specie be forthwith restored. . . .

6. That the lords and gentlemen, commissioners of array, before the 8th January next, procure from his majesty a letter thereby declaring, that in regard a peace is made in the county he will send no forces into the county, and if any other person shall, contrary to such declaration, bring forces into the county (passage for forces without doing any hostile act only accepted) the said lords and gentlemen will join to resist them. And if any forces without the consent of the king and both Houses of Parliament shall come into this county (the passages for forces without doing any hostile act only excepted), the said gentlemen nominated deputy lieutenants will join to resist them and use their utmost endeavour therein.

7. . . . it is agreed that the commissioners of array shall not any further put the commission of array in execution, nor the gentlemen nominated deputy lieutenants, the ordinance of the militia, or execute their commission.

8. Lastly . . . that all parties join in a petition to his majesty and both Houses of Parliament, for putting an end to the great distractions and miseries fallen upon this kingdom, by making a speedy peace . . .

Sir Edward Dering, A declaration, 1644

Sir Edward Dering (1599–1644) was a Kent baronet and an MP for the shire in the Long Parliament until February 1642 when he was disabled for printing his speeches. Dering was one of those moderates originally drawn into the royalist camp by the need to defend episcopacy and the prayer book. Yet even before the first major battle of the war he was making overtures to the other side and he surrendered his commission in the royalist army prior to the opening of the 1643 campaign. He was the first to accept parliament's terms for a pardon at the start of 1644 and felt obliged to publish the following justification of his action.
Source: A declaration wherein is full satisfaction given concerning Sir Edward Dering (London, 1644), Thomason Tracts, E. 33/4.

The declaration of the two kingdoms of England and Scotland[23] have produced some effects in giving time to those who have stepped out of the way to come in by the first of March, as appeareth by Sir Edward Dering, Mr Murry and others, who submitting themselves to the mercy of the parliament accordingly do receive the benefit of the declaration. And no doubt there will be many more here before that time, in the meantime here is presented a declaration of what hath proceeded against Sir Edward Dering.

Whereas malignants, and some evil disposed people have censured this return from Oxford to the parliament, to be either because to be pricked sheriff[24] of Kent could not be obtained, nor yet the deanery of Canterbury, and last of all to be turned out of the parliament at Oxford,[25] it is nothing but the malice of the envious brood that feigns these false calumnies to blemish by unjust reports.

The true reasons of this return from that unfortunate army, (unfortunate indeed, by misleading just intentions, to walk out of the way) are these.

1. That because it was so clearly manifest, that whatsoever resolutions or advice the nobility and gentry had taken and given to his majesty to follow, he from time to time was led the contrary way by a secret junto of popishly affected counsels, who continually crossed the designs of the moderate party about the king.

2. For advising his majesty to show some mark of disfavour upon the papists, and not to put them in trust in places of such concernment, as he doth, but found no acceptance.

3. For declaring plainly at Oxford how to take up arms under the earl of Essex was better grounded upon better reason, for satisfaction of conscience: than to take up arms against the parliament, and to join with the papists and prelates in their cavalry.

4 For saying at Oxford before the sitting of the juntos, that if they offered to sit there as a parliament, that it were just with God to throw some judgement down upon them.

Sir Edward Dering, considering the ways of the enemy, as is expressed in the declaration, laid down his commission in November last.

On Wednesday, February the seventh, Sir Edward Dering presented an humble petition to the House of Commons, for every one that comes in by virtue of the aforesaid declaration, must petition the parliament, and thereby claimed what is promised by the same.

1. Sir Edward Dering did acknowledge it a great weakness in him, that he had deserted the parliament: and leave that just and legal way which he was in with them to join with the wicked proceedings of the enemy.

2. That he is fully convinced that the enemy seeks all possible ways to destroy the liberty of the subject involved in parliaments.

3.   That he hath been much troubled in conscience, for that he having formerly taken the Protestation to maintain and defend this parliament, hath been so far deluded to appear in arms against it, and could not be in quiet until he had returned.

4.   That although he will not tax his majesty with breach of promise, yet he sees there is a deficiency somewhere, since the papists are not only in arms against the parliament, but in chief commands in the king's army.

5.   That the preferring of papists before Protestants in the king's army, hath been a great grief to him to see.

6.   That whereas there he see them about to affront the parliament, by forging a pretended one at Oxford, which proceedings were clean against his approbation, he was exceedingly desirous to leave them.

7.   That he thought it a great happiness to see the declaration published, the benefit whereof he was now returned to claim.

And accordingly he took the covenant, and is at liberty.

4

THE IMPACT OF WAR

LEVIES AND DISTRAINTS

An assessment ordinance, 1642

Faced with the urgent need to finance their respective war efforts, both sides quickly moved over from voluntary appeals to compulsory demands for loans and contributions. A parliamentary ordinance of 29 November 1642 provided for the assessment of all inhabitants of London and its suburbs who had not already made a sufficient voluntary contribution to the parliamentarian war effort. The ordinance below completed the arrangements for an effective implementation of the new compulsory levies, backed up by the threat to distrain and sell the goods of those failing to meet their assessments and possible imprisonment.
Source: C. H. Firth and R. S. Rait (eds.), *Acts and Ordinances of the Interregnum, 1642–60*, 2 vols (London, 1911), i, 40–1.

Whereas a late ordinance is passed by both Houses of Parliament for the reasons therein declared, for the assessing of all such persons within the cities of London and Westminster, and the suburbs thereof, with the borough of Southwark, as have not contributed upon the propositions of both Houses of Parliament, for raising of money, plate, horse, horsemen, and arms, for the defence of the king, parliament and kingdom, or have not contributed proportionably to their estates and abilities. And whereas it is though fit that some additions be made for further explanation and better execution of the said ordinance: be it further ordained and declared by the Lords and Commons assembled in parliament, that such persons as shall be assessed by respective assessors in the said ordinance appointed, and shall within six days next after notice given to them, or left at their several houses within the said cities, suburbs, or borough, pay in the one moiety of the said sums of money so assessed and within twelve days after the said notice given as aforesaid, the other moiety thereof, unto the treasurers of money and plate in Guildhall, London, or unto the collectors appointed by the said ordinance, respectively to receive the same, that then the said treasurers, or collectors, shall give acquittances for the same, as hath been done to such who have lent monies or plate, upon the propositions of both Houses as aforesaid. And the said monies so paid to the said treasurers, or to the said several collectors, shall be repaid upon the public faith, as all other monies lent upon the said propositions of both Houses. And as for those who shall so far discover their disaffection, as not to bring in the several sums of money so assessed upon them to the persons before appointed, within the times limited, that then their goods shall be distrained and sold according to the said ordinance. And if no sufficient distress be found, that then the said collectors, shall respectively have power to enquire of any sum or sums of money due, or to be due unto them respectively so assessed from any person or persons for any rents, tithes, goods, or debts, or for any other thing or cause whatsoever.

And the said respective collectors shall have power by virtue of this ordinance, to receive all or any part of the said sums due, or to be due unto them or any of them so assessed, until the full value of the sum or sums so assessed, and the charges in levying and recovering of the same shall be received and satisfied, and the said respective collectors shall have further power to compound for any of the said rents, tithes, goods, or debts, due unto the said persons so assessed respectively as aforesaid, with any person or persons by whom the said rents, tithes, goods, or debts, are or shall be owing, as also to give full and ample discharge for the money by them so received, upon composition or otherwise, which discharges shall be good and effectual to all intents and purposes. And if the sum or sums of money so assessed cannot be levied by any of these means or ways, then the persons so respectively assessed, shall be imprisoned in such places of this kingdom, and for so long time as the committee of the House of Commons for the examinations shall appoint and order: and the families of all such persons so imprisoned, shall no longer remain within the cities of London or Westminster, the suburbs, and the counties adjacent.

And be it further ordained, that all and every the assessors and collectors of the said several sums, shall have the protection of both Houses of Parliament, for their indemnity in this service, and receive such reasonable allowances for their pains taken and charges disbursed therein, as the committee of Lords and Commons for advance of money and other necessaries for the army, raised by the parliament, shall apportion and appoint.

Distraints in London for nonpayment of assessments, 1643

An offensive was launched in February 1643 against Londoners who had not paid their assessments. They were visited by collectors to ascertain whether there was sufficient property to distrain and military assistance was on hand for the collectors if needed. A systematic record was kept of the identity of the defaulter, the amount of the assessment and the value of the property or income that could be seized.
Source: PRO, state papers domestic 19/37/125.

Bishopsgate

£400	Henry Boothby At Oxford £1000 p.a.
£200	Nicholas Backhouse
£500	Sir William Cooper. 24th February committed to Ipswich in the interim to custody of the sergeant.
£200	Mr Cooper his son. Profits of assurance office in question.
£50	William Crowther
£500	Robert Vallence Rents distrained 21 tenants.

Broad Street Ward

£250	John Batty Gone away and inventory taken of his goods for the value of them. Captain Underwood in Bucklersbury is responsible.
£1500	Sir Peter Richaut seized divers debts.
£1000	Robert Austen distress made 21 February; £678–9–8 produced of it. 10 March £700 more made of goods distrained.
£250	William Garway distrained and sold for £245–15–00.
£250	Sir Robert Mansell
£150	Ralph Long Gone away long since.

Grievances over parliamentary assessments in Essex and Devon, 1644–6

The amount of the assessment arrived at was sometimes challenged by those assessed as being excessive, especially in view of other charges on their estates, such as the free quartering of soldiers, and debts incurred as a result of the war. On the other hand, others might claim that the rating of assessments had been uneven and some individuals had been under-assessed, with local feuds occasionally lying behind the accusation. The committee for advance of money was responsible for adjudicating on all such cases.

Source: M. A. E. Green (ed.), *Calendar of the Committee for Advance of Money*, 3 vols (London, 1888), i, 364–5; ii, 720.

John Radley, Shenfield, Essex.

26 March 1644. The inhabitants of Shenfield petition the county commissioners. There have been differences in the parish, which hinder service, now when religion and laws are at stake, and we should be united against the common adversary. John Radley has occasioned much strife by a rate for raising 3 dragoons, which he has levied on those who never denied payment, but were only hoping to be righted. He also suppressed a poor-rate legally made, and raised one unequally rated, without consent of the churchwardens and his fellow overseers. There being no sessions of the peace, we present these disorders to you and beg relief. . . .

3 June 1644. William Angell informs the committee for advance of money that the taxation for the 1/5 and 1/20[1] has been very uneven, and that Radley has a good estate and stock, and should have paid £120 instead of £43–16–00.

3 June. Radley to be brought up in custody to answer matters objected against him.

14 March 1645. He having a greater estate than is expressed in his affidavit, as appears by his confession and by testimony of the inhabitants – order that on paying £156–4–00 more, he be left to the mercy of the ordinance to pay a double assessment.

31 March. Angell gives further details of Radley's misdoings; his stock was worth £2000 and is now worth £1000. Has travelled much, but never met so wicked and malicious a man.

4 April 1645. John Radley paying £4 for his son's lands, his assessment to be discharged, any former order notwithstanding.

18 April. Note of his payment and discharge.

19 August 1646. Earl of Warwick to Sir David Watkins. My tenant, Radley, has done good service for the state, and proved before the commissioners for sequestrations that he has lent to the best of his ability, and been active for the public good. I know not by what bad instruments he has been put to the charge of appearing before you, but pray procure his discharge, and let not parliament's friends be prejudiced.

John Gifford, Brightley, Co. Devon.

21 August 1646 assessed at £800.

16 October 1646. He petitions that though he is assessed at £800, his estate, as filed in Goldsmiths' Hall, is only £366 a year in land, and £100 personalty. That he was assessed in the county, and being unable to pay, goods value £350 (being more than his proportion) were taken from him. That he has a wife and 9 children, gave free quarters to parliament soldiers, to the cost of £500, is much in debt and cannot procure more than £100 to pay this assessment. Begs that this may be accepted, and be questioned no further for his assessment.

16 October. Ordered to make up $1/2$ his assessment of £800 for his $1/20$ in 14 days.

18 December 1646. His assessment to be discharged, he having paid £400, the moiety thereof.

Resistance to the royalist excise in Somerset, 1644

The royalists followed the example of the parliamentarians and introduced the excise, or sales tax, to help finance their war effort. In both cases the new tax was extremely unpopular and excise officers could encounter determined resistance to its collection. The following document is a relatively rare surviving account of the problems faced by officials in trying to impose the tax on a county nominally under royalist control.
Source: 'Papers concerning the commissioners for excise, Somerset, November 1644', British Library, Harleian Ms. 6804, ff. 284–7.

... we first repaired to Bridgewater. We showed our commission to Mr [Humphrey] Walrond the deputy governor (the governor[2] himself being then before Taunton) who readily promised us all needful assistance whenever we should require it. The mayor also expressed his readiness to publish the proclamation, and to encourage his neighbours to yield all due obedience to our commission. The townsmen for the most part came in very freely to us and our business went on with as much smoothness. We met not with any rubs in our way neither perceived we any show of opposition until the market day but then upon the refusal of divers people to enter their commodities which they brought to sell, and to pay excise for the same we were fain to send to the deputy governor to require his promised aid to assist us in distraining the goods and wares of the refusers. Instead of sending us aid, he sent for us, and making known the emptiness and weakness of the garrison, most of the soldiers being drawn out to lie before Taunton, desired us to forbear the market for that day, and the next market day he promised us a good guard of musketeers to attend our officers. In the meantime he doubted not but we might with much ease settle it fully and effectually amongst the townsmen. By his persuasions we forbore for that market day but notwithstanding our forbearance we found the townsmen apt to abuse those they conceived to be our officers, while they only walked along the streets not doing anything in the execution of their office, insomuch that some of the soldiers whom we took for our protectors, without the least provocation picked a quarrel with one whom we employed violently haled him out of the inn where he lay, struck him to the ground, and would we fear have murdered him had he not been happily rescued by Sergeant Major Buskyn, the major for the garrison. What punishment was inflicted upon the ringleaders of this riot we have not yet heard. The same night some of the soldiers were heard to make their boast how they had saved the market £20 that day, and they would save them as much the next, or it should cost them their lives. The next day the butchers and some other of the townsmen would needs ride to Taunton to the governor to crave his advice. When they returned from him we found them much more obstinate and far more ready to slight us than before, insomuch that one Pitts a draper who had formerly promised to pay us the excise due for his commodities refused afterwards to pay it and remains still a debtor to his majesty for it, and as we are informed grounds his refusal upon the governor's advice. The governor himself came home at last, upon whom we waited making known our business to him. He demanded whether we had order to pay the moneys we should receive unto him, when we answered we had no such order, he required time of consideration till the next day. We then waited upon him again, he then promised us the best assistance he could give us, desiring us only to go on with as much gentleness as might be. But there was present at that time Mr [John] Coventry, one of the commissioners for the affairs of the county, this gentleman declared his opinion that it was not fit we should carry any money out of the garrison, neither could he perceive how the governor or any other could afford us such assistance as might shield us from the fury of the discontented and overburthened people, unless we could produce a real assurance that the contribution should abate in an equal proportion to the growth of the excise. . . . Thus were we fain to pack from Bridgewater leaving the business half undone . . . . [W]hen we came to Wells . . . divers of the commissioners hearing of it sent for us, whereupon one of us repairing to them was entertained with a kind of chiding for that we would offer to go on in this so distasteful a service and not rather persuade his majesty to lay it quite down. Notwithstanding this we showed our commission to the mayor[3] requiring his aid in the execution of it, who called together his brethren, they presently run to the commissioners for advice without whom they said they would do nothing. What advice the commissioners gave we know not but upon their return the mayor refuses to publish the proclamation, pretending want of a writ authorising him thereunto, when as the high sheriff and under-sheriff were both in town and could either of them easily have satisfied him in that particular if he had desired any satisfaction. The aldermen his brethren were no less obstinate than himself one of them speaking openly in the market place to the people that he would pay no excise, and another, that we came to rob and devour the people. Thus resolved came the mayor and aldermen from the commissioners, neither indeed did we much marvel at it, when we remembered that one of the commissioners had formerly told us to our faces, that if we would go on in the execution of our commission the country would certainly drive us out with stones: this was our best encouragement. Notwithstanding this we were urgent with the mayor to publish the proclamation, and required the under sheriff to give him a warrant for it. . . . We waited three or four days for his certain answer, who at last produced the writ, and showed it to the mayor. The mayor notwithstanding this refused to publish the proclamation saying he had been with the commissioners of the county to advise with them about it, and he knew well enough what they said of our business. When we required his aid he gave us uncertain answers, and at last hid himself, and would not be found. The truth is we plainly discovered a practice not only to delude but oppose us, and we have good reason to believe not only Mr [Edward] Kirton but many of the gentlemen of the county are privy to it by whom the people have been so animated and set against us that no man will obey us, but every man is ready to resist us. Without better encouragement and more assurance of assistance it is not for us to proceed in it. Thus have we spent more than half a year, and that remnant of our estates which we have preserved from the rebels, and yet have not done his majesty that service which perhaps may be expected from us. . . .

Christopher Milton
John Blythe

PLUNDERING

A Commons order to prevent pillaging by soldiers, 1642

Parliament took early action to try to prevent pillaging by soldiers raised for its army by making it a capital offence. Not only had the homes of papists and others identified as enemies been ransacked over the summer by both soldiers and over-zealous agents, but even some of parliament's friends had suffered. Source: *Commons' Journals* (1642), ii, 738.

26 August 1642

Whereas divers soldiers have, in a tumultuous and violent manner, broken into divers of the king's subjects houses, pillaged and ransacked them, under pretence and colour that they are papists' houses, or the houses of persons disaffected; the Lords and Commons taking the premises into consideration, do declare and order, that whatsoever soldier or soldiers shall, without the command of the captains of their respective companies, or the officers of the field, attempt upon, or break open, any house whatsoever, or pillage or ransack any house, shall be pursued and punished according to law as a felon: and the said Lords and Commons do require all officers of the armies to employ their best endeavours for the bringing of any such soldiers that shall commit any of the insolences aforesaid, to condign punishment; that they may be severely and effectually proceeded against according to law. And the lord general is desired, that this order may be duly published in the army, in the head of each particular company.

Plundering by royalist forces in Worcestershire, 1643

The armies of both sides plundered civilians when the need arose but the royalists generally had the worst record. Horses were in constant demand for the cavalry but they were also essential for the livelihood of the civilian

population. A county under royalist control, Worcester bore a heavy burden of royalist exactions.
Source: British Library, Harleian Ms. 6804, f. 140.

To the honourable the governor and other the king's majesty's commissioners for the safeguard of the county of Worcester.

The humble petition of divers the inhabitants especially of Armscote and Blackwell within the parish of Tredington in the said county.

Sheweth that (according to our late information) upon Saturday the third of June instant we were plundered and bereft of 40 of our best horses, but as then we had not found out the authors of our said loss. Now may it please you further to be informed that upon our diligent and chargeable search and enquiry we have found out our horses in the regiment of Colonel Sir Thomas Aston at their quarters about a place called Blackbourton near Burford in the county of Oxford. But so incommiserate and unreasonable are these plunderers that (not content with the wrongful taking our said horses, beating and abusing us for only requesting to buy them again, and at their departure wilfully trooping away near a quarter of a mile over a furlong of our beans and peas in a body of 7 or 8 score horse; when a fair highway of 30 yards broad lay all along by the said furlong) but when our messengers and servants whom we employed in seeking after our horses with 4 or 5 days expense of time found them in the said regiment at Blackbourton aforesaid the soldiers there that were possessed of our said horses (in continuance of their mischievous practices) did imprison and threaten our said messengers and servants and rob them and pick their pockets and take away and deprive them of all their moneys which they took with them for their necessary expenses, so that we dare proceed no further in pursuance of our said horses except you will be pleased honourably to afford us your assistance and aid herein.

We therefore humbly beseech you that (for as much as we your petitioners have made full payment of all our monthly contribution money) you will be pleased to certify these great wrongs and oppressions that we suffer as aforesaid unto that most honourable council of war at Oxford, that by them and you we may receive such satisfaction and reparation for our wrongs as our cause requires and as to their and your honourable and grave wisdoms (to whom we shall humbly herein refer ourselves) shall seem meet.

And we shall always pray for your happiness both here and hereafter.

Nathaniel Brent [and thirteen other signatories].

SEQUESTRATION OF ROYALIST ESTATES

A Commons order concerning sequestered estates, 1643

Both parties sequestered the estates and rental incomes of their enemies

despite initial qualms about violating property rights and later extracted fines, or compositions, from many for their return. Sequestrators and auditors were appointed in each county thereby adding further officials to the bureaucratic burden.
Source: *Commons' Journals* (1643), iii, 231.

Ordered, that the committees of the several counties do respectively forthwith prepare rentals of all the rents of all the lands and estates that are seized, or to be seized, and paid to the state, by force of any order or ordinance; and to send them up to the committee for accounts appointed to receive the same: the which committee is likewise to take care of the putting of this order in execution, in all points and circumstances, to the best advantage, for the bringing in of all monies that are payable to the state, upon any order or ordinance of sequestration, or otherwise: and that, in all such counties where the ordinance of sequestration is not yet put in execution, that the respective committees do forthwith put the same in execution; and that they give public notice to all the tenants of all such persons whose estates are sequestrable, and payable to the state, that they do detain, in their hands, all such rents. And it is further referred to this committee, to appoint agents and auditors for the several counties, for the better managing of this business of bringing in all monies upon any order or ordinance: and that the sequestrators in the several and respective counties do send up a list of all the estates and lands in the several and respective counties, that they have sequestered; and an account of such sales they have made of any goods, and of all such monies as they have received; and that they take care that all the goods sequestered be presently sold: and that they appoint men of trust and credit to see the goods sold.

IMPRESSMENT

An impressment ordinance and its unpopularity, 1643

The foot soldiers of both armies relied heavily for their recruitment on pressed, or conscripted, men. The poor were particularly targeted by the press gang which could frequently face resistance. Gathering together and guarding conscripted men was an arduous and costly task and soldiers recruited in this way were particularly liable to desert or change sides as it suited them.
Sources: *Commons' Journals* (1643), iii, 194; P. Thomas (ed.), *Oxford Royalist Newsbooks*, 4 vols (London, 1971), i, 490.

Forasmuch as the true Protestant religion, the laws and liberties of the subject, and the parliament, are in danger to be subverted, idolatry and tyranny like to be introduced, by the force and power of several armies raised by pretence of the king's authority, consisting of papists, and other dangerous and ill-affected persons of this kingdom, and Irish rebels, and of divers popish soldiers, and others of foreign kingdoms and nations, being not under the king's obedience, for the ruin and destruction of this kingdom, unless the same be prevented by a considerable power of forces to be suddenly raised by both Houses of Parliament; being, with God's blessing and assistance, the most probable way to preserve this kingdom, our religion and liberty; be it therefore ordained, by the Lords and Commons, assembled in parliament, and by the authority of the same, that the committees of the militia for the City of London, the deputy lieutenants and committees of parliament, in every county, city, or place, within this realm, or any two or more of them, within their several limits and jurisdictions, shall, and are hereby authorized, from time to time, until other order be taken by both Houses of Parliament, to raise, levy, and imprest such number of soldiers, gunners, and surgeons, for the defence of the king, parliament and kingdom, as shall be appointed by both Houses of Parliament, or by my lord general; and to command all constables, and other officers to be aiding and assisting to them in the said service of impresting: all which persons, so to be imprested, and every of them, shall have such imprest money, coat and conduct money, wages and entertainment, and other necessary charges and allowances, as shall be fit and convenient, according to the discretion of the said committees and deputy lieutenants, or any two or more of them respectively. And if any person, or persons, shall wilfully refuse so to be imprested for the said service, that then it shall and may be lawful to and for the said persons so authorized as aforesaid to commit them to prison, until they shall yield obedience, or pay the sum of ten pounds to the said committees, or deputy lieutenants, to be employed for the supply of the said service.

Provided always, that this ordinance shall not extend to the pressing of any clergyman, scholar, or student in any of the universities, inns of court, or chancery, or houses of law; or any the trained bands, in any county, city, or place; or any person rated in the last subsidies granted by this parliament; or the son of any person rated at five pounds goods, or three pounds lands, in the subsidy books; or of any person of the rank or degree of an esquire, or upwards, or the son of any such person, or the son of the widow of any such person; or to the pressing of any person under the age of eighteen, or above the age of fifty years; or of the members or officers of either House of Parliament; or of the menial servants of the members or officers of either of the said Houses; or any the assistants of the Lords' House, or any of their menial servants; or any the inhabitants of the Isles of Wight, or Anglesey, or cinque ports; or of any mariner, seaman, or fisherman.

Mercurius Aulicus, Saturday, August 26 [1643].

It was this day signified by letters from London, that the tumults there do daily increase, occasioned chiefly by their daily pressing men to serve in their rebellious army, seizing poor men many times in their beds, and taking them from their wife and children to fight in spite of their hearts they know not why. . . .

114

COMMITTEES

The committee for advance of money

The committee for advance of money established at Haberdashers' Hall, London, at the start of hostilities earned great unpopularity. Its membership and agents were subjected to fairly frequent verbal abuse and its chairman, Lord Howard of Escrick, was accused of corruption. As it transpired, the accusation was correct for he was eventually exposed as having accepted bribes from royalists.
Source: M. A. E. Green (ed.), *Calendar of the Committee for Advance of Money*, 3 vols (London, 1888), i, 297; ii, 669.

Basset Cole, near Charing Cross.

9 July 1645. Deposition that when he was summoned for his assessment, he said that Mr Strode[4] sat as a prince at Haberdashers' Hall, and that he was an unjust, unworthy man, and would undo all the gentlemen in the country, and that he had trusted in Lord Howard,[5] but now saw he was as unworthy as Strode and the rest.

Robert Lowther, merchant, Lothbury.

November [1646?]. Note that on 4 February 1645, Lowther was very discontented about his assessment, and said in passion that the City was abused and cozened, and some of the commissioners had £60 a week, and named Lord Howard of Escrick, as well known in Yorkshire, and not having above £1200 a year.

17 December 1646. The earl of Warwick to report to the House of Lords Lowther's abusive words concerning this committee in general, and Lord Howard in particular.

Sir John Oglander on the Isle of Wight committee

Sir John Oglander (1585–1655) of Nunwell in the Isle of Wight, an ardent royalist, could trace his family back to the Norman conquest. He sneered at the allegedly modest social composition of the local parliamentarian committee which had pushed aside the traditional gentry. However, he has probably exaggerated the real extent of the shift in the social basis of local power.
Source: F. Bamford (ed.), *A Royalist's Notebook: The Commonplace Book of Sir John Oglander Knight of Nunwell* (London, 1936), pp. 110–11.

. . . we had a thing here called a committee, which overruled deputy lieutenants and also justices of the peace, and of this we had brave men: Ringwood of Newport, the pedlar: Maynard, the apothecary: Matthews, the baker: Wavell and Legge, farmers, and poor Baxter of Hurst Castle. These ruled the whole island and did whatsoever they thought good in their own eyes.

The order book of the Staffordshire county committee, 1643–5

County committees, like this parliamentarian example, came to assume wide-ranging powers and as their demands increased so did their unpopularity. The following extracts are taken from one of the few surviving order books of such committees.
Source: D. H. Penington and I. A. Roots (eds), *The Committee at Stafford 1643–5: The Order Book of the Staffordshire County Committee* (Manchester, 1957), pp. 194, 236, 282.

21 October 1644 Mrs Broughton

Forasmuch as Mrs Broughton wife of Thomas Broughton of Broughton esquire hath made her composition with the sequestrators of this county for her husband's estate therein for this present year. And whereas it is informed that divers soldiers do quarter at free quarter with the said Mrs Broughton and her tenants whereby they being disenabled to pay her their rents she is also disenabled to pay her composition according to her agreement. It is therefore ordered that from henceforth no officers or soldiers shall quarter upon the said Mrs Broughton or her tenants without an especial order from the commander in chief, the committee at Stafford or quartermaster general.

9 January 1645

Whereas Mr Hunter corporal under Captain Thacker having taken a horse from Mr Hart of Uttoxeter woodlands hath refused to restore the said horse upon the committee's order and given contemptuous words against them saying he neither cared for the committee nor their order. It is ordered that for his contempt of the said order he shall be committed to the marshall till he restore the said horse and give satisfaction to the committee for his contempt.

25 March 1645 Troopers to return.

Whereas divers of Colonel [Simon] Rugeley's and Captain Jackson's troopers which have departed without any order it is therefore ordered that every one of the said troopers do tomorrow morning repair to their command again, and the corporals of each troop are required to call them together and return with them to their command again with all speed and the refusers are to be proceeded against according to martial law. . . .

The letter books of Sir Samuel Luke, 1644–5

Sir Samuel Luke (1603–70) was the parliamentary governor of the strategically important garrison of Newport Pagnell in Buckinghamshire. His highly informative correspondence reveals, amongst other things, the friction that could arise between the governors of garrisons and county committees. Corruption could also occasionally occur at this as well as at more senior levels.

Source: H. G. Tibbutt (ed.), *The Letter Books 1644–45 of Sir Samuel Luke, Parliamentary Governor of Newport Pagnell*, Historical Manuscripts Commission JP 4 (1963), pp. 31–2, 450–1.

Sir Samuel Luke to the earl of Essex, 18 October 1644.

I put you in mind what ill fate is like to hang over our heads and how little good we may expect in those divisions and distractions which are amongst us. The committees in all places oppose themselves to the governors, who are so discontented that they are either retired from their charges, or little useful there. Colonel [Edward] Massey of Gloucester has had bitter articles put up against him, wherewith he is so discontented that he is returned again to Monmouth, having sent a gentleman on purpose by here to parliament to crave that right might be done him. . . . Coventry and Warwick are in like condition. . . . Colonel [John] Hutchinson and Colonel [Francis] Thornhagh are gone up discontented from Nottingham and resolve to come down no more till right be done them for the injuries they suffered from Mr [Gilbert] Millington and the rest of the committee there. . . . My own condition here is little better, being slighted by all the committees of the [eastern] association, who refused that assistance that was allotted me by ordinance of parliament. This troubles me not much because I have found the readiness both of parliament and the committee of both kingdoms[6] to redress it. The letters and orders made by the committee at Aylesbury,[7] wherein they seem very unwilling to allow me so much air as is within my trenches, troubles me more than all the rest. Though I am a member of the House of Commons, by whom they were delegated and to whom they are to give an account of all their actions, yet they are so peremptory as to make such orders and that in such language as I never knew parliament do so much. If I had done amiss, they might have complained of me either to parliament or to you, but to proclaim into the king's quarters that I, though governor of Newport [Pagnell], have not power for the use of parliament to do that there which every ordinary soldier is allowed to do by the king's authority, seems very strange to me, so that rather than I must send for labourers the works at Newport must lie undone: rather than send for victuals the soldiers must starve. This is my condition. . . .

Sir Oliver Luke[8] to Sir Samuel Luke, [London] 19 February 1645.

. . . there was a warrant procured from [Mr Miles] Corbet to apprehend him [i.e. Captain James Pinckney, collector for Newport Pagnell garrison] and to bring him to the committee [of examinations] which was done, but he promising to pay £400 I gave order first to receive that money and after to arrest him which was done accordingly. Upon his examination he confessed he had received £1,000 more than he had paid to the garrison and being demanded what was done with that money he confessed he had paid it to satisfy some debts of his own but said he would not be long before he gave full satisfaction, and promised to bring good sureties to secure within a month, yet his security is not tendered so he remains in custody. I fear most of that money will be in hazard and much more had been if there had not been more in looking after him than was in employing him: but I hope it will warn them. . . .

PEACE SENTIMENT

The London peace petition of 22 December 1642

An organised peace campaign got off the ground in the capital in December 1642 to counter militant calls for a more vigorous prosecution of the war. Petitions were drawn up and signatures canvassed in London, Westminster and the surrounding suburbs. The petition below drew fairly wide support from Londoners of respectable social standing with relatively conservative religious and political leanings, including some who were later to become prominent royalists, but others may have been more clearly motivated by a genuine desire for peace.
Source: House of Lords record office, main papers, 22 December 1642 petition of divers citizens and other inhabitants of the City of London.

To the right honourable the Lords in this present parliament assembled

The humble petition of divers citizens and other inhabitants of the City of London.

Your petitioners most sadly weighing the present wretched condition of this divided nation; and having too just cause to fear the bitter and fatal consequences of a civil war already broken out amongst us even to the effusion of abundance of blood in several parts of this kingdom, out of piety towards God and pity towards men; do humbly represent unto your lordships the great and unhappy divisions both in church and state of which the bloody rebels in Ireland take advantage, the common safety is infested and endangered, the face of religion is greatly disfigured, commerce and trade the only support of this City exceedingly impaired, whereof none can be equally sensible with us; those with whom we trade in most parts of this, and the kingdom of Ireland much disabled and impoverished by the violence and rapine of soldiers, some of them totally despoiled, others fearing the like measure, the multitude of poor people in and about this City (who by reason of cessation of trade want employment and consequently bread) infinitely abound; sadness of heart, famine, misery, and utter ruin attend us and the whole nation in this condition; besides two great armies being almost at an interview in the bowels of the kingdom ready for another fearful encounter unless a happy mutual concurrence of his majesty, your lordships, and the honourable House of Commons speedily intervene.

The duty therefore which we owe to God the father of peace, and to his church the mother of peace, the honour we bear to a most gracious king, and his great council, and lastly the charity which is due from us to our native Christian country (now ready without the great mercy of God to be sacrificed) hath importuned this most humble petition from us.

That your lordships for the timely prevention of those fearful approaching evils which inevitably wait upon such times of distemper, will be pleased whilest the opportunity is yet in your hands to use such means for an accommodation and procurement of a happy peace in this kingdom without further effusion of blood as to your lordships' wisdom shall seem fit, to effecting whereof your petitioners shall attend your honourable consultation with their most hearty prayers, and not only we and ours, but children unborn shall have cause to bless you and your memorial to the end of time.

The like petition to the honourable House of Commons *mutatis mutandis*.[9]

Three looks over London, or plain dealing is a jewel, *1643*

The anonymous author of this tract claimed that the early material demands involved in raising an army for parliament had transformed public opinion in London. Those who had previously urged for reforms in Church and state, he argues, saw past grievances in a new light as they experienced these new demands. There is certainly evidence that some parliamentarian-inclined Londoners later moved in the king's direction in the hope of a quick return to prewar normality.
Source: Thomason Tracts E. 88/11.

That man that shall look seriously upon this City, and weigh maturely the present condition of it, as it is now, may discern easily that it is in a very deplorable and sad estate, being divided against itself, having both a potent enemy without which labours to destroy it, and an unruly power within it, (a giddy-headed multitude) that labours to bring to destruction both it, and all those that any way endeavour to stand in the defence of it.

That this is apparent is manifested two ways.

First in respect of a potent army abroad, who pretend a maintenance of the Protestant religion, and by that pretence abuse the authority of our king, and altogether destroy the religion, the law of the land, with the property of the subject.

Secondly, in respect of a malignant party within the confines of the said City, who seemingly pretend to take part with the said army, under a notion of standing for the king, by which pretence they gain power to promote many desperate designs, tending to the subversion of religion, and the destruction of that City which by their oath they are bound to preserve, when on the contrary I will make it apparent, the said malignants (notwithstanding their pretences) have promoted the said designs, for particular respects to themselves, and have been for, and against the parliament, as their own ends and profit swayed them, and not any respect or aim at the public good.

You may remember when projectors was voted out of the House, then every man having suffered under their tyranny, with one consent cried them down, looking upon their former sufferings, and then every man gave God public thanks for the parliament so much they thought they were engaged for their delivery from the pressure of those insulting tyrants, but this is forgotten now.

Likewise you might observe how readily the commands of the parliament was obeyed in every particular that concerned the removal of anything that might seem prejudicial to their profit, as the ship-money, star chamber, and high commission, with many other things very fresh in all men's memories, and likewise when the high court of parliament went about to remove the bishops, many men, nay a multitude of men which had suffered under their papist jurisdiction, with one voice, nay with a zealous violence, cried out 'No bishops, no bishops!' But it seems it was the sense of their temporary sufferings, and not that spiritual bondage, that made them so zealous of the cause.

Also when the Protestation was imposed, you may remember with what willingness and cheerfulness the said Protestation was taken by all sorts of men, they would live and die with the parliament etc. but I believe all those men that now are opposers, (and as far as in them lies destroyers) of that power which they then protested to defend, had a mental reservation, to protect them with their tongues, but their hearts should be far from them, this is apparent by the actions of many eminent men that then outwardly seemed both religious toward God, loyal to our king, and loving to their brother, but coming to the test the mantle of hypocrisy being taken off by the touch stone of truth, and the finger of the law, they have been found atheists in religion, traitors in disloyalty, and devils in their dealings with their neighbours. But to my first discourse, when the five members were accused by his majesty, then with a joint consent (so great they conceived their duty to the parliament) they declared that they would spend their lives in their just defence, by all which it appears that so long as the commands of the parliament entrenched not upon their purses, they were as obedient as might be, they were as well affected as any, would the parliament have undertook to maintain the religion and laws of the land at their own charge, then this malignant crew, would have declared them just and honourable in all their actions.

But when his majesty had by the counsel of the Lord [George] Digby, withdrawn himself from his great council, and privately contrived the raising of an army, and when the necessity of the kingdom begun to enforce the parliament to make use of their lawful authority, for the suppressing of that authority so unlawfully employed (the raising of such an army being destructive to the religion and laws of the land, from whence that power had its first derivation) then a discovery was made of their intentions, for when the parliament made propositions touching a contribution for the raising of an army, to oppose the aforesaid army raised against the parliament, then they began to draw their heads out of the fraternity.

So long as they could serve the parliament with a good word, (or a 'God preserve the parliament') they were as obedient as might be, but when they were desired to contribute towards the maintenance of an army for the defence of religion, the laws of the land, and the liberty of the subject, against a crew of popish bishops, flattering courtiers, knavish projectors, and desperate cavaliers, all which they had formerly clamoured against, 'No bishops, no projectors, no Lunsford'[10], etc. now they are of another mind, now they cry out 'What hurt did the bishops? We lived better when there were projectors, the ship-money was not so bad as our taxes now', etc. these are the common phrases among them.

Yet notwithstanding so long as there was only a voluntary contribution of plate and money, they were very well content to live and enjoy that security which others had purchased at so dear a rate, but when an ordinance was made by both Houses, that every man that had not contributed according to his estate, should pay the twentieth part of their estates, then they could find no way to slip their heads out of the collar, but by endeavouring to raise a commotion in the City, which was done under a notion of peace, then they stuck not to declare themselves open enemies to the proceedings of the parliament, then the note was altered, instead of 'God preserve the parliament', bitter curses and reproachful revilings, 'the parliament has undone us, taken away our servants, spoiled our trading, brought the kingdom to destruction by a civil war', see how the case was altered in a little time, see what power a little money has over carnal minded men, 'let them have what religion you please, let the laws be destroyed, let all go how he will, so they may keep their money it makes no matter'. 'Pish', says one that has more hair than wit, 'we shall never have peace except the papists may have freedom of conscience', then says another of the same crew, 'we shall never have peace till all the roundheads' throats are cut; why should we not be content with that religion which was established in Queen Elizabeth's days, and maintained by King James'.

Then a third crowns the catastrophe with a thundering oath, and sums up all their learned censures in this little sentence, 'would all the City were of my mind, we would all rise and cut the throats of these roundheads, and then we should have peace', and these are the champions of peace, of professed Protestants, indeed professed Protestants they may be, but true Protestants they cannot be, they desire peace abroad, and cannot keep peace at home. . . .

WAR

The full and last relation of all things concerning Basing House, 1645

Basing House in Hampshire was one of the most steadfast royalist garrisons, having held out through three sieges before it finally fell to the parliamentarians in October 1645. Its storming was exceptionally bloody partly because the garrison had refused to surrender but also, more importantly, because of its strong Catholic associations. It was a small foretaste of what Irish Catholics could expect in 1649. Hugh Peter (1598–1660), the fiery Independent minister and army chaplain, reported to the Commons on the fall of Basing House.
Source: Thomason Tracts E. 305/8.

The rifling of Basing: or, Mr Peter's report to Mr Speaker, and other members of the House of Commons:

That Mr Peter came into the house of Basing some time after the storm: on Tuesday the 14 October 1645 and took a view, first of the works which were many, though not finished, and of too great a compass, for so few men to keep. Sir Robert Peake the governor swearing to him that they had but 300 fighting men in all, the circumwallation being above a mile and a half about . . . the house stood in its full pride, and the enemy was persuaded that it would be the last piece of ground that would be taken by the parliament, because they had so often failed our forces, that had formerly appeared before it. In the several rooms, and about the house, there were slain, in view 74 and only one woman, the daughter of Dr Griffith, who came forth railing against our soldiers for their rough carriages towards her father, who indeed did remember to him his former malignancy, there lay upon the ground slain by the hands of Major [Thomas] Harrison (that godly, and gallant gentleman), Major Cuffle a man of great account amongst them, and a notorious papist, and Robinson the player, who a little before the storm, was known to be mocking, and scorning the parliament, and our army, 8 or 9 gentlewomen of rank running forth together were entertained by the common soldiers somewhat coarsely, yet not uncivilly, they left them with some clothes upon them, their plunder continued till Tuesday night in this manner,

1. For the goods, the soldiers seized upon the first goods of which there were several sorts; one soldier had sixscore pieces in gold for his share, others plate, others jewels, amongst the rest one got 3 bags of silver; who (being not able to keep his own counsel) it grew to be common pillage amongst the rest, the fellow himself had but one half crown left for himself at last.

There were some cabinets of jewels, and other rich treasure next to that, the soldiers sold the wheat to the country people. . . . After that they sold the household stuff, whereof there was good store, and they loaded away many carts. . . . And the last work of all was the lead, and by Thursday morning, they had hardly left one gutter about all the house.

2. For the fire, what the soldiers left the fire took hold on, joy was more than ordinary, leaving nothing but bare walls and chimneys in less than 20 hours, and occasioned by the neglect of the enemy in quenching a fire ball of ours.

We know not how to give a just account of all that was within, for we have not 200 prisoners, and it may be 100 slain, whose bodies some being covered with rubbish, came not to our view, only riding to the house on Tuesday night, we heard divers crying in vaults for quarter, but our men could neither come to them, nor they to us. . . . there was in all (in the house) about 500 besides some that before got out of the house.

And it is reported there are some vaults that are far underground for their popish priests, of which cattle there were divers, but none came to our hands, how many of them we killed we know not.

3. Mr Peter spend some time in conference with the Marquis of Winchester,[11] and Sir Robert Peake the governor. . . . The marquis being pressed by him, by way of argument, broke out and said that, 'if the king had no more ground in England but Basing House, he would adventure as he did, and so maintain it to his uttermost' (meaning with those papists) and the marquis said himself 'that Basing House was called loyalty'. But he was soon silent on the question between the king, and parliament, only hoping that the king might have a day again.

4. We see who are his majesty's dear friends, and trusty, and well beloved cousins, and counsellers; the marquis being the pope's devoted vassal.

5. And thus the Lord was pleased in a few hours to show us, what mortal seed all earthly glory grow upon, and how just and righteous the ways of God are, who takes sinners in their own snares, and lifteth up the heads of his despised people. . . .

An Irish diary of the Confederate wars, 1646

The war in Ireland was to last from 1641 to 1649. The defeat of the Scottish army in Ulster at the battle of Benburb on 5 June 1646 was a major setback for the Protestant cause in Ireland, and the slaughter that accompanied it continued to set the Irish war apart in the scale of its viciousness. This extract is taken from an English translation of a diary of the Confederate wars kept in Irish by Father O Mellan, OSF, of the Brantry Friary, county Tyrone, who served as a chaplain in the armies of Sir Phelim and Owen Rowe O Neill.
Source: 'An Irish diary of the Confederate wars', *County Louth Archaeological Journal*, vii, pp. 247–9.

A great muster of the forces of the enemy, under General Lord Montgomery, Lord Blaney, Lord Hamilton and Robert Monro. With them were the whole levies of Trian Congail [Clannaboy], 80 horsemen and 300 foot of the levies of O Kane's country near Dungannon, and the levies of Tir Conaill who had reached the Closagh. . . . Montgomery himself had 14 troops of cavalry and nine regiments of foot. The leaders were of opinion that they should make the

The Effigias of his Thomas Fairfax the Parliaments   Exellence Sir Captin Generall of Armie

Nazby

Figure 9 A victorious Fairfax at Naseby, 14 June 1645

attack by the short cut that leads from Armagh to Benburb. But Monro advised against this, and said that they should go round by Tynan, Lisnafeeda, Caledon and thence back to Knocknacloy, so that they might have the advantage of the sun and wind. His counsel prevailed. They left their carriages in Muintir Beirn, with 1,500 soldiers to guard the supplies – for they were carrying seven week's provisions for every soldier. There were stores of white bags, sacks of large meal biscuits, plenty of beer, wine, whiskey, flour, sugar, poultry and a consignment of tents. They displayed their silken banners throughout Muintir Beirn.

The general [Owen Rowe O Neill] sent three troops under Brian O Neill, son of Conn Ruadh, to watch the levies from O Kane's country, and he sent a hundred men against the enemy at Kilgowney so that they took a fright out of them. After that they beat a strategic retreat back to their own camp.

The general was in the midst of his host, instructing his men. Here is the substance of what he said:

'Before you are your oppressors and the enemies of your souls. Be brave against them today. Remember how they drove out your chiefs, plundered your families, oppressed both your spiritual and temporal interests, robbed you of your estates and drove you into exile, etc.'

The two hosts attacked each other at Drumfliuch . . . and the heretics were driven back after great slaughter from the cannon, for five field-guns had been trained on them. The Irish pursued them, and captured their arms, great and small. Then, grasping their pikes and heavy swords, they began cutting down the fugitives in this bloody rout.

Then there came into the fight the famous hero himself – Owen O Neill – the brave champion and fearless protector of the children of Pope Innocent X. The three troops that had been sent out at break of day to cut off reinforcements from Dungannon direction, also joined in the pursuit, and were aided by the fact that the enemy mistook them for the long-expected reinforcements. At the head of his brave company, Sir Phelim [O Neill] also joined in, and made wide gaps in the retreating forces. Lord Blaney was killed, and Lord Montgomery himself was captured by Cormac O Neill. Unhorsed and disarmed, he was taken into custody. The retreat developed into a demoralised and bloody rout. It was then that the Irish let loose their battle-cry. At times in the lead, at times in their midst, the general was encouraging and inciting his men. The slaughter continued until the final disappearance of the last ray of twilight made further pursuit impossible. Numbers of the enemy were drowned in the Blackwater and in the lake of Knocknacloy.

The general and his hosts returned to their camp. They were merry and joyful over the defeat of the enemy. Apart from those struck down in the battle, few of the others reached their homes – they lost their lives in the wilds. . . . The booty included over two thousand muskets, several field-guns, 37 flags, with a large amount of pikes, pickaxes and drums. The general sent Boetius MacEgan, diffinitor of the Franciscans, and his own attendant, Hugh Buidhe MacMahon, to the Council of Kilkenny, to present 26 of the flags to the nuncio[12] as a token of the victory. With them he sent some extraordinary letters taken on the bodies of the heretics, to the effect that no one was to be spared except the general. . . . Those killed within a space of three hours, between Drumfliuch and Lisnafeeda – God be praised for the victory – numbered 3,548. This does not include those killed in the wilds, in Toaghy, the Fews, Orior and Iveagh, most of whom were found dead without even a scratch on them.

TRADE

William Lithgow, The present survey of London and England's state,
1643

William Lithgow (1582–1645?) was a Scotsman who travelled extensively in
Europe and further afield and wrote accounts of his observations and experiences. In May 1643 he arrived in London to find money scarce, trade decayed,
merchant ships lying idle on the Thames and coal in very short supply, all as a
result of the war. Nevertheless, there was no shortage of food. He confirms
that the tax burden to support parliament's army was very heavy.
Source: *Somers' Tracts* (1750), iv, pp. 536–7.

. . . And now, truly, I never saw London, these forty years past, so populous as
now it is; only there is a general muttering that money is hard to come by, and
that is, because all kind of trades and trading begin to decay, and they who have
money keep it close; for common employments are lately metamorphosed in
flying colours, toucking of drums, enveloping scarves, and Pandedalian
feathers. . . . Indeed, for victuals they have abundance, and plenty of all things,
and at any easy rate, and want for nothing as yet, save only peace.

But it may truly be feared, that if these their general combustions draw to a
winter leaguer, that both the city and kingdom shall smart for it: and why?
Because both the great armies, and also the petty armies in every county, do so
sack and spoil the grounds, of horses, bestial, grass, corn, and hay, and also
pitifully plunder the people of moneys, victuals, and domestic furniture, that
the continuing of it in a short time shall ruin all.

. . . I found the river, from Ratcliffe upwards, full of merchant ships, and
they lying two and two, and side to side, with a pretty distance from couple to
couple, resembled as though they had been to make a sea fight; but indeed
they lie at their guard, and are well provided. The first lamentation their
tongues offered me here was, the dearth and scarcity of coals; and notwithstanding of the daily relief they get from Scotland, yet they are loath to part
with money, and, in a wringing way, and grudging at their infranchised lot,
heavily bewail the loss of their advantageous Tyne. I confess their weekly taxes
are great, levied to maintain the parliament's army, besides many other
burthens that daily depend upon their purses; and for all this (besides the
monthly contributions of the nine circumjacent counties) the army's pay falls
daily short, and they can neither march nor fight for lack of moneys, the want
whereof being the main and chiefest cause of their slow proceedings: which
weekly collections, according to that multipotent place, and the country
about, is truly supposed to amount (per annum) to three millions of money.
But how it is disposed, either by the hands of corruption, or if reserved policy,
for future respects, be the main restraint, I cease to discern it, though many
thousands daily gape at it. . . .

GODLY REFORMATION

Commons orders concerning scandalous and malignant ministers, 1643

The purge of parish clergy begun earlier gathered momentum in 1643. The Commons in effect invited complaints against ministers on religious or political grounds which were to be investigated locally before being transmitted to the committee for plundered ministers. The House also issued individual orders for sequestered livings to be filled by godly divines many of whom had fled from royalist areas.
Source: *Commons' Journals*, iii, 231, 233.

6 September 1643

Ordered, that the deputy lieutenants and committees of parliament, in any county of this kingdom, or any five or more of them, shall have power to take the examinations of all witnesses against any ministers that are scandalous, either in life, or doctrine, or any others that have deserted their cures, and joined themselves actually with, and are assistant unto, the forces raised against the parliament: and, to the end that those, who will appear, may have the witnesses examined in their presence,

It is further ordered, that the summons (with sufficient warning of the time and place, when and where the charge against them shall be proved) be either given to their persons, or left at their houses; and (if they desire it) they shall have a copy of the articles against them, within convenient time, to give in their answers under their hands; which, together with their charge, and the proofs upon every particular of it, the said deputy lieutenants, and committees of parliament, shall send up to the committee of this House, appointed for to provide for plundered ministers:[13] which committee shall from time to time transmit them to this House.

8 September 1643

An order for sequestering the vicarage of Dallington, in the county of Sussex, whereof Zachary Tutsham is now vicar, to the use and benefit of John Zachary, Master of Arts, a godly, learned, and orthodox divine; who is thereby authorised and required to officiate the said cure, and to preach diligently to the parishioners; and to receive the profits thereof; was this day read; and, by vote upon the question, assented unto.

William Dowsing's iconoclasm in East Anglia, 1643–4

An ordinance of August 1643 ordered the demolition of all altars and 'superstitious' objects in churches and chapels. William Dowsing (1596–1668), a man of respectable Suffolk yeoman stock, was appointed to carry out this destruction in East Anglia, which he did with great determination and vigour in

1643–4, keeping a systematic record of each building visited and what was destroyed. He also appointed deputies to carry out the work in places he was unable to visit himself.
Source: J. G. Cheshire (ed.), 'William Dowsing's destructions in Cambridge-shire', *Transactions of the Cambridgeshire and Huntingdonshire Archaeological Society*, vol. 3 (1914), p. 84.

Swaffham Bulbeck in Cambridgeshire 1643. 4 crucifixes and Christ nailed to them and God the Father over one of them, and we brake down a 100 superstitious pictures, and 2 crosses we took off the steeple, and 2 on the church and chancel. . . . We digged down the steps, 20 cherubims. . . .

At Babraham in Cambridgeshire, January 5, 1644. We brake down 3 crucifixes and 60 superstitious pictures, and brake in pieces the rails.

January 5 at Linton, we took up 8 inscriptions, we brake down 3 crucifixes and 80 superstitious pictures and brake the rails, and gave order to deface 2 grave stones, with 'pray for our souls'.

At Horseheath January 5, we brake down 2 crucifixes and 6 prophets. Pictures, Malachi, Daniel and Ezekiel and Sophany and 2 more, and 40 superstitious pictures.

January 5 at Withersfield [in Suffolk], we brake down 3 crucifixes and 80 superstitious pictures.

At Chesterfield [in Essex] February 6, we gave order to take down 14 crosses on the steeple and 2 on the porch, we brake down 40 superstitious pictures, and gave order to take down 50 more at least and the level the steps in the chancel. . . .

The solemn league and covenant, 1643

Adoption of the solemn league and covenant was the price the parliamentarians paid for urgently needed Scottish military assistance in the war. The document was mainly prepared by Alexander Henderson (1583?–1646), a leading Scottish Presbyterian divine, but the Westminster assembly and English parliament subsequently made some important alterations to it. It was both a 'civil league', a military alliance with the Scots aimed at preserving constitutional liberties in both kingdoms, and a 'religious covenant', a pledge to work for the unity of all three of Charles's kingdoms in the reformed faith. It was intended to have the covenant sworn throughout both England and Scotland and, had the religious articles been fully implemented, Presbyterianism would have been imposed on England and Ireland.
Source: J. Rushworth, *Historical Collections*, 8 vols (London, 1721), v, 478–9.

A solemn league and covenant for reformation and defence of religion, the honour and happiness of the king, and the peace and safety of the three kingdoms of England, Scotland and Ireland.

We noblemen, barons, knights, gentlemen, citizens, burgesses, ministers of the gospel, and commons of all sorts in the kingdoms of England, Scotland and Ireland, by the providence of God living under one king, and being of one reformed religion, having before our eyes the glory of God, and the advancement of the kingdom of our Lord and Saviour Jesus Christ, the honour and happiness of the king's majesty and his posterity, and the true public liberty, safety and peace of the kingdoms, wherein every one's private condition is included, and calling to mind the treacherous and bloody plots, conspiracies, attempts and practices of the enemies of God against the true religion and professors thereof in all places, especially in these three kingdoms, ever since the reformation of religion, and how much their rage, power and presumption are of late and at this time increased and exercised, whereof the deplorable estate of the church and kingdom of Ireland, the distressed estate of the church and kingdom of England, and the dangerous estate of the church and kingdom of Scotland, are present and public testimonies, we have (now at last) after other means of supplication, remonstrance, protestations and sufferings, for the preservation of ourselves and our religion from utter ruin and destruction, according to the commendable practice of these kingdoms in former times, and the example of God's people in other nations, after mature deliberation, resolved and determined to enter into a mutual and solemn league and covenant, wherein we all subscribe, and each one of us for himself, with our hands lifted up to the most high God, do swear.

I. That we shall sincerely, really and constantly, through the grace of God, endeavour in our several places and callings the preservation of the reformed religion in the Church of Scotland, in doctrine, worship, discipline and government, against our common enemies, the reformation of religion in the kingdoms of England and Ireland, in doctrine, worship, discipline and government, according to the word of God, and the example of the best reformed churches; and we shall endeavour to bring the churches of God in the three kingdoms to the nearest conjunction and uniformity in religion, confessing of faith, form of church government, directory for worship and catechising, that we, and our posterity after us, may, as brethren, live in faith and love, and the Lord may delight to dwell in the midst of us.

II. That we shall in like manner, without respect of persons, endeavour the extirpation of popery, prelacy (that is, church government by archbishops, bishops, their chancellors and commissaries, deans, deans and chapters, archdeacons, and all other ecclesiastical officers depending on that hierarchy), superstition, heresy, schism, profaneness, and whatsoever shall be found to be contrary to sound doctrine and the power of godliness, lest we partake in other men's sins, and thereby be in danger to receive of their plagues, and that the Lord may be one, and His name one in the three kingdoms.

III. We shall with the same sincerity, reality and constancy, in our several vocations, endeavour with our estates and lives mutually to preserve the rights and privileges of the parliaments, and the liberties of the kingdoms, and to preserve and defend the king's majesty's person and authority, in the preservation and defence of the true religion and liberties of the kingdoms, that the world may bear witness with our consciences of our loyalty, and that we have no thoughts or intentions to diminish his majesty's just power and greatness.

IV. We shall also with all faithfulness endeavour the discovery of all such as have been or shall be incendiaries, malignants, or evil instruments, by hindering the reformation of religion, dividing the king from his people, or one of the kingdoms from another, or making any faction or parties amongst the people, contrary to the league and covenant, that they may be brought to public trial, and receive condign punishment, as the degree of their offences shall require or deserve, or the supreme judicatories of both kingdoms respectively, or others having power from them for that effect, shall judge convenient.

V. And whereas the happiness of a blessed peace between these kingdoms, denied in former times to our progenitors, is by the good providence of God granted unto us, and hath been lately concluded and settled by both parliaments, we shall each one of us, according to our places and interest, endeavour that they may remain conjoined in a firm peace and union to all posterity, and that justice may be done upon the wilful opposers thereof in manner expressed in the precedent articles.

VI. We shall also, according to our places and callings, in this common cause of religion, liberty and peace of the kingdom, assist and defend all those that enter into this league and covenant, in the maintaining and pursuing thereof, and shall not suffer ourselves directly or indirectly, by whatsoever combination, persuasion, or terror, to be divided and withdrawn from this blessed union and conjunction, whether to make defection to the contrary part, or give ourselves to a detestable indifferency or neutrality in this cause, which so much concerneth the glory of God, the good of the kingdoms, and the honour of the king, but shall all the days of our lives zealously and constantly continue therein, against all opposition, and promote the same according to our power against all lets and impediments whatsoever; and what we are not able ourselves to suppress or overcome, we shall reveal and make known, that it may be timely prevented or removed; all which we shall do as in the sight of God.

And because these kingdoms are guilty of many sins and provocations against God, and His Son Jesus Christ, as is too manifest by our present distresses and dangers, the fruits thereof, we profess and declare before God and the world our unfeigned desire to be humbled for our sins, and for the sins of these kingdoms, especially that we have not as we ought valued the inestimable benefit of the gospel, that we have not laboured for the purity and power thereof, and that we have not endeavoured to receive Christ in our hearts, nor to walk worthy of him in our lives, which are the causes of other sins and transgressions so much abounding amongst us, and our true and unfeigned purpose, desire and endeavour for ourselves, and all others under our power and charge, both in public and in private, in all duties we owe to

God and man, to amend our lives, and each one to go before another in the example of a real reformation, that the Lord may turn away his wrath and heavy indignation, and establish these churches and kingdoms in truth and peace; and this covenant we make in the presence of Almighty God, the searcher of all hearts, with a true intention to perform the same, as we shall answer at that great day, when the secrets of all hearts shall be disclosed, most humbly beseeching the Lord to strengthen us by His Holy Spirit for this end, and to bless our desires and proceedings with such success as may be a deliverance and safety to his people, and encouragement to the Christian churches groaning under, or in danger of the yoke of Antichristian tyranny, to join in the same or like association and covenant, to the glory of God, the enlargement of the kingdom of Jesus Christ, and the peace and tranquillity of Christian kingdoms and commonwealths.

The register book of the fourth classis in the province of London, 1646

The attempt to impose Presbyterianism on England was a dismal failure. Parliament ensured that ultimate authority in the Church remained in lay hands, Presbyterianism generated only limited popular support, and in London, Essex and Lancashire only was anything approaching a full Presbyterian structure erected. Presbyterian church government required each parish to send ministers and lay elders to *classes*, which in turn sent representatives to provincial assemblies (one for London and each county), and the whole structure was crowned by a national synod acting alongside parliament. The following extract from the register book of the fourth classis in the province of London records some of the initial moves to establish Presbyterian discipline.
Source: C. E. Surnam (ed.), *The Register Book of the Fourth Classis in the Province of London 1646–59*, Harleian Society, lxxxii and lxxxiii (1952–3), p. 4.

Saturday, November 7th 1646.
A note for the convention of elders, at Mary Hill [St Mary at Hill].

Sir,
It is thought necessary and seasonable by those who have most frequently met, for the setting up of the Presbyterial government of the church, that since the greater number of parishes in this fourth classis have chosen their elders and such as are chosen have been for the most part, examined and approved by the triers, that there be a preparatory assembly at the church at Mary at Hill on Wednesday November 18th at three of the clock, in the afternoon, and that it begin with a sermon, punctually at that hour. Where at all the triers and elders of every parish are desired to be present, that the sermon ended, they may consult and conclude of some expedient course for the execution of such orders and ordinances of parliament as tend to the increase of knowledge and godliness;

131

and particularly to the holy administration and receiving of the sacrament of the Lord's Supper. And you are desired to give notice hereof in your congregation the next Sabbath-day, and the Sabbath-day following, that all may have notice both of the time and occasion of this meeting, as also to publish the names of the elders of your parish which are approved being these.

Sent to every congregation in the same classis.

THE NEW MODEL ARMY

Joshua Sprigge, Anglia rediviva, *1647*

Joshua Sprigge (1618–84) was an Independent minister who served as a chaplain to the New Model Army and afterwards published an account of its military campaigns from April 1645 to June 1646, from which the following extract is taken. In his interpretation of the army's success, God was showing His approval of its good Christian officers and soldiers, and their godly diversity which had not prevented them from uniting together to be an effective force. Sprigge pays an idealised tribute to the New Model Army and its conduct and organisation.
Source: Joshua Sprigge, *Anglia rediviva* (London, 1647), pp. 323–5.

The officers of this army, as you may read, are such, as knew little of war, than our own unhappy wars had taught them, except some few, so as men could not contribute much to this work: indeed I may say this, they were better Christians than soldiers, and wiser in faith than in fighting, and could believe a victory sooner than contrive it; and yet I think they were as wise in the way of soldiery as the little time and experience they had could make them.

These officers, many of them with their soldiery, were much in prayer and reading scripture, an exercise that soldiers till of late have used but little, and thus then went on and prospered: men conquer better as they are saints, than soldiers; and in the countries where they came, they left something of God as well as of Caesar behind them, something of piety as well as pay.

They were much in justice upon offenders, that they might be still in some degree of reformation in their military state. Armies are too great bodies to be found in all parts at once.

The army was (what by example and justice) kept in good order, both respectively to itself, and the country: nor was it their pay that pacified them; for had they not had more civility than money, things had not been so fairly managed.

They were many of them differing in opinion, yet not in action nor business; they all agreed to preserve the kingdom; they prospered more in their unity, than uniformity; and whatever their opinions were, yet they plundered none with them, they betrayed none with them, nor disobeyed the state with them, and they were more visibly pious and peaceable in their opinions, than many we call more orthodox.

132

They were generally constant and conscientious in duties, and by such soberness and strictness conquered much upon the vanity and looseness of the enemy; many of those fought by principle as well as pay, and that made the work go better on, where it was not made so much matter of merchandise as conscience: they were little mutinous or disputing commands; by which peace the war was better ended.

There was much amity and unity amongst the officers, while they were in action, and in the field, and no visible emulations and passions to break their ranks, which made the public fare better. That boat can go but slowly where the oars row several ways; the best expeditions is by things that go one way.

The army was fair in their marches to friends, and merciful in battle and success to enemies, by which they got love from enemies, though more from friends.

This army went on better by two more wheels of treasurers and a committee; the treasurers were men of public spirits to the state and the army, and were usually ready to present some pay upon every success, which was like wine after work, and cheered up the common spirits to more activity.

The committee, which the House of Commons formed, were men wise, provident, active and faithful in providing ammunition, arms, recruits of men, clothes: and that family must needs thrive that hath good stewards.

Thus you have a copy of our army; we will not say they have no faults, but those they have, we wish rather reformed than read by the world.

CLUBMEN

The desires and resolutions of the clubmen of the counties of Dorset and Wiltshire, 1645

Two years' experience of plundering and free quarter by the rival armies, and the heavy financial burdens and frequent outside interference in local communities, led to the clubmen risings of 1645. Local peasants, often with the approval of local gentry, organised to defend their property and communities against the armies of both sides. Their aims were essentially localist and conservative, and they represented a profound yearning for peace and a return to normality. They were numerically strong, often outnumbering the available armed forces of either side, and for a time posed a real threat to both sides.
Source: Thomason Tracts (1645) E. 292/24.

The desires and resolutions of the clubmen of the counties of Dorset and Wiltshire.

We the miserable inhabitants of the said counties being too too deeply touched with the apprehension, and sense of our past, and present sufferings, occasioned only by these civil, and unnatural wars within this kingdom: and finding by sad experience, that by means thereof, the true worship of Almighty God, and our religion are almost forgotten, and that our ancient laws, and liberties, contrary to the great charter of England, and the petition of right,[14] are altogether swallowed up in the arbitrary power of the sword. And foreseeing that destruction, famine, and utter desolation will inevitably fall upon us, our wives, and children (unless God of his infinite mercy shall upon our true humiliation be graciously pleased to impose a period to these sad distractions) are unanimously resolved, wherein we desire the concurrence of all the garrisons of this county to join in petitioning his majesty, and the two houses of parliament for an happy peace, and accommodation of the present differences, without further effusion of Christian blood. Without which accommodation, we cannot expect the enjoyment of our religion, liberties, or properties. And lest any false aspersion of endeavouring, or desiring to introduce popery, or arbitrary government should be cast on all, or any of us, we do all with one heart and mind, profess before God, and the world, ourselves enemies to both. And that we aim at nothing herein, save only the glory of God, and the good of the church and state. And for that purpose we do here declare, that we really intend to the utmost of our lives, and fortunes:

First, to maintain, and defend the true reformed Protestant religion, and the inheritance of the crown.

Secondly, to join with, and assist one another in the mutual defence of our liberties, and properties against all plunderers, and all other unlawful violence whatsoever.

Thirdly, we do hereby resolve, and faithfully promise each to other, that if any person or persons whatsoever, who shall concur with, and assist us in these our resolutions, happen to suffer in his person or estate in the execution of the premises, that shall be accounted as the suffering of the generality, and reparation shall be made to the party suffering, according to his damages; and in case of loss of life, provision shall be made for his wife and children, and that at the country's charge.

Fourthly, we do hereby declare all such unworthy of our assistance, as shall refuse to join with us in the prosecution of these our just intentions.

Certain directions for present behaviour, made, and agreed on at a meeting of the inhabitants of Dorset and Wiltshire at Gorehedge-corner, May 25, 1645.

Whereas by the articles of our association, we challenge unto ourselves no other freedom for the present from the burden of war than to preserve ourselves from plunder, and all other unlawful violence: it is therefore advised by the generality, that until such time as we receive answer to our petitions from his majesty, and the houses of parliament:

[Nine directions follow providing for the selection of local leaders, organisation of the watch, action to be taken against plundering or violent soldiers and the arming of the population. Legally sanctioned contributions of money and provisions for the armies, or quarters for the soldiers, were to be met taking into account each person's ability to contribute and the soldiers' behaviour.]

If any inconvenience shall be found to ensue on the observation of these directions, it is desired to be made known at the next general rendezvous, that upon consultation had, it may be amended.

5

COUNTER-
REVOLUTIONARIES AND
REVOLUTIONARIES

POLITICAL PRESBYTERIANISM

The City remonstrance of 26 May 1646

The political Presbyterian City remonstrance of May 1646 was drawn up by London's governing body for presentation to both Houses. It combined religious with political demands and enlisted support from both religious Presbyterians and those who were simply anxious for a return to peace and normality. Among its principal demands were an exclusive Presbyterian church settlement, a swift peace agreement with the king, continuing close relations with Scotland, the reconquest of Ireland, some relief from financial burdens and the re-establishment of the City's control over its militia. The Lords gave it a generally favourable reception while the Commons were distinctly cool towards it. Eight thousand respectable citizens subsequently signed a petition backing the remonstrance.
Source: *Lords' Journals* (1646), viii, 332–4.

26 May 1646

To the right honourable the Lords assembled in the high court of parliament.

The humble remonstrance and petition of the lord mayor, aldermen, and commons of the City of London, in common council assembled.

Our duty in the first place doth lead us to begin all our addresses, as we most heartily and humbly do these, with all due and humble acknowledgement of the great labours and endeavours which your lordships have these many years employed in reformation both of the church and commonwealth, and in preservation of both; with the humble tender of our constant devotion to serve the parliament, according to our covenant made before ALMIGHTY GOD: in the next place, we most humbly crave pardon, although we do presume again to return unto your lordships, and humbly yet plainly lay open the sorrows and fears of our hearts, even in this season, when as GOD hath blessed our armies with the greatest successes, and that man might persuade himself that the war is almost at an end.

For, first, when we remember that it hath been long since declared to be far from any purpose or desire to let loose the golden reins of discipline and government in the church, or to leave private persons or particular congregations to take up what form of divine service they please; when we look upon what both Houses have resolved against Brownism and Anabaptism properly so called; when we mediate on our Protestation and covenant; and lastly, when we pursue the directory and other ordinances for Presbyterial government; and yet find private and separate congregations daily erected in divers parts of the City and elsewhere, and commonly frequented; and Anabaptism, Brownism, and almost all manner of heresies, schisms, and blasphemies, boldly vented and maintained by such as to the point of church government profess themselves Independent; we cannot but be astonished at the swarm of sectaries which discover themselves everywhere, who, if by their endeavours they should get into places of profit and trust in martial and civil affairs, it might tend much to the disturbance of the public peace both of the church and commonwealth.

We cannot but also call to mind what vows we have made to GOD in the same covenant, as well as our former Protestation, to preserve the rights and privileges of parliament, and the liberties of the kingdoms, and to preserve and defend the king's majesty's person and authority, in the preservation and defence of the true religion and liberties of the kingdoms; that the world may bear witness of our loyalty, and that we have no thoughts or intentions to diminish his majesty's just power and greatness; and do humbly rest in the assurances we have received, in the many former declarations of both Houses, concerning their intentions towards his majesty, his royal posterity, and the peace of this kingdom; which we doubt not but your lordships will pursue with all speedy dispatch of propositions to his majesty, now whilst GOD doth so mercifully and miraculously go along with our armies in all the parts of the kingdom.

We may not, in the next place, forget our brethren of Scotland, how first they were invited to engage with this kingdom in GOD'S cause, when yet they were at peace at home; in what covenant this nation is mutually linked with them; at what time, in relation both to the weak condition of our forces then, and the season of the year, they adventured upon an enemy warmly lodged, and well armed and prepared; what they have since suffered for this cause in their own kingdom; how successful ever since GOD hath made our forces, in suppressing the common enemies of both nations; and what present hopes we have of a well-settled peace, while we continue in this mutual amity: and then cannot but lament the many jealousies which the enemies of our peace, union, and good government, do now strive to beget between both nations, and tremble at the sad effects thereof, if not timely prevented by the wisdom of the parliaments of both kingdoms.

We cannot also omit humbly to represent to your lordships' consideration, how many citizens have already suffered, and how many more will be undone, if your lordships shall still make use of that ancient privilege, to protect yourselves, the assistants of this honourable House, and the servants of both, and others, from being proceeded against in any course of law for debt; which now, because this parliament hath already sat so long, and is likely by reason of the unsettledness of affairs to sit much longer, would especially require some expedient, for relief of so many as otherwise must daily suffer under this privilege.

And now that the kingdom is almost reduced, by which means the revenues of the kingdom will be unburthened, and the customs and excise increase, and the public charge of the kingdom decrease; now that delinquents do daily come in and compound; and now that the enemy hath but few holds left: we hope that the great and extraordinary taxes and burthens on the City and their trade shall be in the future abated; that the debts owing to the City and citizens of London, either by particular assurances of the parliament, or upon the public faith of the kingdom, be taken care for and discharged, as well as those assigned upon the excise, and may not be diverted from the uses appointed by former acts and ordinances.

And we humbly crave leave to present to the consideration of this honourable House the committee of Haberdashers' Hall,[1] as being one of the greatest grievances of this City, and which, so long as it is continued, doth hinder the concourse of people thereunto, and tendeth much to the destruction of the trade and inhabitants thereof.

And now also we doubt not but GOD will give the parliament some better means and opportunity for the relief of our bleeding brethren in Ireland, and the suppressing of those horrid rebels, and reducing of that kingdom, wherein, besides the public and common interest, we are particularly concerned.

Lastly, we should have much to say for this City, if we could imagine that its fidelity and constant services and devotion to the parliament could either be questioned or forgotten. That little we shall express on the part of the City is, not to repeat how zealous we have been in the cause of GOD and this parliament; how we have spilt our blood, and spent and laid out ourselves and our estates, in maintenance thereof; how many public acknowledgements we have by us of the favourable acceptance of them, and promises to leave testimonies thereof to all future ages: but only to beseech your lordships to consider, how much our hearts may justly be dejected, now that GOD hath followed your endeavours and our prayers with so many successes, and brought this war to a probable period (as to the sense of man), that the enemies of our peace should strive now to sow jealousies between the parliament and this City, as hath been too evident of late; and particularly should so far prevail as to be able to render the chief magistrate of this City, the lord mayor,[2] suspect; unto whom we cannot but give this just testimony, that he in his place hath faithfully behaved himself, and carefully discharged his office.

We could add much more, of the daily invectives against us from the pulpit, and other places where the boutefeus[3] of these sectaries are admitted; the scurrilous and seditious pamphlets daily broached in and against the City; and the great contempt of, and discouragement unto, the ministers of the gospel who adhere to the Presbyterial government: but we shall conclude with this brief and humble representation of our petitions and desires to your lordships, in the name of the whole City:

[the suppression of all separatist churches and prosecution of their members, enforced conformity to the Presbyterian church government settled by parliament and exclusion from public office of its opponents, the hastening of peace negotiations with the king, the preserving of unity between England and Scotland, action on parliamentary protections, measures to reduce the tax burdens on the City and repay the large sums owing to its citizens, the immediate dissolution (or stringent reform) of the committee at Haberdashers' Hall, the reduction of Ireland and the vindication of Mayor Adams.]

And lastly, and above all, that your lordships will be pleased not to look upon any expression of this our remonstrance and petition as charging anything upon your lordships, or as is intended to entrench upon any privilege of this honourable House; but favourably to accept thereof, and so to interpret the same, as from a single and humble heart it is sincerely, and without any by-ends, or to comply with any party whatsoever, intended and breathed forth from the sad hearts of the petitioners, who are overwhelmed with many fears on all sides, and who call GOD the searcher of all hearts to witness, that, according to their covenant and duty, their zeal, devotion, and obedience, is as fervent and prostrate as ever to serve the parliament, with their lives and estates, against all the enemies of our peace, and to conjoin the City more and more to the parliament, and to maintain the union of both nations against all opposers whatsoever.

All which we humbly submit unto the wisdom of this honourable House.

Robert Baillie, Letters, 1646–7

Robert Baillie (1599–1662) was a leading Scottish Presbyterian divine and former covenanter who spent much of the early 1640s in London where he was a member of the Westminster assembly of divines. He also maintained close contact in London with English enthusiasts for a Presbyterian church settlement and his correspondence provides an important Scottish perspective on English domestic politics during these years. He advocated an exclusive and coercive Presbyterian Church which would vanquish the Independents and the sects and was disgusted with the Erastian nature of the church settlement eventually arrived at in England. He finally returned to Scotland in 1646 where he continued to make grave pronouncements on the situation in the southern kingdom and the possibility of yet another Scottish military intervention.

Source: D. Laing (ed.), The Letters and Journals of Robert Baillie, 3 vols (Edinburgh, 1841), ii, 361; iii, 9–10.

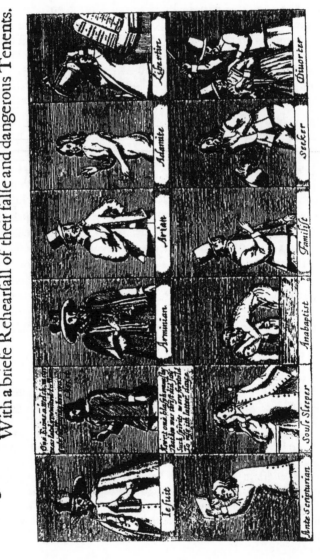

Figure 10 A catalogue of sects in England, 1647

Baillie to Mr Dickson,[4] London, 17 March 1646.

. . . The Independents has [sic] the least zeal to the truth of God of any men we know. Blasphemous heresies are now spread here more than ever in any part of the world; yet they are not only silent, but are patrons and pleaders for liberty almost to them all. We and they have spent many sheets of paper upon the toleration of their separate churches. At the last meeting we concluded to stop our paper-debates, and on Thursday next to begin our verbal disputation against the lawfulness of their desired separation. When we have ended, the Houses will begin to consider this matter. The most there, and in the army, will be for too great a liberty; but the assembly,[5] the City, and the body of all the ministry in the kingdom, are passionately opposite to such an evident breach of our covenant. What the Lord will make the issue, a little time will now declare. We had great need of your prayers: we were never more full of weighty business and perplexed solicitude of mind. . . .

Baillie to William Spang, Edinburgh, 13 July 1647.

. . . These matters of England are so extremely desperate, that now twice they have made me sick: except God arise, all is gone there. The imprudence and cowardice of the better part of the City and parliament, which was triple or sextuple the greater, has permitted a company of silly rascals, which calls themselves yet no more than fourteen thousand, horse and foot, to make themselves masters of the king, and parliament, and City, and by them of all England; so that now that disgraced parliament is but a committee to act all at their pleasure, and the City is ready to fright the parliament, at every first or second boast from the army. No human hope remains but in the king's unparalleled wilfulness, and the army's unmeasurable pride. As yet they are not agreed, and some writes they are not like to agree: for in our particular I expect certainly they will agree well enough, at what distance soever their affections and principles stand. Always if the finger of God in their spirits should so far dement them as to disagree, I would think there were yet some life in the play; for I know the body of England are overweary long ago of the parliament, and ever hated the sectaries, but much more now for this their unexpected treachery and oppression. On the other part, the king is much pitied and desired; so if they give him not contentment, he will overthrow them. If he and they agree, our hands are bound: we will be able, in our present posture and humour of our highly distracted people, to do nothing; and whom shall we go to help, when none calls but the king? Parliament and City, as their masters command, are ready to declare against us if we should offer to arm: but if the king would call, I doubt not of rising of the best army ever we had, for the crushing of these serpents, enemies to God and man. . . .

LONDON AND THE ARMY

Thomas Juxon's diary, 1647

Thomas Juxon (1614–72) was a London merchant of strong Independent sympathies who kept a diary from 1643 to 1647. The diary is an invaluable source for studying political and religious developments within London, and the interaction of City and parliamentary politics during these years and provides a useful counter-balance to the Presbyterian analysis of Robert Baillie. In the piece below, Juxon gives an account of the force upon the Houses on 26 July 1647, and the events leading up to it, and reveals the complicity of some senior City figures in it.
Source: Dr Williams's Library, Ms. 24.50 diary of Thomas Juxon, ff. 112–4.

The impeached members[6] absent from the House but come into the City and hold private meetings with all sort of persons: for to countermine the army: and in short do procure a petition to the common council joined with an engagement to bring the king to London upon his granting what he did offer the 12 of May:[7] and this in the name of covenanters, citizens, apprentices, seamen and others, and with their utmost to oppose whoever should act contrary to this their engagement copies hereof were dispersed in all the wards and many of the trained band officers and others were engaged in it. The parliament having notice hereof do vote it traiterous: and in case they do not desist to be proceeded against. The conspiracy was so strong that as twas cried in the streets they in disdain tore it: and go on amain in getting hands.

Sir Thomas [Fairfax] desires the militia may be put into safe hands, alleging many things considerable against the present [London militia committee]. Twas granted and the old [committeemen] put in again with an addition of others. They meet at the accustomed place at Guildhall but were quickly attended by a company of young men who came boldly into them and wished them to be gone and not to sit there, telling them if they caught them there again they would hang their guts about their ears: and never left them till they had compelled them to rise and as they went followed them with ill language. Then went the aldermen together with the common council with a petition to the parliament desiring the former militia [committee] might be restored and reinvested. The answer of both Houses was that they could not alter what they had done: upon which several of them told the apprentices and others who were there in great numbers that they had done what they could: and that now it rested in them to play their parts: who presently repaired to both Houses' doors. The Lords were threatened in case they did not vote the other [committee] in again and so much that they condescended: and yet were fain to shift for themselves out at the back door. Then they come to the Commoners' House force open the door: tell the Speaker they would not nor should they stir till they had done it: cause them to put it to the vote, themselves standing at the bar: and proposed what they would have voted: and though desired would not withdraw to permit them liberty of voting: when the Commons voted the prentices voted with them and when there appeared some difficulty in the negative and affirmative desired them to withdraw that they might divide the House: but told them they would not but they should do it where they were. And then they were not contented but would see it entered in the journal. All this while there was in the Palace Yard Alderman Bunce[8] with some common councilmen and others as a committee for to give direction for the management of this business: to whom there came continually some from the Commons' door to give them account what was done and to receive directions what to do. This force upon the House remained till nine at night. In the meanwhile the parliament sent to my lord mayor[9] to send down some of the trained bands for their guard: but he refused, called a common council and then when they understood the House had done the thing twas ordered that some of them that were gracious with the multitude should go to Westminster and quiet them: where they no sooner came but they were quiet and departed every one home: but with the general acclamation to return the next day. The next day the Houses met but neither of the Speakers viz. earl [of] Manchester and [William] Lenthall came: sent to their houses, were not there but gone to the army who upon the news of these things sent out orders for the army with all speed (who were dispersed upon and down the kingdom upon the granting of the old militia) to march up to a general rendezvous at Hounslow.

The army's declaration and the City's submission, 1647

Prior to the army's march on London, Fairfax and the council of war prepared a declaration justifying its action. The declaration recalled the moves made in the City of London and parliament to bring about a counter-revolution culminating in the force upon the Houses and the flight of both Speakers and many members to the army. The intention, therefore, was to bring to trial the eleven Presbyterian MPs responsible for these manoeuvres and to restore those members who had fled their seats. Facing up to political reality, the City's government immediately despatched a letter of submission to the army. The army entered the capital on 6 August, and passed through the City the following day, without a single shot being fired or blow exchanged. The soldiers' exemplary conduct won them applause and praise from many citizens.
Source: Corporation of London records office, journals of common council, vol. 40, ff. 248–50.

August 3, 1647.

A declaration of his excellency Sir Thomas Fairfax and his council of war on behalf of themselves and the whole army; showing the grounds of their present advance towards the City of London.

When this army was formerly led by the manifold dispensations of God's providence, and the grounds then declared, to advance towards the City of London;[10] we held it our duty to yield the kingdom the sum of those desires which we had to propose on behalf of it ourselves, wherein we should acquiesce: and having received from the parliament some hopes of due satisfaction therein; and some assurance from the lord mayor, aldermen, and common council of the City of London, of their ready concurrence with us in those things; and also great resolution professed by them of their care and tenderness to preserve all the rights and privileges of parliament; safe, free and inviolate from attempts of all kind; we do appeal to God, to the City and to all men, what a speedy compliance to their desires for our removal to a further distance, found in this army for preventing all fears, jealousies and other inconveniences to the City; and to give clear testimony that we had nothing in our breasts but thoughts of peace, and the good and welfare both of parliament, City and kingdom. . . . Having then upon the aforesaid confidence so withdrawn, and out of a just sense of the country's suffering (by quartering) removed the headquarters of the army above forty miles from London,[11] and dispersed the rest well nigh two hundred miles, for the more ease of all parts, and that we might give the better satisfaction to the kingdom. And being in this secure way, and labouring after the sudden settlement of the kingdom, we had even brought to perfection the particular proposals (included in the generals of our first representation) to be sent to the parliament for a final conclusion of all our troubles.[12] And also had made good progress towards the present relief of distressed Ireland, by assigning a competent force, both of horse and foot, forthwith to have advanced for that service.

But the kingdom's and our enemies being most vigilant and active to prevent and frustrate those good intentions and endeavours of ours, that they might carry on their former evil designs and underhand practices, and also preserve themselves from the hand of justice, they have endeavoured to cast the kingdom into a new and bloody war. And for that end have procured the underhand listing of several reformadoes, and others; have contrived, promoted, and caused to be entered into by several persons, a wicked and treasonable combination;[13] as it is sufficiently manifested by a declaration passed thereupon by both Houses of parliament the 23 July last, for the prevention of the disturbances that were like to ensue thereupon; from which kind of disorders the City had been well preserved, during the space of almost four years, whilst the militia was in the hands of the old commissioners; whereby it appears, there was cause for the army to entreat the parliament, that the militia might be returned into the hands it was in before; as also for divers other good reasons.

1. The old commissioners of the militia (that have been since left out) were not only persons without all exceptions, having been formerly chosen and approved by the parliament and City, but also men of whom the City, parliament, and kingdom have had above four years experience in the faithful discharge of their trust. . . . Now that on a sudden this trust which they had so

faithfully discharged so long, should be taken out of their hands, and put into the hands of others, some whereof (at the best) have been very cool in the service of the parliament at the beginning of this war: that this should be pressed, and in a manner forced upon the parliament, with such importunity from the common council. . . . That they would not be contented with the militia of the City of London only, unless they might have power also over that of the suburbs and out-parts: and all this before the peace of the kingdom was settled, or the propositions sent to the king for that purpose.

. . . At the same time that the alteration of the militia of London was set on foot, the same persons with as much earnestness pressed for the disbanding of this army, before anything was settled for the security and liberty of the kingdom. At the same time the common council was new modellized, and a lord mayor chosen[14] that might suit with the present design in hand. At the said time (under colour of differences in some circumstances of church government) it was earnestly endeavoured, that such as had been constantly true, and most faithful to the interest of the kingdom, should be disabled to have any employment in church and commonwealth, either in England or Ireland, and without any such colour or pretence, divers persons were left out of the common council and militia of eminent deserts and fidelity, and others brought into their rooms, that had either testified an ill affection, or little affection to the parliament and their cause: and such as seeking to withdraw themselves from all employment in the beginning of this war, now at the winding up thereof, are ambitious to thrust themselves into employment, with a design (as may justly be suspected) to frustrate and overthrow, in the close of all, the fruit and effect of all the cost and blood that hath been spent and spilt in this cause: and after that with difficulty, and not without reluctancy in the Houses of parliament, they had obtained the power of the militia in the City of London, and also in the out-parts, for the space of one year, many officers and under-officers in the trained bands, of known trust and fidelity were displaced, and others of more doubtful affections placed in their rooms, little care was taken of the honour of the parliament, which was continually trampled under foot, and their authority affronted by every rabble of women, apprentices, reformadoes, and soldiers; which latter sort of persons were thereby so encouraged to rise higher and higher in their tumultuous carriages against the Houses, till at length it is risen to the height of barbarous and monstrous violence against the parliament, that they might set themselves on work, and the kingdom on fire again. And now at length the design appears open-faced, and though the militia be made as the principal ground of the quarrel, yet by the late vows and engagements set on foot before any alteration of the militia, and the pressing so much the message of the 12th of May,[15] and the king's coming to London to confirm the same, show, that the militia is desired but in order to that design, and to force the parliament (being wholly in their power) to such terms of peace as they pleased.

2. In the next place, when the interest of the common council, in their

change of the militia shall be claimed as the birthright of the City of London. . . . It is time for all the kingdom to look to their birthrights, if such a claim shall be held up against both the Houses of parliament: that upon no occasion whatsoever, nor in no time of danger and distraction whatsoever, they may appoint those that shall have the power of the militia of London, without the consent of the common council; especially when as the Houses shall sit under their power. . . .

3. Lastly, the army discerning how intimate some of the new militia were with some of the eleven accused members,[16] how forward they were to comply and act with them in their endeavours to raise a new war; how they made eighteen or nineteen votes in order thereunto, together with them in one night.

All which the common council and parliament disliked and revoked; how notwithstanding afterwards they secretly promoted their designs by private listings, which now appears to have been still working under ground.

The army . . . observing this . . . found it necessary to desire, that the militia might be put into the hands wherein it was formerly. . . .

To the intent that the army being secured by that means from that danger, might with the more confidence retire further from the City, enlarge their quarters, for the greater ease of the kingdom, and intend wholly the settling of a secure peace in this kingdom, and a speedy and effectual relief of Ireland, which was almost brought to a period, and nothing in the sight of man could have hindered, but this cursed practice of violence upon the parliament, under pretence of the militia; which, according to our desire, being restored again into the hands of the old commissioners, by an ordinance of both Houses, dated the 21st of July (in pursuance of the aforesaid treasonable combination) several petitions were presented to the common council of the City of London, in the name of the apprentices and others, importing their desires, that the militia of the City might continue in the hands of the former commissioners, according to the ordinance of the 4th of May last.

Whereupon, Monday July 26, the common council of the City presents their petitions to both Houses for changing the militia, wherein the House of Lords refuse to alter their resolutions; the House of Commons answered, they would take it into consideration the next morning; notwithstanding which, the City and kingdom cannot be ignorant with what rage and insolency the tumult of apprentices the same day forced both Houses. . . .

After this, the Houses being adjourned till Friday following, upon the Thursday the apprentices printed and posted a paper in several places of the City, requiring all their fellows to be early at the parliament the next morning, for that they intended to adjourn by seven of the clock, and that for a month. Thus the Speakers, with many of the members were driven away from the parliament. . . .

These things being seriously considered by us, we have thought fit in the name of the army to declare, that all such members of either House of parliament as are ready with the army for the security of their persons, and for the ends aforesaid, are forced to absent themselves from Westminster . . . we invite them to make repair to this army to join with us in this great cause, we being resolved, and do hereby faithfully oblige ourselves to stand by them therein, and to live and die with them against all opposition whatsoever; and in particular we do hold ourselves bound to that honourable act of the Speaker of the House of Commons, who upon the grounds he himself expressed in his declaration sent unto us, hath actually withdrawn himself; and hereupon we do further engage to use our utmost and speedy endeavours, that he and those members of either House that are thus enforced away from their attendance at Westminster, may with freedom and security sit there, and again discharge their trust as a free and legal parliament: and in the meantime we do declare against that late choice of a new Speaker by some gentleman at Westminster, as contrary to all right, reason, law, and custom: and we profess ourselves to be most clearly satisfied in all our judgements; and are also confident the kingdom will herein concur with us, that as things now stand, there is no free nor legal parliament sitting, being through the aforesaid violence at present suspended; and that orders, votes, or resolutions forced from the House on Monday the 26th of July last, as also such as shall pass in this assembly of some few lords and gentlemen at Westminster, under what pretence and colour soever, are void and null, and ought not to be submitted unto by the freeborn subjects of England.

. . . we hold ourselves bound by our duty to God and the kingdom, to bring to condign punishment the authors and fomenters of that unparalleled violence done to the parliament . . . and therefore we are resolved to march up towards London, where we do expect that the well-affected people of that City will deliver up unto us (or otherwise put into safe custody, so as they may be reserved to a legal trial) the eleven members impeached, that have again thrust themselves into the management of public affairs by this wicked design.

And that all others will give us such assistance therein, that the members of both Houses may receive due encouragement to return to Westminster, there to sit with all freedom, and so to perform their trust, as shall conduce to the settlement of this distracted kingdom; and to inflict such punishments upon these late offenders as shall deter any for the future to make the like attempt. . . .

This morning, being Wednesday August the 4th, another letter was presented to the general at Thistleworth,[17] from the lord mayor, aldermen, etc. of London, in these words:

Right honourable,

We have, by some of that committee, which we sent down unto your excellency this morning received the declaration of your excellency, and your council of war, on the behalf of yourselves, and the whole army, as we were sitting in council, about five of the clock in the afternoon, and have heard the same read, and considered seriously thereupon; and by our committee we have had a full relation of all passages between your excellency and them; and forasmuch as we observe from the said declaration, of the chief cause that hath drawn your excellency and your army thus near the City, is to bring home those noble and honourable members of both Houses; who, because of the tumults at Westminster the 26th past, have retired themselves, to the end they may be placed in safety, and in free parliament at Westminster, we cheerfully and heartily join with your excellency therein; and according as we shall find directions from your excellency, they shall find all ports and passes open to receive you and them, as also such guards of two or three regiments as your excellency shall think fitting, for their conduct to the two Houses of parliament; and the parliament being sat with peace and safety, we shall humbly submit to their direction, what forces of yours and ours to continue for their future guard; in which service, we humbly offer the whole strength of this City, all other matters which in this straight of time we cannot go through, we wholly refer and submit to be determined by both Houses, when they shall be set in safety at Westminster, as aforesaid, and in confidence that God will give a blessing to these our endeavours, for the taking away all offences and misunderstandings, we have recalled our late declaration, published in the name of the lord mayor, aldermen, and commons of the City of London, in common council assembled:[18] and now we well hope, that your excellency will receive such satisfaction hereby, as that you will withhold the soldier from doing any offence or prejudice to the City, or lines of communication.

London, August 3, 1647. By command of the lord mayor, aldermen, and commons at London, in common council assembled.

THE LEVELLERS

The first Agreement of the People, 1647

The *Agreement of the People* was the Levellers' blueprint for a written constitution for England. It was written before the end of October 1647, possibly by William Walwyn, and had been approved by a meeting of army radicals and civilian Levellers. It provided for the dissolution of the Long Parliament on 30 September 1648, a redistribution of the electorate according to population, biennial parliaments and a one-chamber parliament. Neither the king nor the House of Lords are mentioned. Parliaments were not to enjoy unlimited legislative sovereignty because certain powers, such as those concerned with religion and conscription, were to be reserved to the people alone. The Levellers planned to circulate the document among the adult males of England for their signatures and those refusing to sign it would be excluded from voting and politics. The *Agreement* was tabled for discussion by the General Council of the Army at Putney on 28 October in the hope of gaining army endorsement for it and was published in early November.
Source: D. M. Wolfe (ed.), *Leveller Manifestoes of the Puritan Revolution* (New York, 1944), pp. 225–8.

An Agreement of the People, for a firm and present peace, upon grounds of common-right.

Having by our late labours and hazards made it appear to the world at how high a rate we value our just freedom, and God having so far owned our cause, as to deliver the enemies thereof into our hands: we do now hold ourselves bound in mutual duty to each other, to take the best care we can for the future, to avoid both the danger of returning into a slavish condition, and the chargeable remedy of another war: for as it cannot be imagined that so many of our countrymen would have opposed us in this quarrel, if they had understood their own good; so may we safely promise to ourselves, that when our common rights and liberties shall be cleared, their endeavours will be disappointed, that seek to make themselves our masters: since therefore our former oppressions, and scarce yet ended troubles have been occasioned, either by want of frequent national meetings in council, or by rendering those meetings ineffectual; we are fully agreed and resolved, to provide that hereafter our representatives be neither left to an uncertainty for the time, nor made useless to the ends for which they are intended: in order whereunto we declare,

I

That the people of England being at this day very unequally distributed by counties, cities and boroughs, for the election of their deputies in parliament, ought to be more indifferently proportioned, according to the number of the inhabitants: the circumstances whereof, for number, place, and manner, are to be set down before the end of this present parliament.

II

That to prevent the many inconveniences apparently arising from the long continuance of the same persons in authority, this present parliament be dissolved upon the last day of September, which shall be in the year of our Lord, 1648.

III

That the people do of course choose themselves a parliament once in two years, viz. upon the first Thursday in every 2nd March, after the manner as shall be prescribed before the end of this parliament, to begin to sit upon the first Thursday in April following at Westminster, or such other place as shall be appointed from time to time by the preceding representatives; and to continue till the last day of September, then next ensuing, and no longer.

IV

That the power of this, and all future representatives of this nation, is inferior only to theirs who choose them, and doth extend, without the consent or concurrence of any other person or persons; to the enacting, altering, and repealing of laws; to the erecting and abolishing of offices and courts; to the appointing, removing, and calling to account magistrates, and officers of all degrees; to the making war and peace, to the treating with foreign states: and generally, to whatsoever is not expressly, or impliedly reserved by the represented to themselves.

Which are as followeth,

1. That matters of religion, and the ways of God's worship, are not at all entrusted by us to any human power, because therein we cannot remit or exceed a tittle of what our consciences dictate to be the mind of God, without wilful sin: nevertheless the public way of instructing the nation (so it be not compulsive) is referred to their discretion.

2. That the matter of impressing and constraining any of us to serve in the wars, is against our freedom; and therefore we do not allow it in our representatives; the rather, because money (the sinews of war) being always at their disposal, they can never want numbers of men, apt enough to engage in any just cause.

3. That after the dissolution of this present parliament, no person be at any time questioned for anything said or done, in reference to the late public differences, otherwise than in execution of the judgements of the present representatives, or House of Commons.

4. That in all laws made, or to be made, every person may be bound alike, and that no tenure, estate, charter, degree, birth, or place, do confer any exemption from the ordinary course of legal proceedings, whereunto others are subjected.

5. That as the laws ought to be equal, so they must be good, and not evidently destructive to the safety and well-being of the people.

These things we declare to be our native rights, and therefore are agreed and resolved to maintain them with our utmost possibilities, against all opposition whatsoever, being compelled thereunto, not only by the examples of our ancestors, whose blood was often spent in vain for the recovery of their freedoms, suffering themselves, through fraudulent accommodations, to be still deluded of the fruit of their victories, but also by our woeful experience, who having long expected, and dearly earned the establishment of these certain rules of government are yet made to depend for the settlement of our peace and freedom, upon him that intended our bondage, and brought a cruel war upon us.

William Clarke's record of the army debates at Putney, 1647

William Clarke (1623?–66), as secretary to the General Council of the Army, kept a remarkably full record of its debates held in Putney church in late October and early November 1647. The Army Council was composed of two

(The manner of His Excellency Sir *Thomas Fairfax*, and the Officers of His Armie fitting in C O V N C E L L.

Figure 11 The General Council of the Army (chaired by Fairfax) in 1647

representatives of the ranks and two officers from each regiment and the army's most senior officers. Two civilian radicals from London were also allowed to take part in the Putney discussions. Cromwell chaired the meetings in the absence of Fairfax who was ill, but it was his son-in-law, Commissary-General Henry Ireton (1611–51), a Nottinghamshire gentleman, who dominated the debates. The extract below is from the second day's debate when Ireton interpreted the first article of the Leveller *Agreement of the People*, which was tabled for discussion, as implying universal manhood suffrage. He defended the existing arrangement whereby the franchise was restricted to property-owners and independent traders, and predicted that giving votes to the propertyless would result in the abolition of property. His position was supported by Colonel Nathaniel Rich (d. 1701) one of the most conservative army officers. Ireton's principal opponent was Colonel Thomas Rainsborough (1610?–48), the only senior officer to side with the radicals in the debates, who defended a democratic position. He was supported by Edward Sexby (1616?–58), the most articulate of the agitators. Maximilian Petty (1617–62?) served with John Wildman as a civilian spokesmen at Putney. Later, the Levellers were prepared to exclude servants, apprentices and alms-takers from the franchise and at no stage, of course, did they or anybody else contemplate giving women a vote.

Source: A. S. P. Woodhouse (ed.), *Puritanism and Liberty: Being the Army Debates (1647–9) from the Clarke Manuscripts* (London, 1951), pp. 52–71.

Putney, 29 October 1647

The paper called the Agreement read. Afterwards the first article read by itself.

COMMISSARY-GENERAL HENRY IRETON The exception that lies in it is this. It is said, they are to be distributed according to the number of the inhabitants: 'The people of England,' etc. And this doth make me think that the meaning is, that every man that is an inhabitant is to be equally considered, and to have an equal voice in the election of those representers, the persons that are for the general representative; and if that be the meaning, then I have something to say against it. But if it be only that those people that by the civil constitution of this kingdom, which is original and fundamental, and beyond which I am sure no memory of record does go –

[COMMISSARY NICHOLAS COWLING (*interrupting*)] Not before the conquest.[19]

IRETON But before the conquest it was so. If it be intended that those that by that constitution that was before the conquest, that hath been beyond memory, such persons that have been before [by] that constitution [the electors], should be [still] the electors, I have no more to say against it. . . .

MAXIMILIAN PETTY We judge that all inhabitants that have not lost their birthright should have an equal voice in elections.

COLONEL THOMAS RAINSBOROUGH I desired that those that had engaged in it [might be included]. For really I think that the poorest he that is in England hath a life to live, as the greatest he; and therefore truly, sir, I think it's clear, that every man that is to live under a government ought first by his own consent to put himself under that government; and I do think that the poorest man in England is not at all bound in a strict sense to that government that he hath not had a voice to put himself under; and I am confident that, when I have heard the reasons against it, something will be said to answer those reasons, insomuch that I should doubt whether he was an Englishman or no, that should doubt of these things.

IRETON That's [the meaning of] this, ['according to the number of the inhabitants']?

Give me leave to tell you, that if you make this the rule I think you must fly for refuge to an absolute natural right, and you must deny all civil right; and I am sure it will come to that in the consequence. . . . For my part, I think it is no right at all. I think that no person hath a right to an interest or share in the disposing of the affairs of the kingdom, and in determining or choosing those that shall determine what laws we shall be ruled by here – no person hath a right to this, that hath not a permanent fixed interest in this kingdom, and those persons together are properly the represented of this kingdom, and consequently are [also] to make up the representers of this kingdom, who taken together do comprehend whatsoever is of real or permanent interest in the kingdom. . . . I am sure if we look upon that which is the utmost (within [any] man's view) of what was originally the constitution of this kingdom, upon that which is most radical and fundamental, and which if you take away, there is no man hath any land, any goods, [or] any civil interest, that is this: that those that choose the representers for the making of laws by which this state and kingdom are to be governed, are the persons who, taken together, do comprehend the local interest of this kingdom; that is, the persons in whom all land lies, and those in corporations in whom all trading lies. This is the most fundamental constitution of this kingdom and [that] which if you do not allow, you allow none at all. This constitution hath limited and determined it that only those shall have voices in elections. . . . And if we shall go to take away this, we shall plainly go to take away all property and interest that any man hath either in land by inheritance, or in estate by possession, or anything else – [I say], if you take away this fundamental part of the civil constitution.

RAINSBOROUGH Truly, sir, I am of the same opinion I was, and am resolved to keep it till I know reason why I should not. . . . I do hear nothing at all that can convince me, why any man that is born in England ought not to have his voice in election of burgesses[20]. . . . I do think that the main cause why Almighty God gave men reason, it was that they should make use of that reason, and that they should improve it for that end and purpose that God gave it them. . . . I think there is nothing that God hath given a man that any [one] else can take from him. And therefore I say, that either it must be the law of God or the law of man that must prohibit the meanest man in the kingdom to have this benefit as well as the greatest. I do not find anything in the law of God, that a lord shall choose twenty burgesses, and a gentleman but two, or a poor man shall choose none: I find no such thing in the law of nature, nor in the law of nations. But I do find that all Englishmen must be subject to English laws, and I do verily believe that there is no man but will say that the foundation of all law lies in the people, and if [it lie] in the people, I am to seek for this exemption.

And truly I have thought something [else]: in what a miserable distressed condition would many a man that hath fought for the parliament in this quarrel, be! I will be bound to say that many a man whose zeal and affection to God and this kingdom hath carried him forth in this cause, hath so spent his estate that, in the way the state [and] the army are going, he shall not hold up his head, if when his estate is lost, and not worth forty shillings a year, a man shall not have any interest. . . . And therefore I do [think], and am still of the same opinion, that every man born in England cannot, ought not, neither by the law of God nor the law of nature, to be exempted from the choice of those who are to make laws for him to live under, and for him, for aught I know, to lose his life under. And therefore I think there can be no great stick in this.

Truly I think that there is not this day reigning in England a greater fruit or effect of tyranny than this very thing would produce. Truly I know nothing free but only the knight of the shire,[21] nor do I know anything in a parliamentary way that is clear from the height and fullness of tyranny, but only [that]. As for this of corporations [which you also mentioned], it is as contrary to freedom as may be. For, sir, what is it? The king he grants a patent under the Broad Seal of England to such a corporation to send burgesses, he grants to [such] a city to send burgesses. When a poor base corporation from the king['s grant] shall send two burgesses, when five hundred men of estate shall not send one, when those that are to make their laws are called by the king, or cannot act [but] by such a call, truly I think that the people of England have little freedom.

IRETON I think there was nothing that I said to give you occasion to think that I did contend for this, that such a corporation [as that] should have the electing of a man to the parliament. I think I agreed to this matter, that all should be equally distributed. But the question is, whether it should be distributed to all persons, or whether the same persons that are the electors [now] should be the electors still, and it [be] equally distributed amongst *them*. I do not see anybody else that makes this objection; and if nobody else be sensible of it I shall soon have done. . . .

All the main thing that I speak for, is because I would have an eye to property. I hope we do not come to contend for victory – but let every man consider with himself that he do not go that way to take away all property. For here is the case of the most fundamental part of the constitution of the kingdom, which if you take away, you take away all by that. Here men of this and this quality are determined to be the electors of men to the parliament, and they are all those who have any permanent interest in the kingdom, and who, taken together, do comprehend the whole [permanent, local] interest of the kingdom. . . . Now I wish we may all consider of what right you will challenge that all the people should have right to elections. Is it by the right of nature? If you will hold forth that as your ground, then I think you must deny all property too, and this is my reason. For thus: by that same right of nature (whatever it be) that you pretend, by which you can say, one man hath an equal right with another to the choosing of him that shall govern him – by the same right of nature, he hath the same [equal] right in any goods he sees – meat, drink, clothes – to take and use them for his sustenance. He hath a freedom to the land, [to take] the ground, to exercise it, till it; he hath the [same] freedom to anything that any one doth account himself to have any propriety in. Why now I say then, if you, against the most fundamental part of [the] civil constitution (which I have now declared), will plead the law of nature, that a man should (paramount [to] this, and contrary to this) have a power of choosing those men that shall determine what shall be law in this state, though he himself have no permanent interest in the state, [but] whatever interest he hath he may carry about with him – if this be allowed, [because by the right of nature] we are free, we are equal, one man must have as much voice as another, then show me what step or difference [there is], why [I may not] by the same right [take your property, though not] of necessity to sustain nature . . . if you do, paramount [to] all constitutions, hold up this law of nature, I would fain have any man show me their bounds, where you will end, and [why you should not] take away all property.

RAINSBOROUGH   . . . to say because a man pleads that every man hath a voice [by right of nature], that therefore it destroys [by] the same [argument all property – this is to forget the law of God]. That there's a property, the law of God says it; else why [hath] God made that law, 'Thou shalt not steal'? I am a poor man, therefore I must be [op]pressed: if I have no interest in the kingdom, I must suffer by all their laws be they right or wrong. Nay thus: a gentleman lives in a country and hath three or four lordships, as some men have (God knows how they got them); and when a parliament is called he must be a parliament-man; and it may be he sees some poor men, they live near this man, he can crush them – I have known an invasion to make sure he hath turned the poor men out of doors; and I would fain know whether the potency of [rich] men do not this, and so keep them under the greatest tyranny that was [ever] thought of in the world. And therefore I think that to that it is fully answered: God hath set down that thing as to propriety with this law of his, 'Thou shalt not steal.' And for my part I am against any such thought, and, as for yourselves, I wish you would not make the world believe that we are for anarchy.

OLIVER CROMWELL I know nothing but this, that they that are the most yielding have the greatest wisdom; but really, sir, this is not right as it should be. No man says that you have a mind to anarchy, but [that] the consequences of this rule tends to anarchy, must end in anarchy; for where is there any bound or limit set if you take away this [limit], that men that have no interest but the interest of breathing [shall have no voice in elections]? Therefore I am confident on't, we should not be so hot one with another.

RAINSBOROUGH I know that some particular men we debate with [believe we] are for anarchy.

IRETON I profess I must clear myself as to that point. I would not desire, I cannot allow myself, to lay the least scandal upon anybody. And truly, for that gentleman that did take so much offence, I do not know why he should take it so. We speak to the paper – not to persons – and to the matter of the paper . . . I have, with as much plainness and clearness of reason as I could, showed you how I did conceive the doing of this [that the paper advocates] takes away that which is the most original, the most fundamental civil constitution of this kingdom, and which is, above all, that constitution by which I have any property. If you will take away that and set up, as a thing paramount, whatever a man may claim by the law of nature, though it be not a thing of necessity to him for the sustenance of nature; if you do make this your rule, I desire clearly to understand where then remains property. . . .

RAINSBOROUGH To the thing itself – property [in the franchise]. I would fain know how it comes to be the property [of some men, and not of others]. . . . And I would fain know what we have fought for. [For our laws and liberties?] And this is the old law of England – and that which enslaves the people of England – that they should be bound by laws in which they have no voice at all!

IRETON . . . I do not speak of not enlarging this [representation] at all, but of keeping this to the most fundamental constitution in this kingdom, that is, that no person that hath not a local and permanent interest in the kingdom should have an equal dependence in election [with those that have]. But if you go beyond this law, if you admit any man that hath a breath and being, I did show you how this will destroy property. It may come to destroy property thus. You may have such men chosen, or at least the major part of them, [as have no local and permanent interest]. Why may not those men vote against all property? . . .

RAINSBOROUGH I desire to know how this comes to be a property in some men, and not in others.

COLONEL [NATHANIEL] RICH I confess [there is weight in] that objection that the commissary-general [i.e. Ireton] last insisted upon; for you have five to one in this kingdom that have no permanent interest. Some men [have] ten, some twenty servants, some more, some less. If the master and servant shall be equal electors, then clearly those that have no interest in the kingdom will make it their interest to choose those that have no interest. It may happen, that the majority may by law, not in a confusion, destroy property; there may be a law enacted, that there shall be an equality of goods and estates. I think that either of the extremes may be urged to inconveniency; that is, [that] men that have no interest as to estate should have no interest as to election [and that they should have an equal interest]. . . .

EDWARD SEXBY I see that though liberty were our end, there is a degeneration from it. We have engaged in this kingdom and ventured our lives, and it was all for this: to recover our birthrights and privileges as Englishmen; and by the arguments urged there is none. There are many thousands of us soldiers that have ventured our lives; we have had little propriety in the kingdom as to our estates, yet we have had a birthright. But it seems now, except a man hath a fixed estate in this kingdom, he hath no right in this kingdom. I wonder we were so much deceived. If we had not a right to the kingdom, we were mere mercenary soldiers. . . . I shall tell you in a word my resolution. I am resolved to give my birthright to none. Whatsoever may come in the way, and [whatsoever may] be thought, I will give it to none . . . I do think the poor and meaner of this kingdom – I speak as in relation [to the condition of soldiers], in which we are – have been the means of the preservation of this kingdom. I say, in their stations, and really I think to their utmost possibility; and their lives have not been [held] dear for purchasing the good of the kingdom. [And now they demand the birthright for which they fought.] Those that act to this end are as free from anarchy and confusion as those that oppose it, and they have the law of God and the law of their conscience [with them]. . . .

IRETON   . . . For my part, rather than I will make a disturbance to a good constitution of a kingdom wherein I may live in godliness and honesty, and peace and quietness, I will part with a great deal of my birthright. . . .

Now let us consider where our difference lies. We all agree that you should have a representative to govern, and this representative to be as equal as you can [make it]. But the question is, whether this distribution can be made to all persons equally, or whether [only] amongst those equals that have the interest of England in them. That which I have declared [is] my opinion [still]. I think we ought to keep to that [constitution which we have now], both because it is a civil constitution – it is the most fundamental constitution that we have – and [because] there is so much justice and reason and prudence [in it] – as I dare confidently undertake to demonstrate – that there are many more evils that will follow in case you do alter [it] than there can [be] in the standing of it. . . .

RAINSBOROUGH   Sir, I see that it is impossible to have liberty but all property must be taken away. If it be laid down for a rule, and if you will say it, it must be so. But I would fain know what the soldier hath fought for all this while? He hath fought to enslave himself, to give power to men of riches, men of estates, to make him a perpetual slave. We do find in all presses that go forth none must be pressed that are freehold men. When these gentlemen fall out among themselves they shall press the poor scrubs to come and kill [one another for] them.

John Rushworth's account of the Corkbush Field mutiny, 1647

The first of three post-Putney army rendezvous was held on 15 November in Corkbush Field near Ware, Hertfordshire, at a time when the senior officers' political grip on the army appeared to be slipping. Seven regiments were authorised to attend the rendezvous but a further two (Harrison's and Lilburne's regiments) also turned up uninvited and without their officers with printed copies of the Leveller *Agreement* pinned to their hats. Colonel Thomas Rainsborough, whose presence at the rendezvous was also highly irregular, headed a delegation which presented a petition in favour of the *Agreement* to Fairfax when he arrived at the field. The following official account to parliament by John Rushworth (1612–90), the historian and Fairfax's secretary, does not mention Cromwell's presence yet other sources confirm that he helped Fairfax put down the mutiny and restore order. One mutineer was summarily executed and several key figures were taken into custody. The other two rendezvous were entirely trouble free.

Source: J. Rushworth, *Historical Collections*, 8 vols (London, 1721), vii, 875–6.

Tuesday, November, 16 [1647].

This day both Houses received letters from his excellency Sir Thomas Fairfax, giving account of a rendezvous of part of the army yesterday between Hertford and Ware; the particulars as thus certified:

'Monday the 15th instant, according to appointment, the rendezvous of the first brigade of the army was held in Corkbush Field between Hertford and Ware, Hertford being the headquarters, Saturday and Sunday. The general went from thence to the rendezvous; where according to order, there met, of horse, the general's regiment, Colonel [Charles] Fleetwood's, Colonel [Nathaniel] Rich's and Colonel [Philip] Twisleton's; of foot, the general's, Colonel [Robert] Hammond's, and Colonel [Thomas] Pride's: and besides these, upon the seducements of the new agents,[22] Colonel [Thomas] Harrison's, and Colonel [Robert] Lilburne's regiments. The general expressed himself very gallantly at the head of every regiment, to live and die with them for those particulars which were contained in a remonstrance[23] read to every regiment; and notwithstanding the endeavours of Major [Thomas] Scot and others to animate the soldiers to stand to a paper, called, *The Agreement of the People*, they generally, by many acclamations, declared their affections and resolutions to adhere to the general; and as many as could in a short time they had allowed, signed an agreement drawn up for that purpose, concerning their being ready from time to time to observe such orders as they should receive from the general and council of the army.

But it may not be forgot, that upon the general's coming into the field, Colonel [William] Eyre, Major Scot, and others, were observed insinuating divers seditious principles unto the soldiers, incensing them against the general and general officers; upon which order was given for the commitment of Colonel Eyre and others into the marshal's hands, Major Scot committed to the custody of Lieutenant [Edmund] Chillenden, and sent up to the parliament, he being a member of the House of Commons. Some inferior persons were likewise committed for dispersing factious papers, as the *Agreement of the People*, etc. among the private soldiers, and finding those people who pretend most for the freedom of the people, had dispersed divers of those papers amongst Colonel Lilburne's regiment of foot, the most mutinous regiment in the army, strict command was given for them, to tear them, and cast them away, which was done; and Captain-Lieutenant [William] Bray, who was the only officer above a lieutenant left among them, the rest being driven away by the mutinous soldiers, and one of them wounded, was taken from the head of that regiment, and committed to custody; it being alleged, that he had led on the soldiers to that rendezvous, contrary to orders. And afterwards, a council of war being called in the field, divers mutineers, for example sake, were drawn forth, three of them were tried and condemned to death; and one of them whose turn it fell to by lot, was shot to death at the head of the regiment, and others are in hold to be tried.

Colonel [Thomas] Rainsborough and some others, presented a petition, and the *Agreement of the People*, to his excellency, at his first coming. Colonel Harrison's regiment, who had papers in their hats, with this motto, *England's freedom*, and *Soldiers' rights*, when they understood their error, by the general's severe reproof, of their so doing, tore them, and expressed their resolution to be obedient to his excellency's commands.

There is to be a further rendezvouz of the army Wednesday and Thursday next about Windsor, and at Kingston.'

Both Houses had a conference upon the general's letters; and the Lords recommended several votes to the Commons for concurrence: as, that a letter of thanks be sent to the general; for which they named a committee of four: also that the late proceedings in London and elsewhere, tending to the dividing the army, and to so much sedition, be examined.

That they will think of sudden pay for the army also for the future; that they will cause a satisfactory way for arrears to be declared, and make the act of indemnity full; that Major Scot might give an account of his doings, and that Colonel Rainsborough may not go to sea until he have cleared himself.[24]

The Leveller petition of 11 September 1648

With the second civil war over, parliament was still intent on trying to reach a negotiated settlement with the king and the petition of 11 September was the Levellers' response to this. The petition denounced the forthcoming negotiations with Charles, called in effect for his trial and provided the most comprehensive statement of Leveller policy since the 'large' petition of March 1647. The Levellers were also astute enough to include in the document demands for the settlement of the army's main grievances and, in subsequent weeks, army militants would appear to have combined with Levellers in organising support for its programme in the army. Like other anonymous Leveller petitions, it was a composite work probably drafted in this instance by Walwyn and Overton. The Commons gave the petition a non-committed

reception and were later lobbied by London Levellers accompanied by some lower army officers.
Source: G. E. Aylmer (ed.), *The Levellers in the English Revolution* (London, 1975), pp. 132–8.

To the right honourable, the Commons of England in parliament assembled.

The humble petition of divers well affected persons inhabiting the City of London, Westminster, the borough of Southwark, Hamlets, and places adjacent.

With parliament's answer thereunto.

Showeth,

That although we are as earnestly desirous of a safe and well-grounded peace, and that a final end were put to all the troubles and miseries of the common-wealth, as any sort of men whatsoever: yet considering upon what grounds we engaged on your part in the late and present war, and how far (by our so doing) we apprehend ourselves concerned, give us leave (before you conclude as by the treaty in hand[25]) to acquaint you first with the ground and reason which induced us to aid you against the king and his adherents. Secondly, what our apprehensions are of this treaty. Thirdly, what we expected from you, and do still earnestly desire.

Be pleased therefore to understand, that we had not engaged on your part, but that we judged this honourable House to be the supreme authority of England, as chosen by, and representing the people; and entrusted with abso-lute power for redress of grievances, and provision for safety: and that the king was but at the most the chief public officer of this kingdom, and accountable to this House (the representative of the people, from whom all just authority is, or ought to be derived) for discharge of his office: and if we had not been confident hereof, we had been desperately mad to have taken up arms or to have been aiding and assisting in maintaining a war against him; the laws of the land making it expressly a crime no less than treason for any to raise war against the king.

But when we considered the manifold oppressions brought upon the nation, by the king, his lords, and bishops; and that this honourable House declared their deep sense thereof; and that (for continuance of that power which had so oppressed us) it was evident the king intended to raise forces, and to make war; and that if he did set up his standard, it tended to the disso-lution of the government: upon this, knowing the safety of the people to be above law, and that to judge thereof appertained to the supreme authority, and not to the supreme magistrate, and being satisfied in our consciences, that the public safety and freedom was in imminent danger, we concluded we had not only a just cause to maintain; but the supreme authority of the nation, to justify, defend, and indemnify us in time to come, in what we should perform by direction thereof; though against the known law of the land, or any inferior authority, though the highest.

And as this our understanding was begotten in us by principles of right reason, so were we confirmed therein by your proceedings, as by your condemning those judges who in the case of ship-money had declared the king to be judge of safety; and by your denying him to have a negative voice in the making of laws; where you wholly exclude the king from having any share in the supreme authority: then by your casting the bishops out of the House of Lords, who by tradition also, had been accounted an essential part of the supreme authority; and by your declaring to the Lords, that if they would not join with you in se[tt]ling the militia, (which they long refused) you would settle it without them, which you could not justly have done, and they had any real share in the supreme authority.

These things we took for real demonstrations, that you undoubtedly knew yourselves to be the supreme authority; ever weighing down in us all other your indulgent expressions concerning the king or Lords. It being indeed impossible for us to believe that it can consist either with the safety or freedom of the nation to be governed either by 3 or 2 supremes, especially where experience hath proved them so apt to differ in their judgements concerning freedom or safety, that the one hath been known to punish what the other hath judged worthy of reward; when not only the freedom of the people is directly opposite to the prerogatives of the king and Lords, but the open enemies of the one, have been declared friends by the other, as the Scots were by the House of Lords.

And when as most of the oppressions of the commonwealth have in all times been brought upon the people by the king and Lords, who nevertheless would be so equal in the supreme authority, as that there should be no redress of grievances, nor provision for safety, but at their pleasure. For our parts, we profess ourselves so far from judging this to be consistent with freedom or safety, that we know no great cause wherefore we assisted you in the late wars, but in hope to be delivered by you from so intolerable, so destructive a bondage, so soon as you should (through God's blessing upon the armies raised by you) be enabled.

But to our exceeding grief, we have observed that no sooner God vouchsafeth you victory, and blesseth you with success, and thereby enables you to put us and the whole nation, into an absolute condition of freedom and safety: but according as ye have been accustomed, passing by the ruin of a nation, and all the blood that hath been spilt by the king and his party, ye betake yourselves to a treaty with him, thereby putting him that is but one single person, and a public officer of the commonwealth, in competition with the whole body of the people, whom ye represent; not considering that it is impossible for you to erect any authority equal to yourselves; and declared to all the world that you will not alter the ancient government, from that of king, Lords, and Commons: not once mentioning (in case of difference) which of them is supreme, but leaving that point (which was the chiefest cause of all our public differences, disturbances, wars and miseries) as uncertain as ever.

Insomuch as we who upon these grounds have laid out ourselves every way to the uttermost of our abilities: and all others throughout the land, soldiers and others who have done the like in defence of our supreme authority, and in opposition to the king, cannot but deem ourselves in the most dangerous condition of all others, left without all plea of indemnity, for what we have done; as already many have found by loss of their lives and liberties, either for things done or said against the king; the law of the land frequently taking place, and precedency against and before your authority, which we esteemed supreme, and against which no law ought to be pleaded. Nor can we possibly conceive how any that have any ways assisted you, can be exempt from the guilt of murders and robbers, by the present laws in force, if you persist to disclaim the supreme authority, though their own conscience do acquit them, as having opposed none but manifest tyrants, oppressors and their adherents.

And whereas a personal treaty,[26] or any treaty with the king, hath been long time held forth as the only means of a safe and well-grounded peace; it is well known to have been cried up principally by such as have been disaffected unto you; and though you have contradicted it: yet it is believed that you much fear the issue; as you have cause sufficient, except you see greater alteration in the king and his party than is generally observed, there having never yet been any treaty with him, but was accompanied with some underhand dealing; and whilst the present force upon him (though seeming liberty) will in time to come be certainly pleaded, against all that shall or can be agreed upon: nay, what can you confide in if you consider how he hath been provoked; and what former kings upon less provocations have done, after oaths, laws, charters, bonds, excommunications, and all ties of reconciliations, to the destruction of all those that had provoked and opposed them: yea, when yourselves so soon as he had signed those bills in the beginning of this parliament, saw cause to tell him, that even about the time of passing those bills, some design or other was one fact which if it had taken effect would not only have rendered those bills fruitless, but have reduced you to a worse condition of confusion than that wherein the parliament found you.

And if you consider what new wars, risings, revolting invasions, and plottings have been since this last cry for a personal treaty, you will not blame us if we wonder at your hasty proceedings thereunto: especially considering the wonderful victories which God hath blessed the army withall.

We profess we cannot choose but stand amazed to consider the inevitable danger we shall be in, though all things in the propositions were agreed unto, the resolutions of the king and his party have been perpetually, violently and implacably prosecuted and manifested against us; and that with such scorn and indignation, that it must be more than such ordinary bonds that must hold them.

And it is no less a wonder to us, that you can place your own security therein, or that you can ever imagine to see a free parliament any more in England.

The truth is (and we see we must either now speak it [or] for ever be silent,) we have long expected things of another nature from you, and such as we are confident would have given satisfaction to all serious people of all parties:

[Twenty-seven articles follow detailing their demands: the ending of the veto of the king or Lords over the Commons; automatic yearly elections of MPs to parliaments of fixed duration; freedom of religious belief, worship and expression; abolition of impressment; law reforms stressing the equality of all before the law, trial by jury, freedom from self-incrimination and arbitrary law, and quicker and cheaper proceedings; the end of all trading monopolies; the abolition of the excise and all other taxes except for subsidies; the reversal of all recent enclosures of common land or their enclosure 'only or chiefly to the benefit of the poor'; reforms of imprisonment for debt, begging and punishment for felony; the abolition of tithes; compensation for parliamentarians out of confiscated royalist estates; an absolute prohibition on 'abolishing propriety, levelling men's estates, or making all things common'; strict definition of the powers of both king and Lords; electoral reform in the City of London; compensation for former victims of prerogative courts or monopolists; the abolition of committees; justice to be done on 'the capital authors and promoters of the former or late wars' and doubts about an act of oblivion; and settlement of the army's grievances over pay and indemnity.]

These and the like we have long time hoped you would have minded, and have made such an establishment for the general peace and contentful satisfaction of all sorts of people, as should have been to the happiness of all future generations, and which we most earnestly desire you would set yourselves speedily to effect; whereby the almost dying honour of this most honourable House, would be again revived, and the hearts of your petitioners and all other well affected people, be afresh renewed unto you, the freedom of the nation (now in perpetual hazard) would be firmly established, for which you would once more be so strengthened with the love of the people, that you should not need to cast your eyes any other ways (under God) for your security: but if all this availeth nothing, God be our guide, for men showeth us not a way for our preservation.

The House received this petition, and returned answer thereunto which was to this effect viz. that the House gave them thanks for their great pains, and care to the public good of the kingdom, and would speedily take their humble desires into their serious consideration.

THE SECOND CIVIL WAR

A letter from a gentleman to a friend in London, 1648

The king secured Scottish military assistance in the new war by signing an 'engagement' promising to confirm Presbyterianism in England for three years. The Scots were deeply divided over the wisdom of invading England as

former covenanters fell out among themselves. Their army was late in arriving, ill-provided for, and hence forced to resort to plunder, and the promised mass uprising of royalists never occurred. The Scottish and northern royalist forces were devastatingly defeated near Preston on 17 August.
Source: Thomason Tracts, 669 f. 12/3.

Kind Sir, I thank you for yours of the 5th of April, though I am troubled to find by it the distempers of England, which indeed (with grief I speak it) are paralleled here. The [Scottish] parliament hath deserted the clergy, refuses all conference with them, have this day resolved breaches upon every branch of the covenant, and immediately are to put themselves into a posture of defence (but it is thought) on purpose to enter England with 40,000 men to redeem the king (as they call it) and re-establish the covenant. But what most troubles, is, they receive the first and great adversaries of peace and religion, the cavaliers converse and communicate counsels with them, desire their assistance, and doubtless will raise great bodies of men in the north of England, the whole northern quarter being nothing else but a mass of malignancy. Our commissioners are and have been active to suppress this rising monster, both by reason and reward, but now almost despair the effect; pray God they may not be prejudiced in their return, for they meet not with respect due to their qualities. Nothing remains to confirm this bad work, but choice of officers, which tomorrow will be done (they say). Good David Leslie is almost mad to see his army desert him and his petition, to follow the idol of a king. Argyll and his confederates stand stiff to God's cause, our religion and country's good, but are all overswayed by the power and faction of Hamilton. Balmerino this day voted a war to redeem the king, to the great wonder of others, he having till now been a faithful labourer in God's vineyard; the effect of all this will doubtless appear in England, and suddenly. God strengthen you and all good men to oppose such invasions, which is the prayer of your most affectionate friend and servant.

Edinburgh, April 11, 1648.

The declaration of the county of Dorset, 1648

This declaration of June 1648 shows the continuing importance of localism, and its continuity with the earlier clubman movement, in helping to deliver provincial support for the king in the second civil war. The grievances expressed in other parts of the country in the summer of 1648 followed a similar pattern. Yet the war was more than simply a localist revolt against oppressive centralism; there was a royalist commitment to the restoration of the king and the Church of England as an absolute necessity if harmony and normality were to be recovered.
Source: Thomason Tracts, E. 447/26.

The declaration of the county of Dorset, showing their consent to join with other counties in this loyal work of redeeming his majesty and settling the kingdom.

We the surviving inhabitants of the much despised and distressed county of Dorset, having like the rest of the kingdom, long groaned under the oppressing tyranny of those whom we deputed for our redeemer. And being formerly too impatient, sought ways of redress, but proved unsuccessful. Nor could we now imagine any hopes of a Jubilee,[27] did we not see our fellow counties (who have formerly been too insensible of our misery and their own dangers) throwing down their Issachar's burthen[28] and unanimously lending their hands to wrest our sovereign from the jaws of rebellion and treason; and vindicating our gasping laws and liberties, from the unrelenting tyranny of those that would bury both in the Golgotha of their lawless wills.

And though distance and remoteness hinder us from performing the ceremony of a petition, to travel so far for a few dissembled thanks from a member of the House . . . we thought fit to declare to the world what we mean to do for ourselves, and the kingdom.

1 Therefore we demand a speedy retroduction of our imprisoned king to sit personally in the House of Peers, that the supreme court of the kingdom may not be any longer . . . called a master without a head.

2 That the government of the Church may be first settled by the advice of a new assembly of Protestant divines to be indifferently chosen by the clergy of each county or diocese, and this synod that have sat so long to so little purpose, unless to act the wills of those that packed them, may be sent home to their lectures, and the 4 sh[illings] per diem conferred on those that have more need of it, and better deserve it.

3 That the common birthright of us all, the laws, may be restored to their former purity, and that we may enjoy them without the corrupt glosses and comments of their arbitrary power, or the unequal ordinances and practices between them and their committees.

4 That our liberties (the purchase of our ancestors' blood) may be redeemed from all former infringements, and preserved henceforth inviolable, and that our ancient liberties may not lie at the mercy of those that have none, nor be enlarged and repealed by the votes and revotes of those that have taken too much liberty to destroy the subjects.

5 That we may have a speedy and just account of all our monies and estates cheated or wrested from us by loans, contributions, taxes, fines, excise, or plunder, and that the estates of committees, sequestrators and all state officers (being lately purchased and raised out of the ruins of honest and loyal subjects) may be re-sequestered, and be made liable to give us and the kingdom satisfaction.

6 That our knights and burgesses may be recalled, as having broken their trust reposed by us in them, and that we may have free power and liberty

to make a new choice of such patriots, as we shall have just cause to repose things of such moment, as our lives and fortunes, and the power of making the kingdom happy, or miserable, into their hands.

7   That we may no longer subjugate our necks to the boundless lusts, and unlimited power of beggarly and broken committees, consisting generally of the tail of gentry, men of ruinous fortunes, and despicable estates, whose insatiate desires, hungry with their frequent wants, prompts them to continual projects of pilling and stripping us, to repair themselves. Nor be awed by their emissaries who are generally the most shirking and cunning beggars that can be picked out of a county.

8   That instead thereof we may be governed in military affairs, and civil, by men of visible estates, and of unquestioned repute, well beloved by us; such whose degree and condition may make them assume places of authority and trust, out of nobleness of mind and love to their country, and not to re-edify their delapidated fortunes.

9   That the late imperious governor of Lyme and other of his office, and broken condition, may be no more sheltered under the wings of a membership to glory in the innocent blood of well-meaning countrymen he hath so unjustly spilt, nor live upon the estates which they have thievishly taken from the right owners, but that they may be exposed to the equal justice of the known laws, that we may freely right ourselves, and each of us fetch back a stolen feather.

10   And lastly, that all those among us who have been sequestered, imprisoned, plundered, or fined, or any way abused, and stripped of our estates, for our allegiance and loyal adherence to his majesty, may be restored to our estates, without any more compositions, and may have leave to take any legal course for due reparation.

These are our joint desires which we would have moulded into a petition but that we hear of the success of unnatural usage of our fellow subjects on the like occasion; of which the king cannot in duty but be sensible. This made us turn our petitionary resolves into resolute demands and propositions, of which we expect satisfactory grants, and do hereby declare, that as heretofore on less encouragement we engaged our lives, liberties, and estates, on the same grounds, under the slighted and unprosperous notion of clubmen. Notwithstanding our sufferings therefore, our ends are still the same, and our endeavours shall be now vigorous and active, and we doubt not (by God's and your assistance) more prosperous and successful.

Subscribed by above 10,000 inhabitants of that county.

6

REVOLUTION

CHARLES STUART, THAT MAN OF BLOOD

William Allen's account of the Windsor prayer meeting of 1 May 1648

On 29 April 1648, senior officers and agitators met in Windsor Castle for three days of prayer and discussion as they faced the start of a new war. On the third day, 1 May, as news of hostilities was confirmed, the meeting came to the conclusion that if God once again gave the army victory, they should bring the king to justice as a 'man of blood'. The concept of blood-guilt that cried out for justice was derived from the Old Testament. The extract below is from the account of William Allen (fl. 1642–67), one of the agitators present at the meeting, which was published in 1659.
Source: W. Allen, *A Faithful Memorial of that Remarkable Meeting of Many Officers of the Army in England, at Windsor Castle, in the Year 1648* (London, 1659), Thomason Tracts, E 979/3, pp. 4–5.

. . . [the Lord] did direct our steps, and presently we were led, and helped to a clear agreement amongst ourselves, not any dissenting, that it was the duty of our day, with the forces we had, to go out and fight against those potent enemies, which that year in all places appeared against us, with an humble confidence in the name of the Lord only, that we should destroy them; also enabling us then, after serious seeking his face, to come to a very clear and joint resolution, on many grounds at large then debated amongst us, that it was our duty, if ever the Lord brought us back again in peace, to call Charles Stuart, that man of blood, to an account, for that blood he had shed, and mischief he had done, to his utmost, against the Lord's cause and people in these poor nations: and how the Lord led and prospered us in all our undertakings this year, in this way, cutting his work short in righteousness, making it a year of mercy equal, if not transcendent to any since these wars began, and making it worthy of remembrance by every gracious soul, who was wise to observe the Lord and the operations of his hands; I wish may never be forgotten . . . the king's armies in all places broken, his strongholds most of them taken: he himself all that time treating with the then parliament, and both of them desirous to conclude; yet by an overruling providence hindered, and the king so infatuated, as he stands disputing punctilios till he loses all, and himself with it, and is fetched away from his place of treaty to a prison, in order to execution, which suddenly followed accordingly; and all this done within less than three-quarters of a year, even to the astonishment of ourselves, and other beholders both at home and abroad; yea our very enemies then were made to say, God was amongst us of a truth, and therefore they could not stand against us. . . .

The parliament under the power of the sword, 1648

The purge of parliament by soldiers under the command of Colonel Thomas Pride on 6 December 1648 immediately followed a Commons resolution the previous day that the king's latest answer to peace proposals provided a basis for a settlement. From a sizeable list of MPs marked out for arrest, over forty MPs were taken into custody and many more were either prevented from entering the House or stayed away. A greatly depleted House of Commons was subsequently to vote in favour of setting up a high court of justice for the king's trial.

Source: Thomason Tracts, 669 f. 13/52.

Wednesday the 6 of December 1648 before eight in the morning, the army sent a party of horse and foot to beset all passages and avenues to the two houses of parliament to frighten away the members; yet many members of us repairing to the House, were seized upon, and carried prisoners by the soldiers into the queen's court; nothing being objected against us; nor no authority vouched for it: Colonel [John] Birch and Master Edward Stephens were pulled out of the House of Commons, as they looked out at the door: at last the number shut up prisoners in the queen's court amounted to 41. And Hugh Peter came to us and avowed this as the act of the general, and lieutenant general:[1] so did Colonel [John] Hewson, about 4 of the clock that day we were told by an officer, that we must be carried to Wallingford House, and so put into coaches: but before this happened, I should have told you, that the sergeant of the House of Commons was sent with his mace from the House to command our attendance there; and came into the queen's court to us, but the guard would not let us out: he was sent again with his mace for us, but then the guards upon the House would not let the sergeant come to us; at last the coaches aforesaid (to put the greater scorn upon the parliament) carried us all to Master Duke's alehouse in *Hell*,[2] and there thrust us in to spend the night without any accommodation of beds, etc. only Colonel Hewson came to us, and offered it as a courtesy, that some of the eldest should be suffered to lie at home that night, engaging to render themselves the next morning by 9 of the clock at Colonel Hewson's lodgings in Whitehall, which was refused, it not being thought fit we should so far own an usurped authority. All this is done in pursuance of the army's last *Remonstrance* and *Declaration*,[3] and in subversion of the king, and his posterity, parliament, city, and kingdom; the utter extirpation of all law, government, and religion: and the converting of our well-regulated monarchy into a military anarchy, with a popular parliament of the meanest of the commons, only at the beck of the army: I appeal to heaven and earth whether the attempt of Jermyn, Goring, etc. to bring up the northern army to London to over-awe the parliament; which attempt only was then voted treason: whether the tumult of apprentices at the parliament door,[4] so severely prosecuted against the city, were comparable to this rebellion: the members so surprised are almost all such as have lost for their constant service to the parliament, and have gotten nothing.

A COMMONWEALTH WITHOUT A KING OR HOUSE OF LORDS

The act abolishing the office of king, March 1649

The 'act' of 17 March, which had been enacted by the Commons acting alone, abolished the institution of monarchy as judged to be unnecessary, burdensome and dangerous to the people and their liberty and freedom. It also promised to bring to an end the present parliament as soon as it was feasible and provide for free elections to a new representative assembly. Radical hopes that the end of monarchy would usher in social revolution

Figure 12 The execution of Charles I outside the Banqueting House in Whitehall, 30 January 1649

were also soon disappointed. The Rump was eventually dissolved by
Cromwell and the army in April 1653.
Source: S. R. Gardiner, *The Constitutional Documents of the Puritan
Revolution, 1625–1660*, 3rd edn (Oxford, 1906), pp. 384–7.

Whereas Charles Stuart, late king of England, Ireland, and the territories and
dominions thereunto belonging, hath by authority derived from parliament
been and is hereby declared to be justly condemned, adjudged to die, and put
to death, for many treasons, murders, and other heinous offences committed
by him, by which judgement he stood, and is hereby declared to be attainted
of high treason, whereby his issue and posterity, and all others pretending title
under him, are become incapable of the said crowns, or of being king or queen
of the said kingdom or dominions, or either or any of them; be it therefore
enacted and ordained, and it is enacted and ordained, and declared by this
present parliament, and by authority thereof, that all the people of England
and Ireland, and the dominions and territories thereunto belonging, of what
degree or condition soever, are discharged of all fealty, homage and allegiance
which is or shall be pretended to be due unto any of the issue and posterity of
the said late king, or any claiming under him. . . .

And whereas it is and hath been found by experience, that the office of a
king in this nation and Ireland, and to have the power thereof in any single
person, is unnecessary, burdensome, and dangerous to the liberty, safety, and
public interest of the people, and that for the most part, use hath been made of
the regal power and prerogative to oppress and impoverish and enslave the
subject; and that usually and naturally any one person in such power makes it
his interest to encroach upon the just freedom and liberty of the people, and to
promote the setting up of their own will and power above the laws, that so
they might enslave these kingdoms to their own lust; be it therefore enacted
and ordained . . . that the office of a king in this nation shall not henceforth
reside in or be exercised by any one single person; and that no one person
whatsoever shall or may have, or hold the office, style, dignity, power, or
authority of king of the said kingdoms and dominions, or any of them, or of
the prince of Wales, any law, statute, usage, or custom to the contrary thereof
in any wise notwithstanding. . . .

And whereas by the abolition of the kingly office provided for in this act, a
most happy way is made for this nation (if God see it good) to return to its just and
ancient right, of being governed by its own representatives or national meetings
in council, from time to time chosen and entrusted for that purpose by the people,
it is therefore resolved and declared by the Commons assembled in parliament,
that they will put a period to the sitting of this present parliament, and dissolve
the same so soon as may possibly stand with the safety of the people that hath
betrusted them, and with what is absolutely necessary for the preserving and
upholding the government now settled in the way of a commonwealth; and that
they will carefully provide for the certain choosing, meeting, and sitting of the

next and future representatives, with such other circumstances of freedom in choice and equality in distribution of members to be elected thereunto, as shall most conduce to the lasting freedom and good of this commonwealth. . . .

An act abolishing the House of Lords, March 1649

The House of Lords was condemned as useless and dangerous, and hence abolished on 19 March. Although the peers were to lose their distinctive legal privileges, they retained their titles and were eligible to sit in future representative assemblies if they secured election. They subsequently maintained a low political profile, attending to the reconstruction of their damaged estates, and were ready to recover their political power at the Restoration.
Source: Gardiner, *The Constitutional Documents of the Puritan Revolution*, pp. 387–8.

The Commons of England assembled in parliament, finding by too long experience that the House of Lords is useless and dangerous to the people of England to be continued, have thought fit to ordain and enact, and be it ordained and enacted by this present parliament, and by the authority of the same, that from henceforth the House of Lords in parliament shall be and is hereby wholly abolished and taken away; and that the Lords shall not from henceforth meet or sit in the said House called the Lords' House, or in any other house or place whatsoever, as a House of Lords; nor shall sit, vote, advise, adjudge, or determine of any matter or thing whatsoever, as a House of Lords in parliament: nevertheless it is hereby declared, that neither such lords as have demeaned themselves with honour, courage, and fidelity to the commonwealth, nor their posterities who shall continue so, shall be excluded from the public councils of the nation, but shall be admitted thereunto, and have their free vote in parliament, if they shall be thereunto elected, as other persons of interest elected and qualified thereunto ought to have. And be it further ordained and enacted by the authority aforesaid, that no peer of this land, not being elected, qualified and sitting in parliament as aforesaid, shall claim, have, or make use of any privilege of parliament, either in relation to his person, quality, or estate, any law, usage, or custom to the contrary notwithstanding.

An act declaring England to be a commonwealth, May 1649

England was declared to be a commonwealth and free state in which supreme authority rested in the representatives of the people in parliament without a king or House of Lords. The term 'republic' was avoided because of its radical associations in favour of the term 'commonwealth'. The latter term had been in use in England for well over a century and conveyed the idea of a country united in the pursuit of the welfare of all. By no means, of course, could what was left of the present parliament claim a popular mandate.
Source: Gardiner, *The Constitutional Documents of the Puritan Revolution*, p. 388.

Be it declared and enacted by this present parliament, and by the authority of the same, that the people of England, and of all the dominions and territories thereunto belonging, are and shall be, and are hereby constituted, made, established, and confirmed, to be a commonwealth and free state, and shall from henceforth be governed as a commonwealth and free state by the supreme authority of this nation, the representatives of the people in parliament, and by such as they shall appoint and constitute as officers and ministers under them for the good of the people, and that without any king or House of Lords.

REVOLUTION HALTED

Richard Overton, The Hunting of the Foxes, *March 1649*

A burning sense of betrayal, deception and hypocrisy experienced at the hands of Cromwell, Ireton and their fellow officers radiates from this pamphlet written by Richard Overton (fl. 1631–64), the Leveller leader. The immediate occasion of it was the punishing and cashiering of five soldiers on 6 March 1649 for breaching new rules governing petitioning in the army. The pamphlet signalled a final breach between the Levellers and their former senior allies in the army.
Source: D. M. Wolfe (ed.), *Leveller Manifestoes of the Puritan Revolution* (New York, 1944), pp. 369–72.

. . . O Cromwell, O Ireton, how hath a little time and success changed the honest shape of so many officers! Who then would have thought the [army] council would have moved for an act to put men to death for petitioning? Who would have thought to have seen soldiers (by their order) to ride with their faces towards their horse tails, to have their swords broken over their heads, and to be cashiered, and that for petitioning, and claiming their just right and title to the same?. . . .

Was there ever a generation of men so apostate so false and so perjured as these? Did ever men pretend an higher degree of holiness, religion, and zeal to God and their country than these? These preach, these fast, these pray, these have nothing more frequent than the sentences of sacred scripture, the name of God and of Christ in their mouths: you shall scarce speak to Cromwell about anything, but he will lay his hand on his breast, elevate his eyes, and call God to record, he will weep, howl and repent, even while he doth smite you under the first rib. . . .

Thus it is evident to the whole world, that the now present interest of the officers is directly contrary to the interest of the soldiery: there is no more difference betwixt them, than betwixt Christ and Belial, light and darkness: if you will uphold the interest of the one, the other must down; and as well you may let them bore holes through your ears, and be their slaves for ever, for your better distinction from free men: for what are you now? Your mouths are stopped, you may be abused and enslaved, but you may not complain, you may not petition for redress; they are your lords, and you are their conquered vassals, and this is the state you are in. . . .

But now dear friends, that you may see that their conclave of officers at Whitehall hath sucked into it the venom of all former corrupt courts, and interests that were before them, we shall show you how the court of the high commission, the star chamber, the House of Lords, the king and his privy council are all alive in that court, called the general council of the army.

First if you do but remember, the king to his death stood upon this principle, that he was accountable to none but God; that he was above the parliament, and above the people. And now to whom will these be accountable? To none on earth. And are they not above the parliament? They have even a negative voice thereover: formerly the Commons could pass nothing without the concurrence of the Lords, now they dare pass nothing without the concurrence of the conclave of officers: we were before ruled by king, Lords, and Commons; now by a general, a court martial, and House of Commons: and we pray you what is the difference? The Lords were not members both of the House of Lords, and of the House of Commons, but those are members both in the House of Officers, (the Martial Lords,) and in the House of Commons. The old king's person, and the old Lords, are but removed, and a new king and new Lords, with the Commons, are in one House; and so under a more absolute arbitrary monarchy than before. We have not the change of a kingdom to a commonwealth; we are only under the old cheat, the transmutation of names, but with the addition of new tyrannies to the old: for the casting out of one unclean spirit they have brought with them in his stead seven other unclean spirits, more wicked than the former, and they have entered in, and dwell there; and the last state of this commonwealth, is worse than the first. . . .

The Moderate *on the execution of mutineers at Burford, May 1649*

The execution of three mutineers in the churchyard of the parish church of Burford in Oxfordshire on the 17 May 1649 marked the end of the most serious internal challenge to the new regime that year. Large numbers of fellow mutineers had been held prisoner in the church awaiting the decision of the Council of War on their fate after they had confessed their crimes and begged for mercy. They were to witness the executions from the church and its roof. *The Moderate* was a consistently pro-Leveller newsbook and it gave the executed men a sympathetic report. Whether the men were Leveller martyrs, however, is open to dispute.
Source: Thomason Tracts, E 556/3.

Burford, May 19[5]

This day Cornet [James] Thompson was brought into the churchyard (the place of execution). Death was a great terror to him, as unto most. Some say he had hopes of a pardon, and therefore delivered something reflecting upon the legality of his engagement, and the just hand of God upon him; but if he had, they failed him. Corporal Perkins was the next; the place of death, and sight of his executioners, was so far from altering his countenance, or daunting his spirit, that he seemed to smile upon both, and account it a great mercy that he was to die for this quarrel, and casting his eyes up to His Father and afterwards to his fellow prisoners (who stood upon the church leads to see the execution) set his back against the wall, and bid the executioners shoot; and so died as gallantly, as he lived religiously. After him Master John Church was brought to the stake, he was as much supported by God, in this great agony, as the latter; for after he had pulled off his doublet, he stretched out his arms, and bid the soldiers do their duties, looking them in the face, till they gave fire upon him, without the least kind of fear or terror. Thus was death, the end of his present joy, and beginning of his future eternal felicity. Cornet [Henry] Denne was brought to the place of execution, he said, he was more worthy of death than life and showed himself somewhat penitent, for being an occasion of this engagement; but though he said this to save his life, yet the two last executed, would not have said it, though they were sure thereby to gain their pardon. The rest of the prisoners are to be sent to their several homes. Colonel Eyre[6] is removed hence to Oxford Castle, to be tried for his life, in a civil capacity.

KING JESUS

Certain queries, *February 1649*

This was the first Fifth Monarchist petition, a document which was subscribed by its followers throughout Norfolk and published on 19 February 1649. The petition began with a rebuke to the army for having previously tried to reach a settlement with the king. With Charles executed, the way was now clear for King Jesus to come down to earth and commence his thousand-year rule over his saints, and preparations should commence to pave the way for that miraculous event. Revelation and Daniel provided the main biblical sources for this millenarian enthusiasm.
Source: *Certain queries humbly presented in way of petition, by many Christian people, dispersed abroad throughout the county of Norfolk and City of Norwich . . . to the lord general and council of war* (London, 1649), Thomason Tracts, E 544/5, pp. 3–8.

Humbly showeth,

That your petitioners acknowledge themselves unspeakably engaged to the God of heaven and earth, for his great mercy to us, in giving you hearts to offer yourselves so willingly among the people, in the late great undertakings of this nation, against the enemies of the peace thereof, and blessing your faithful endeavours with such glorious and wonderful successes: whereby, as the Lord hath put great honour upon you, crowning your valour with victory, and making you the warlike glory of the world; so He hath no less put great obligations upon you all, to exalt Him that hath exalted you, and to lift up his glory in the world, where He hath given you a name so great and glorious.

And because the great design of God in the falls and overthrows of worldly powers, that have opposed the kingdom of His Son, is (by making Christ's foes His footstool) to lift up Him on high, far above all principality, and powers, and might, and dominion, and every name that is named in this world, that He may be PRINCE of the kings of the earth, and all nations may serve and obey Him, as you shall quickly see, if you make the scriptures your counsellors. . . .

Therefore our daily prayer shall be for yourselves and your noble army, that you may never stumble at the stumbling stone, nor take that honour to yourselves, that is due to Christ, nor be instrumental for the setting up of a mere natural and worldly government, like that of heathen Rome and Athens (as too many late overtures have caused us to fear) whereby the public interest of Jesus Christ will be utterly banished the kingdom in the conclusion: but that you (whom God hath honoured so highly, as to begin the great work of smiting the image on the feet) may show yourselves thankful to Him, that hath given you victory through our Lord Jesus Christ, may honour His Son, and comfort his saints, in whom He reigns spiritually, and by whom He will reign visibly over all the nations of the world. . . .

To which end we humbly crave, that yourselves would take into your serious and grave consideration and debate, the particulars in the papers herewith humbly offered to you, and also present them to the honourable parliament, that they may be improved so far, as found agreeable to the will and word of God; which done, we doubt not but God shall have much glory, the godly party shall be comforted, natural men (enjoying their estates) will be at rest also, and much satisfied; and this commonwealth will be exalted to be both an habitation of justice, and mountain of holiness, even such a people as God will bless. . . .

[Seven queries posed about the imminent establishment of Christ's kingdom, the fifth monarchy, on the earth.]

The brief resolutions of the queries

1. There is a kingdom and dominion, which the church is to exercise on the earth, 2. that extends to all persons and things universally, which is to be externally and visibly administered, 3. by such laws and officers, as Jesus Christ our mediator hath appointed in his kingdom. 4. It shall put down all worldly rule and authority (so far as relates to the worldly constitution thereof) though in the hands of Christians: 5. and is to be expected about this time we live in. 6. This kingdom shall not be erected by human power and authority, but Christ by his spirit shall call and gather a people, and form them into several less families, churches and corporations; and when they are multiplied,

7. they shall rule the world by general assemblies; or church-parliaments, of such officers of Christ, and representatives of the churches, as they shall choose and delegate, which they shall do, till Christ come in person.

Query. What then is the present interest of the saints and people of God?

Reply. To associate together into several church-societies and corporations (according to the Congregational way) till being increased and multiplied, they may combine into general assemblies or church-parliaments (according to the Presbyterian way) and then shall God give them authority and rule over the nations and kingdoms of the world.

For the present to lay aside all differences and divisions amongst themselves, and combine together against the Antichristian powers of the world, Revelations, 15:2, etc. whom they may expect to combine against them universally, Revelations, 17:13–14. . . .

THE DIGGERS

Gerrard Winstanley, The True Levellers' standard advanced, *April 1649*

This was the first of the manifestos written by Gerrard Winstanley (1609–76?), a cloth-trader whose business had failed in 1643, for the Diggers. The inspiration for establishing Digger communities came to Winstanley in a vision which he felt an overwhelming urge to act upon. The first experiment in communal living began on common land on St George's Hill, Surrey, on 1 April 1649, but later that year they moved to nearby Cobham where they planted crops and built several cottages. They were constantly harassed and even attacked by local inhabitants, and the enterprise had come to an end by the following summer. There were nine other similar communities established elsewhere which also ultimately failed.
Source: G. H. Sabine (ed.), *The Works of Gerrard Winstanley* (New York, 1965), pp. 251–66.

A declaration to the powers of England, and to all the powers of the world, showing the cause why the common people of England have begun, and gives consent to dig up, manure, and sow corn upon George Hill in Surrey;[7] by those that have subscribed, and thousands more that gives consent.

In the beginning of time, the great creator reason, made the earth to be a common treasury, to preserve beasts, birds, fishes, and man, the lord that was to govern this creation; for man had domination given to him, over the beasts, birds, and fishes; but not one word was spoken in the beginning, that one branch of mankind should rule over another.

And the reason is this, every single man, male and female, is a perfect creature of himself; and the same spirit that made the globe, dwells in man to govern the globe; so that the flesh of man being subject to reason, his maker, hath him to be his teacher and ruler within himself, therefore needs not run abroad after any teacher and ruler without him, for he needs not that any man should teach him all things.

But since human flesh (that king of beasts) began to delight himself in the objects of the creation, more than in the spirit reason and righteousness, who manifests himself to be the indweller in the five senses, of hearing, seeing, tasting, smelling, feeling; then he fell into blindness of mind and weakness of heart, and runs abroad for a teacher and ruler; and so selfish imagination taking possession of the five senses, and ruling as king in the room of reason therein, and working with covetousness, did set up one man to teach and rule over another; and thereby the spirit was killed, and man was brought into bondage, and became a greater slave to such of his own kind, than the beasts of the field were to him.

And hereupon, the earth (which was made to be a common treasury of relief for all, both beasts and men) was hedged in to enclosures by the teachers and rulers, and the others were made servants and slaves: and that earth that is within this creation, made a common store-house for all, is bought and sold, and kept in the hands of a few, whereby the great creator is mightily dishonoured, as if he were a respector of persons, delighting in the comfortable livelihood of some, and rejoicing in the miserable poverty and straits of others. From the beginning it was not so. . . .

But for the present state of the old world that is running up like parchment in the fire, and wearing away, we see proud imaginary flesh, which is the wise serpent, rises up in flesh and gets domination in some to rule over others, and so forces one part of the creation man, to be a slave to another; and thereby the spirit is killed in both. The one looks upon himself as a teacher and ruler, and so is lifted up in pride over his fellow creature: the other looks upon himself as imperfect, and so is dejected in his spirit, and looks upon his fellow creature of his own image, as a lord above him. . . .

But when once the earth becomes a common treasury again, as it must, for all the prophecies of scripture and reason are circled here in this community, and mankind must have the law of righteousness once more writ in his heart, and all must be made of one heart, and one mind.

Then this enmity in all lands will cease, for none shall dare to seek a dominion over others, neither shall any dare to kill another, nor desire more of the earth than another; for he that will rule over, imprison, oppress, and kill his fellow creatures, under what pretence soever, is a destroyer of the creation, and an actor of the curse, and walks contrary to the rule of righteousness: ('do, as you would have others to do to you; and love your enemies, not in words, but in actions'). . . .

O thou powers of England, though thou hast promised to make this people a free people, yet thou hast so handled the matter, through thy self-seeking humour, that thou has wrapped us up more in bondage, and oppression lies heavier upon us; not only bringing thy fellow creatures, the commoners, to a morsel of bread, but by confounding all sorts of people by thy government, of doing and undoing. . . .

We are made to hold forth this declaration to you that are the great council,[8] and to you the great army of the land of England, that you may know what we would have, and what you are bound to give us by your covenants and promises; and that you may join with us in this work, and so find peace. Or else, if you do oppose us, we have peace in our work, and in declaring this report: and you shall be left without excuse.

The work we are going about is this, to dig up George's Hill and the waste ground thereabouts, and to sow corn, and to eat our bread together by the sweat of our brows.

And the first reason is this, that we may work in righteousness, and lay the foundation of making the earth a common treasury for all, both rich and poor, that every one that is born in the land, may be fed by the earth his mother that brought him forth, according to the reason that rules in the creation. Not enclosing any part into any particular hand, but all as one man, working together, and feeding together as sons of one father, members of one family; not one lording over another, but all looking upon each other, as equals in the creation. . . . And we are moved hereunto for that reason, and others which hath been showed us, both by vision, voice, and revelation.

For it is showed us, that so long as we, or any other, doth own the earth to be the peculiar interest of lords and landlords, and not common to others as well as them, we own the curse,[9] and hold the creation under bondage; and so long as we or any other doth own landlords and tenants, for one to call the land his, or another to hire it of him, or for one to give hire, and for another to work for hire; this is to dishonour the work of creation; as if the righteous creator should have respect to persons, and therefore made the earth for some, and not for all: and so long as we, or any other, maintain this civil propriety, we consent still to hold the creation down under that bondage it groans under, and so we should hinder the work of restoration, and sin against light, that is given into us, and so through the fear of the flesh man, lose our peace.

And that this civil propriety is the curse, is manifest thus, those that buy and sell land, and are landlords, have got it either by oppression, or murder, or theft; and all landlords live in the breach of the seventh and eighth commandments, 'thou shalt not steal, nor kill'. . . .

And such as these rise up to be rich in the objects of the earth; then by their plausible words of flattery to the plain-hearted people, whom they deceive, and that lies under confusion and blindness: they are lifted up to be teachers, rulers, and law makers over them that lifted them up; as if the earth were made peculiarly for them, and not for others' weal. . . .

Take notice, that England is not a free people, till the poor that have no land, have a free allowance to dig and labour the commons, and so live as comfortably as the landlords that live in their enclosures. For the people have not laid out their monies, and shed their blood, that their landlords, the Norman power,[10] should still have its liberty and freedom to rule in tyranny in his lords, landlords, judges, justices, bailiffs, and state servants; but that the oppressed might be set free, prison doors opened, and the poor people's hearts comforted by an universal consent of making the earth a common treasury, that they may live together as one house of Israel, united in brotherly love into one spirit; and having a comfortable livelihood in the community of one earth their mother.

If you look through the earth, you shall see, that the landlords, teachers and rulers, are oppressors, murderers, and thieves in this manner; but it was not thus from the beginning. And this is one reason of our digging and labouring the earth one with another, that we might work in righteousness, and lift up the creation from bondage: for so long as we own landlords in this corrupt settlement, we cannot work in righteousness; for we should still lift up the curse, and tread down the creation, dishonour the spirit of universal liberty, and hinder the work of restoration.

Secondly, in that we begin to dig upon George Hill, to eat our bread together by righteous labour, and sweat of our brows; it was showed us by vision in dreams, and out of dreams, that that should be the place we should begin upon; and though that earth in view of flesh, be very barren, yet we should trust the spirit for a blessing. And that not only this common, or heath should be taken in and manured by the people, but all commons and waste ground in England, and in the whole world, shall be taken in by the people in righteousness, not owning any property; but taking the earth to be a common treasury, as it was first made for all.

Thirdly, it is showed us, that all the prophecies, visions, and revelations of scriptures, of prophets, and apostles, concerning the calling of the Jews, the restoration of Israel; and making of that people, the inheritors of the whole earth; doth all seat themselves in this work of making the earth a common treasury. . . .

Fourthly, this work to make the earth a common treasury, was showed us by voice in trance, and out of trance, which works were these, 'work together, eat bread together, declare this all abroad'. Which voice, was heard three times: and in obedience to the spirit, we have declared this by word of mouth, as occasion was offered. Secondly, we have declared it by writing, which others may read. Thirdly, we have now begun to declare it by action, in digging up the common land, and casting in seed, that we may eat our bread together in righteousness. And every one that comes to work, shall eat the fruit of their own labours, one having as much freedom in the fruit of the earth as another. Another voice that was heard was this, 'Israel shall neither take hire, nor give hire.'

And if so, then certainly none shall say, this is my land, work for me, and I'll give you wages: for, the earth is the Lord's, that is, man's, who is lord of the creation, in every branch of mankind. . . . And if the earth be not peculiar to any one branch, or branches of mankind, but the inheritance of all; then it is free and common for all, to work together, and eat together.

And truly, you councillors and powers of the earth, know this, that wheresoever there is a people, thus united by common community of livelihood into oneness, it will become the strongest land in the world, for then they will be as one man to defend their inheritance; and salvation (which is liberty and peace) is the walls and bulwarks of that land or city.

Whereas on the other side, pleading for property and single interest, divides the people of a land, and the whole world into parties, and is the cause of all wars and bloodshed, and contention everywhere.

Another voice that was heard in a trance, was this, 'Whosoever labours the earth for any person or persons, that are lifted up to rule over others, and doth not look upon themselves, as equal to others in the creation: the hand of the Lord shall be upon that labourer: I the Lord have spoke it, and I will do it.' This declares likewise to all labourers, or such as are called poor people, that they shall not dare to work for hire, for any landlord, or for any that is lifted up above others; for by their labours, they have lifted up tyrants and tyranny; and by denying to labour for hire, they shall pull them down again. He that works for another, either for wages, or to pay him rent, works unrighteously, and still lifts up the curse; but they that are resolved to work and eat together, making the earth a common treasury, doth join hands with Christ, to lift up the creation from bondage, and restores all things from the curse.

Fifthly, that which does encourage us to go on in this work, is this; we find the streaming out of love in our hearts towards all; to enemies as well as friends; we would have none live in beggary, poverty, or sorrow, but that every one might enjoy the benefit of his creation: we have peace in our hearts, and quiet rejoicing in our work, and filled with sweet content, though we have but a dish of roots and bread for our food. . . .

Sixthly, we have another encouragement that this work shall prosper, because we see it to be the fulness of time. . . . For whereas the people generally in former times did rest upon the very observation of the sacrifices and types, but persecuted the very name of the spirit; even so now, professors do rest upon the bare observation of forms and customs, and pretend to the spirit, and yet persecutes, grudges, and hates the power of the spirit; and as it was then, so it is now: all places stink with the abomination of self-seeking teachers and rulers: for do not I see that every one preacheth for money, counsels for money, and fights for money to maintain particular interests? And none of these three that pretend to give liberty to the creation, do give liberty to the creation; neither can they, for they are enemies to universal liberty; so that the earth stinks with their hypocrisy, covetousness, envy, sottish ignorance, and pride. . . .

Thus we have discharged our souls in declaring the cause of our digging upon George Hill in Surrey, that the great council and army of the land may take notice of it, that there is no intent of tumult or fighting, but only to get bread to eat, with the sweat of our brows; working together in righteousness, and eating the blessings of the earth in peace. . . .

NOTES

1 THE COLLAPSE OF CHARLES I'S GOVERNMENT

1 George Walker (1581?–1651), a future Presbyterian minister, who was to be imprisoned the following year for preaching a controversial sermon.
2 Henry Burton (1578–1648), radical preacher and writer and future Independent minister.
3 The London livery companies.
4 21 Decenber.
5 William Juxon (1582–1663), bishop of London.
6 John Goodwin (c. 1593–1665), a leading Independent minister and controversialist.
7 'Witness Hicks, apparitor.' An apparitor was the servant or attendant of a civil or ecclesiastical officer.
8 A law officer who acts as vicar-general for the bishop and holds diocesan courts for him.
9 Wooden panel-work used to line walls.
10 Square or rectangular columns or pillars.
11 25 March.
12 Without guilt or blame.
13 John Williams (1582–1650), bishop of Lincoln, leading episcopal opponent of Laud and a prisoner in the Tower.
14 A London street running from Tower Hill to Aldgate.
15 A commercial centre behind St Paul's cathedral.
16 Bond.
17 The gospel.
18 The House of Commons.
19 Sir Thomas Wentworth (1593–1641), who was acting in his other capacity as lord president of the Council in the North.
20 Sir John Finch (1584–1660), created first Lord Finch of Fordwich, 7 April 1640.
21 Alexander Leslie (c. 1580–1661), distinguished soldier and general of all the forces of the covenant.
22 Henry Rich (1590–1649), first earl of Holland.
23 William Laud and Thomas Wentworth (created first earl of Strafford on 12 January 1640).

2 THE LONG PARLIAMENT

1 Thursday.

2 Worcestershire.
3 Ministers who could turn their listeners' painful consciousness of their sins into hope of eventual salvation.
4 Archbishop Laud who was to be executed on 10 January 1645.
5 The Thirty Years War, 1618–48.
6 The one necessary thing.
7 The London root and branch petition of 11 December 1640. .
8 The Tower Hamlets which usually provided a guard for the Tower of London.
9 John Lilburne, the later Leveller leader.
10 Henry Percy, brother of the tenth earl of Northumberland.
11 Cardinal Richelieu.
12 Charles Louis, Elector Palatine, the nephew of Charles I.

3 CHOOSING SIDES

1 The king was in Scotland from 14 August to 17 November 1641.
2 1 October 1641.
3 At the intercession of the French ambassador, the king wanted to pardon seven Catholic priests who had been arrested and convicted in England.
4 A recreational area in the northern suburbs of London.
5 Henry Somerset (1576/7–1646), fifth earl of Worcester, of Raglan Castle (Monmouthshire), head of a pre-eminent Catholic family.
6 Baal was the chief male deity of the Phoenician and Canaanite nations and the name had come to be used generally to denote a false god.
7 Dagon was the god of the Philistines.
8 Those who were not members or officials of parliament.
9 Constantine (AD 274/5–337), the first Christian Roman Emperor.
10 'In these words.'
11 13 January 1641.
12 The 1593 act enforcing attendance at parish churches.
13 'Monday, namely, 18 January 1641.'
14 The Lords' order forbidding disruption of worship according to the book of common prayer.
15 George Kirke was one of Charles I's courtiers who benefited personally from enclosures in fens and forests.
16 Elizabeth, Countess Rivers, née Darcy (1581–1651).
17 Robert Rich, second earl of Warwick (1587–1658). Lord Robert Rich and Charles Rich were his sons.
18 The release from imprisonment, and triumphant return to London, of the three puritan pamphleteers.
19 Sir John Potts of Mannington, one of the Norfolk MPs in the Long Parliament.
20 Warwick was named lieutenant for Norfolk and Essex in the militia ordinance.
21 23 July 1642.
22 1 August 1642.
23 The declaration of 30 January 1644 offering a pardon to former royalists if they took the solemn league and covenant and paid a fine for the restoration of their sequestered estates.
24 To be appointed sheriff.
25 The parliament composed of royalist peers and MPs summoned to meet in Oxford on 22 January 1644.

4 THE IMPACT OF WAR

1 A levy theoretically based upon $1/5$ of the personal, and $1/20$ of the real estate of the person assessed.
2 Edmund Wyndham.
3 Richard Casbeard.
4 William Strode (1599?–1645), a radical MP.
5 Edward, first Lord Howard of Escrick (d. 1675), venal chairman of the committee for advance of money.
6 The central committee set up after Scotland had entered the war on parliament's side to act as a military executive.
7 The county committee for Buckinghamshire.
8 Sir Oliver Luke (1574–c. 1650) the father of Sir Samuel Luke.
9 'With the necessary changes.'
10 Sir Thomas Lunsford (1610?–53?), a royalist colonel whose appointment to the lieutenancy of the Tower of London in December 1641 had produced uproar in the capital.
11 John Paulet, fifth marquess of Winchester (c. 1598–1675), the Catholic owner of Basing House.
12 Jean Baptist Rinuccini, archbishop of Fermo, papal agent in Ireland from 1645.
13 The committee for plundered ministers was originally set up to provide livings for godly clergy expelled in royalist areas, but later acquired a wider clerical role.
14 Magna Carta of 1215 and the petition of right of 1628.

5 COUNTER-REVOLUTIONARIES AND REVOLUTIONARIES

1 The committee for advance of money (the earliest central revenue-raising committee for parliament's war effort).
2 Thomas Adams (1586–1668), lord mayor 1645–6, a leading political Presbyterian.
3 Incendiaries; those who kindle strife.
4 David Dickson (1583?–1663), leading Scottish Presbyterian divine.
5 Westminster assembly of divines set up in 1643 to determine the future shape of the English church.
6 The eleven MPs who had withdrawn from the Commons on 26 June 1647 having earlier been accused by the army of fomenting a new war.
7 The solemn engagement of the City, 21 July 1647. The king had replied to the Newcastle propositions on 12 May.
8 Alderman James Bunce (d. 1670), a staunch political Presbyterian.
9 Sir John Gayre (d. 1649), neo-royalist lord mayor, 1646–7.
10 The army's advance on London in June 1647 which resulted in the restoration to the City's militia committee of its recently purged members.
11 To Bedford.
12 *The Heads of the Proposals*, the army's proposals for a settlement with the king published on 1 August 1647.
13 The solemn engagement of the City.
14 Sir John Gayre.
15 The king's response to the Newcastle propositions.
16 The eleven MPs (in note 6 above).
17 Isleworth in Middlesex.

18 The City's own recent declaration disclaiming any responsibility for the force upon the Houses.

19 The Norman conquest of England from 1066.

20 MPs representing incorporated towns and cities.

21 One of the two MPs representing each county.

22 Representatives who emerged in about a dozen regiments in September and October 1647 who were more radical, and Leveller-influenced, than their equivalents chosen in the previous spring.

23 In his remonstrance Fairfax blamed the new agents and their Leveller associates for the army's current crisis, and threatened to resign. The army's material and other grievances were also addressed, and it was proposed to set a time limit for the present parliament and to provide for free elections for future parliaments set to meet at prescribed times.

24 Major Thomas Scot (d. 1648) was recruiter MP for Aldborough, Yorkshire. Rainsborough had been appointed vice-admiral of the fleet on 27 September 1647 but he was not to receive orders to take up his command until January 1648.

25 Negotiations on the treaty of Newport were to open on 18 September.

26 The king going to London to negotiate directly with parliament.

27 A Jewish festival held every fiftieth year during which all land was restored to those original owners who had lost it within that period, all debts were remitted and all slaves or captives were released.

28 Genesis 49:14. Issachar is a strong ass couching down between two burdens.

6 REVOLUTION

1 Sir Thomas (now Lord) Fairfax and Oliver Cromwell.

2 *Hell* was an alehouse adjoining Westminster Hall.

3 *The Remonstrance of the Army*, 18 November, and *The Declaration of the Lord Fairfax and his General Council*, 30 November 1648.

4 The first army plot of 1641 [ch. 2, pp. 73–5] and the force upon the Houses of 26 July 1647 [ch. 5, pp. 142–3].

5 The executions in fact took place on 17 May.

6 The council of war had no jurisdiction over William Eyre (*fl.* 1647–60) as he was no longer a member of the army.

7 St George's Hill in the parish of Walton-on-Thames, Surrey.

8 The council of state set up in February 1649.

9 The Fall in the Garden of Eden.

10 There was an established radical tradition of viewing the Norman conquest as ushering in tyranny and oppression.

CHRONOLOGY

1625 Accession of Charles I.

1629 End of Charles's third parliament and beginning of eleven years of 'personal rule'.

1633 Thomas Wentworth, lord deputy of Ireland. William Laud, archbishop of Canterbury.

1634 First levy of ship money.

1637 Public mutilation of three puritan pamphleteers. John Hampden's ship money case. Attempt to impose new prayer book on Scotland.

1638 Scottish national covenant.

1639 First bishops' war.

1640 Short Parliament. Second bishops' war. Long Parliament, 1640–53. Impeachment of Wentworth (now earl of Strafford) and Laud. 'Root and branch' petition.

1641 Triennial Act. Act against dissolving present parliament without its own consent. Attainder and execution of Strafford. Abolition of high commission and star chamber, and nonparliamentary taxation. 'Root and branch' bill. The king in Scotland. Irish rebellion. Grand remonstrance. Impeachment of twelve bishops.

1642 Attempt on 'five members'. King leaves London. Militia ordinance. Commission of array. Battle of Edgehill.

1643 Solemn league and covenant. Alliance with the Scots. Westminster assembly of divines. Excise introduced.

1644 Establishment of gathered churches. Presbyterian/Independent divisions appear.

1645 Execution of Archbishop Laud. Directory of public worship. Formation of New Model Army. Battles of Naseby and Langport.

1646 King surrenders to Scots. End of first civil war. Newcastle propositions. Episcopacy abolished. Attempt to impose a Presbyterian church settlement on England. Emergence of the Levellers.

1647 Scots surrender king to parliament and leave England. Crisis over attempts to disband most of the New Model Army. Seizure of the king by the army. Division in parliament. Attempted counter-revolution in London. Army enters London. Putney debates. A Leveller-inspired mutiny is suppressed.

1648   King's treaty with the Scots. Second civil war. The army defeats Scots and royalists. Pride's purge of parliament.

1649   Trial and execution of the king. Abolition of monarchy and House of Lords. England declared a 'commonwealth'. Levellers suppressed. Digger communes established. The reconquest of Ireland begun.

GLOSSARY

acquittances receipts.

agitators the representatives chosen by regiments of the New Model Army over the spring of 1647; the term had not yet acquired its sinister connotation.

amain vehemently, in all haste.

Anabaptists radical Protestants who rejected infant baptism in favour of adult (or believers) baptism.

anno (domini) in the year (of the Lord).

Arminians anti-Calvinist Protestants named after the Dutch theologian, Jacobus Arminius.

array the calling forth of a military force; the arming of the militia.

attainder conviction of treason by act of parliament without a judicial trial.

bestial cattle.

bone-lace lace made by knitting on a pattern marked by pins with bobbins originally made of bone.

Brownists English separatists named after the Elizabethan separatist, Robert Browne, but the term was applied more loosely to all opponents of a national church.

bruit rumour or report.

canons rules, laws or decrees of the Church.

chancel the eastern part of a church where the clergy officiate.

churchwardens senior lay officers of the parish.

classis a Presbyterian assembly of ministers and lay elders from neighbouring parishes which met regularly to supervise parish matters (pl. **classes**).

coat-and-conduct money a local levy to clothe soldiers and feed them on the way to their rendezvous.

composition a fine paid to recover a sequestered estate or property, as in the case of former royalists (**compound** to pay the fine).

constablewick the district under the charge of a constable.

contemn to treat with contempt; to scorn.

conventicles unorthodox religious meetings.

Convocation the Church's representative assembly in the provinces of Canterbury and York.

cozen to cheat, defraud by deceit.

curate a junior or assistant minister.

delinquents royalists (see also **malignants**).

diffinitor or definitor an officer of the chapter in certain monastic orders; **distress** legal seizure and detention of goods; **distrain** to seize by way of distress.

divers several.

elders lay assistants to the minister chosen in parishes under the Presbyterian form of church government.

excise a consumption tax on main domestic goods payable at point of sale.

felony the more serious kinds of crime, usually bringing the death penalty.

font a receptacle, usually of stone, for the water used in baptism.

furlong an area of land containing ten acres.

General Baptists Baptists who broke with Calvinism and believed in the doctrine of general redemption.

high commission an English court set up to hear ecclesiastical cases with powers to impose fines and imprisonment.

hundred a subdivision of an English county.

hurly-burly commotion, tumult.

imprest to impress (or enforce service) in the army or navy.

incommiserate lacking in compassion or feelings of pity.

indemnity exemption from legal proceedings for executing a particular task.

inventory a detailed listing of goods and personal effects.

jealousies suspicions, distrust.

kirk the northern English and Scottish form of 'church'.

leaguer siege.

lecture a sermon.

libels handbills or pamphlets posted up or circulated, especially ones abusing a named individual.

liberties districts beyond the bounds of the city yet subject to municipal authority.

litany a set form of public prayer, in which the clergy lead and the congregation respond, laid down in the book of common prayer.

lordships manors.

lowable desirable, commendable.

malignants royalists (see also **delinquents**).

mark 13s. 4d. or two thirds of a pound sterling.

miscreant vile, depraved.

moiety a half.

muster   assembling of troops for inspection.

ordinance   a piece of legislation claiming the force of law which had passed both Houses of parliament and yet lacked the royal assent.

ordinary   eating-house or tavern.

pandedalian   of curious workmanship.

peculiar   a parish or church exempt from the jurisdiction of the bishop in whose diocese it lies.

prebend   a priest maintained by cathedral revenues.

prog, progging   to search or hunt about for; to forage.

projector   a speculator who forms an enterprise or undertaking for his own personal gain.

propriety   property.

Protestation, the   the 1641 oath to defend the Protestantism of the Church of England against popery.

recusants   those refusing to attend the services of the Church of England (usually Catholics, as in **popish recusants**).

reformadoes   unemployed ex-soldiers.

remonstrance   a formal statement of public grievances.

retroduction   a bringing back.

schismatics   those breaching the unity of the Church.

score   a group of twenty.

sectaries   members of a gathered church or sect rejecting the national church.

sequestration   the seizure or confiscation of estates and property.

ship money   a rate regularly levied by the king in the 1630s, by virtue of his emergency powers, to meet the costs of the navy.

shocks   groups of sheaves of corn set upright to dry and ripen.

star chamber   a leading court composed of councillors and senior judges which derived its powers from the crown's judicial role.

surplice   the standard white linen vestment worn by a minister when conducting church services.

tithes   payments originally designed to support the local church and its clergy which had often fallen into the hands of laymen.

tod   a weight for wool, usually twenty-eight pounds.

toucking   beating.

train bands/trained bands   part-time, partly-trained soldiers of county or city militias.

triers   ministers and laymen appointed within each London classis to vet elders in 1645–6.

vestry   an assembly or meeting of parishioners to conduct parish business.

videlicet (viz.)   that is to say; namely.

visitation   an inspection of a diocese conducted by its bishop.

watch   local street patrol to keep the peace.

SELECT BIBLIOGRAPHY

Adamson, J. S. A. (1990) 'The baronial context of the English civil war', *Transactions of the Royal Historical Society*, 5th series, 40, London.

Ashton, Robert (1994) *Counter-revolution: the Second Civil War and its Origins*, Yale.

Aylmer, G. E. (1975) *The Levellers in the English Revolution*, London.

—— (1987) *Rebellion or Revolution? England from Civil War to Restoration*, Oxford.

Brenner, Robert (1993) *Merchants and Revolution: Commercial Change, Political Conflict and London's Overseas Traders, 1550–1653*, Cambridge.

Carlton, C. (1992) *Going to the Wars: the Experience of the British Civil Wars, 1638–1651*, London.

Cust, R. and Hughes, A. (eds) (1989) *Conflict in early Stuart England: Studies in Religion and Politics 1603–1642*, London.

Dow, F. D. (1985) *Radicalism in the English Revolution 1640–1660*, Historical Association Studies, Oxford.

Fletcher, A. (1985) *The Outbreak of the English Civil War*, London.

Gentles, I. (1992) *The New Model Army in England, Ireland and Scotland, 1645–1653*, Oxford.

Hibbard, C. (1983) *Charles I and the Popish Plot*, Chapel Hill, NC.

Hill, C. (1972) *The World Turned Upside Down: Radical Ideas During the English Revolution*, London.

Hirst, D. (1986) *Authority and Conflict: England 1603–1658*, London.

Holmes, C. (1974) *The Eastern Association in the English Civil War*, Cambridge.

Hughes, A. (1991) *The Causes of the English Civil War*, London.

Hutton, R. (1982) *The Royalist War Effort 1642–1646*, London.

—— (1990) *The British Republic 1649–1660*, London.

Kishlansky, M. (1987) *Parliamentary Selection: Social and Political Choice in Early Modern England*, Cambridge.

Lindley, K. (1972) 'The impact of the rebellion of 1641 upon England and Wales, 1641–45', *Irish Historical Studies*, vol. xviii, no. 70.

—— (1982) *Fenland Riots and the English Revolution*, London.

—— (1997) *Popular Politics and Religion in Civil War London*, Aldershot.

Mac Cuarta, B. (ed.) (1993) *Ulster 1641: Aspects of the Rising*, Belfast.

Manning, B. (1991) *The English People and the English Revolution*, 2nd edn, London.

—— (1992) *1649: The Crisis of the English Revolution*, London.

McGregor, J. F. and Reay, B. (eds) (1986) *Radical Religion in the English Revolution*, Oxford.

Moody, T. W., Martin, F. X. and Byrne, F. J. (eds) (1976) *Early Modern Ireland 1534–1691, A New History of Ireland* vol. 3, Oxford.

Morrill, J. (1980) *The Revolt of the Provinces: Conservatives and Radicals in the English Civil War, 1630–1650*, London.

—— (ed.) (1982) *Reactions to the English Civil War, 1642–1649*, London.

—— (ed.) (1991) *The Impact of the English Civil War*, London.

—— (ed.) (1992) *Revolution and Restoration: England in the 1650s*, London.

—— (1993) *The Nature of the English Revolution*, London.

Porter, S. (ed.) (1996) *London and the Civil War*, London.

Richardson, R. C. (1989) *The Debate on the English Revolution Revisited*, London.

Richardson, R. C. and Ridden, G. M. (eds) (1986) *Freedom and the English Revolution*, Manchester.

Russell, C. (1990) *The Causes of the English Civil War*, Oxford.

—— (1991) *The Fall of the British Monarchies 1637–1642*, Oxford.

Seaver, P. S. (1985) *Wallington's World: A Puritan Artisan in Seventeenth Century London*, London.

Sharpe, K. (1992) *The Personal Rule of Charles I*, Yale.

Stevenson, D. (1973) *The Scottish Revolution 1637–1644: The Triumph of the Covenanters*, Newton Abbot.

—— (1981) *Scottish Covenanters and Irish Confederates*, Belfast.

Stone, L. (1965) *The Crisis of the Aristocracy 1558–1641*, Oxford.

Tolmie, M. (1977) *The Triumph of the Saints: The Separate Churches of London 1616–1649*, Cambridge.

Tyack, N. (1987) *Anti-Calvinists: The Rise of English Arminianism c. 1590–1640*, Oxford.

Underdown, D. (1971) *Pride's Purge: Politics in the Puritan Revolution*, London.

—— (1985) *Revel, Riot and Rebellion: Popular Politics and Culture in England 1603–1660*, Oxford.

Woolrych, A. (1987) *Soldiers and Statesmen: The General Council of the Army and its Debates, 1647–1648*, Oxford.

Wrightson, K. (1982) *English Society 1580–1680*, London.

INDEX